BAZAAR OF OPPORTUNITIES FOR NEW BUSINESS DEVELOPMENT

Bridging Networked Innovation, Intellectual Property and Business

Series on Technology Management*

Series Editor: J. Tidd (University of Sussex, UK) ISSN 0219-9823

*The complete list of the published volumes in the series can be found at
http://www.worldscientific.com/series/stm

SERIES ON TECHNOLOGY MANAGEMENT – VOL. 20

BAZAAR OF OPPORTUNITIES FOR NEW BUSINESS DEVELOPMENT

Bridging Networked Innovation, Intellectual Property and Business

Jaakko Paasi
Katri Valkokari
Tuija Rantala

VTT Technical Research Centre of Finland, Finland

Soili Nystén-Haarala
Nari Lee
Laura Huhtilainen

University of Eastern Finland, Finland

Imperial College Press

ICP

Published by

Imperial College Press
57 Shelton Street
Covent Garden
London WC2H 9HE

Distributed by

World Scientific Publishing Co. Pte. Ltd.
5 Toh Tuck Link, Singapore 596224
USA office: 27 Warren Street, Suite 401-402, Hackensack, NJ 07601
UK office: 57 Shelton Street, Covent Garden, London WC2H 9HE

British Library Cataloguing-in-Publication Data
A catalogue record for this book is available from the British Library.

Series on Technology Management — Vol. 20
BAZAAR OF OPPORTUNITIES FOR NEW BUSINESS DEVELOPMENT
Bridging Networked Innovation, Intellectual Property and Business

Copyright © 2013 by Imperial College Press

ISBN 978-1-84816-891-6

Typeset by Stallion Press
Email: enquiries@stallionpress.com

Printed in Singapore.

Preface

In 2007 one of the authors of this book was repeatedly bombarded with messages and questions from his colleagues in industry such as *"intellectual property (IP) is a difficult issue in inter-organizational innovation"*, *"who should own the results of collaborative innovation?"*, *"how can we manage joint IP?"*, *"how can we manage IP in open innovation?"* As a researcher, he started to explore extant literature about IP and IP management in collaborative and open innovation. He found that many researchers identified the topic as highly important, but that little was written about the topic itself. IP in collaborative and open innovation was almost like a blank slate. What an opportunity for a researcher!

He started to gather a multidisciplinary research team, consisting of experts in innovation management, business network management, business contracting, IP law, and IP valuation, and submitted a proposal for research funding for a large international research project about firms' practices of knowledge and IP management in inter-organizational innovation and new business development. Finally, in Autumn 2008, the research project "Intellectual Property in Open Business Models" (IPOB) took place. The main project partners were VTT Technical Research Centre of Finland (coordinator) and University of Eastern Finland. The project was supported by Tekes — the Finnish Funding Agency for Technology and Innovation. Rotterdam School of Management was closely involved in the design of the project and in the collection of empirical material in the Netherlands through its spin-off company Inpaqt B.V. The title of the research project was inspired by the open innovation paradigm introduced by H. Chesbrough.[1]

The research was based on qualitative business research methods. It had an interpretative orientation and aimed to understand the phenomena from the inside rather than the outside. The empirical material was collected in two parallel ways: by an interview study about inter-organizational innovation that was carried out in 40 innovative organizations in the Netherlands and in Finland; and by active case working in 6 innovative case companies in Finland (Arcusys, Blancco, Medisize, Outotec, Sandvik and Tamlink).

The idea for this book arose from the multidisciplinary nature of the work. We have written several focused papers for scientific journals and conferences about the results of the research (a list of the papers is given in Appendix I), but writing to highly focused scientific journals does not allow us to address the multidisciplinary nature of the work. In real business life, business, legal and network management processes are strongly connected, but little has been written about that. Furthermore, the text and style in the focused scientific papers follows the lingo of the particular discipline and it may be difficult for an expert from another discipline to understand the content of the paper. In this book we have tried to explain the multidisciplinary content of the book in a way that can be understood by people from different backgrounds: technical, business, legal, academic, and industry.

The title of the book was formulated as *Bazaar of Opportunities for New Business Development — Bridging Networked Innovation, Intellectual Property and Business*. With the "Bazaar of Opportunities for New Business Development" we would like to go beyond the paradigm of open innovation and underline the variety of opportunities that firms may have in innovation and new business development with external actors. By the expression "New Business Development" we mean here the development of really new business as well as the renewal of existing business. In the Bazaar of Opportunities firms can interact, innovate, and make business with different known and unknown actors, both formally and informally, and using different levels of openness. External actors mean, however, additional risks for the firm that they should manage. The rest of the title, "Bridging Networked Innovation, Intellectual Property and Business", addresses the guidance and perspectives that the book will give in order to better manage the risks.

The book is a monograph written by a group of authors. The content of the book was formed in numerous group discussions between the authors during the research. For each chapter there is a named person responsible for writing the first draft. In some chapters the responsible person received strong support from a co-author. And in all chapters he or she received input and comments from the other authors of the book. Finally, the coordinator (Jaakko Paasi) made the book a coherent presentation.

Jaakko Paasi was responsible for Chapter 1 "Introduction". Katri Valkokari wrote first drafts of Chapters 2 "Open and Networked Innovation", and 3 "Collaboration Models and Knowledge Management", with support from Jaakko Paasi. The first draft of Chapter 4 "IP in Networks" was written by Soili Nystén-Haarala with support from Nari Lee. Chapter 5 "Contract and IP Management in Networked Innovation" was written by Soili Nystén-Haarala with support from Laura Huhtilainen. Jaakko Paasi wrote first drafts of the remaining chapters: Chapter 6 "IP Strategy and Collaboration"; Chapter 7 "Bridging Networked Innovation, IP and Business"; and Chapter 8 "When is Dealing in the Bazaar of Opportunities Beneficial?" Tuija Rantala (née Luoma) was responsible for the quotations from the interview study (i.e. voices of interviewed managers) throughout the book.

This book will be followed by another book titled *Workbook for Opening Innovation — Bridging Networked Business, Intellectual Property and Contracting*,[2] to be published in the Series on Technology Management by Imperial College Press. The workbook will focus on the implementation of work and theories presented in *Bazaar of Opportunities for New Business Development*. So if readers of *Bazaar of Opportunities* would like to have practical guides, tools, and check-lists to support the implementation of open and networked innovation in their businesses, the *Workbook for Opening Innovation* may give valuable help.

The authors thank Henri Hytönen at VTT and Marko Torkkeli at Lappeenranta University of Technology for useful discussions related to the scientific part of the study; Jari Erkkilä, Vesa Nisula and Johanna Hakulinen at Tamlink Oy; Jussi Hurskainen at Arcusys Oy; Sergey Vasiliev at Blancco Oy; Juha Laiho and Marita Salo at Medisize Oy; Marja Lahonen at Outotec Oyj; Kristina Kirveskoski, Veikko Räisänen, Erkki Ahola, Riku Pulli and Marko Jokinen at Sandvik Mining and Construction Oy; Risto Kuivanen at VTT, Jukka Saarinen at Nokia Research Center and Petri Räsänen at Hermia (New Factory) for useful discussions related to the practical case study part of the study; William Suijkerbuijk, Felix Janszen, Tom Sengers and Willeke Kremer at Inpaqt B.V. for their assistance related to the part of the study carried out in the Netherlands; and all the interviewed managers in the 40 innovative organizations listed in Appendix II who shared their experiences and practices for us during the interview study.

Jaakko Paasi

Katri Valkokari

Tuija Rantala

Soili Nystén-Haarala

Nari Lee

Laura Huhtilainen

Tampere, 13 October 2011

Notes

1. The open innovation paradigm is a concept in business and innovation management literature, originally introduced by Henry Chesbrough in his two books [Chesbrough, H. (2003). *Open Innovation: The New Imperative for Creating and Profiting from Technology*, Harvard Business School Press, Boston; Chesbrough, H. (2006). *Open business models: How to thrive in the new innovation landscape*, Harvard Business School Press, Boston]. The open innovation paradigm is built on empirical findings where innovation processes combine internal and external ideas into architectures and systems and the business models that are used should define the requirements for these architectures and systems. The business model utilizes both external and internal ideas to create value, while defining internal mechanisms to claim some portion of that value. We will present the open innovation paradigm in more detail in Chapter 2 of this book.
2. Paasi, J., Valkokari, K., Hytönen, H., Huhtilainen, L. and Nystén-Haarala, S. (2012). *Workbook for Opening Innovation — Bridging Networked Business, Intellectual Property and Contracting*. Series on Technology Management, Imperial College Press, London.

About the Authors

Jaakko Paasi

Dr. Jaakko Paasi is a Principal Scientist at VTT Technical Research Centre of Finland. His doctoral thesis (in 1995) was in the field of electrical physics. Gradually his career moved towards studying business and technology management, with a special focus on innovation management. He has written about 100 reviewed scientific articles on magnet technology, superconductivity, electrostatics and innovation management.

Katri Valkokari

PhD Katri Valkokari is a Senior Scientist and team leader at VTT Technical Research Centre of Finland. Her research over past ten years has focused on management and development of business networks. In 2009 Katri Valkokari concluded her doctoral thesis on business network development. She has published several international and national articles in the research areas of strategic business networks, collaboration, organizational knowledge, and innovation management.

Tuija Rantala

Tuija Rantala (née Luoma), M.Sc. (Tech.), is a Senior Scientist at VTT Technical Research Centre of Finland. Since 1999 she has been with VTT, working in innovation and risk management projects with industry, applying and developing qualitative risk management methods to different contexts. Her main research interests are related to new business creation, innovation management and open innovation, mergers & acquisitions (M&A) process management, and intellectual property (IP) management.

Soili Nystén-Haarala

Soili Nystén-Haarala, LL.D., M.Sc. (Econ.), is Professor of Civil Law at the University of Eastern Finland. In her doctoral dissertation she compared the logics of contract law applied by courts with logics of business. Since then she has written on proactive law and contracting as well as on developing Russian law in its social, economic and political circumstances. She has led several research projects on these themes. From July 2011 she has also worked as a part-time professor of law at Luleå University of Technology in Sweden.

Nari Lee

Dr. Nari Lee, LL.D, Ph.D, is an Assistant Professor of Intellectual Property Law at Hanken School of Economics, Finland and an affiliated research fellow at the Max Planck Institute for Intellectual Property and Competition Law in Munich, Germany. She has written several publications to scientific journals. Her main research interests are in the intellectual property laws and policy, and international trade both from theoretical and practical perspectives. The research for the book was done while she was a Postdoctoral Research Fellow at the University of Eastern Finland and a program director for Munich Intellectual Property Law Center, Germany.

Laura Huhtilainen

Laura Huhtilainen is a Doctoral Student at the University of Eastern Finland. Her research interests are related to contracting in the context of networked innovation and business.

Contents

Chapter 1

Introduction

Think about a place where you can find the missing piece of knowledge to develop the offering for a new business opportunity. Think about a place where you can create and capture value for your unused ideas and intellectual property (IP) through finding an actor who is interested in applying them in their business offering. Think about a place where you can find other actors who share your vision, who are willing to open and share their knowledge with you to jointly explore new business opportunities and works towards making these identified opportunities happen. Would such a "Bazaar of Opportunities" be a fantastic place to supplement your own business development efforts? In the Bazaar of Opportunities for New Business Development[1] you do not have to do everything by yourself. Instead, you can deal with numbers of known and unknown actors and gain from their knowledge, IP, business relationships, visions, and opportunities. You may not yet be there in your business ecosystem, but with this book you are a step closer.

Many readers may have heard about the Connect and Develop program of Procter & Gamble,[2] where work in research and development (R&D), commercialization and brand strength is shared with the company's innovation partners worldwide. The program works in both inbound and outbound directions within business value chains. Procter & Gamble is searching for partners with promising products, technology, business models, methods, trademarks, packages, designs, or ideas that could be integrated into the company's offering. They are also actively offering their technology and other innovation assets for others through licensing. Most readers may also have heard about the successful strategic movement of IBM where IBM donated closed source code of their operating system (internal IP) to create open source projects and communities in order to fuel adoption of related products and services.[3] The value of the related products and services has exceeded the value of the original IP of the closed source code many times over. These two examples are famous success stories of "business giants". Similar inter-organizational innovation actions take place daily on a smaller scale in thousands of smaller firms and research organizations worldwide. Some of those actions lead to success stories from which we may hear about later on. From most of them, however, we will never hear anything.

You may now ask what is then new in the Bazaar of Opportunities? Is it not so that firms have always been interested in interaction with their customers and other firms in their value chain in innovation? And we have to answer that yes, it is absolutely true that firms have always had interaction with their customers and suppliers in innovation. Innovative endeavour almost always requires a network of independent actors with different competences. Single firms as organizational systems alone do not emerge with innovation, except in a minority of cases. Designs of new innovation, on the other hand, are often developed internally by individual firms that keep strategic control over their designs.[4] However, there are two things that have essentially changed during the past three decades, which have had a major impact on innovation. Firstly, the interaction is no longer restricted to face-to-face meetings in the neighbourhood. The growth of electronic commerce and the internet has expanded the possibilities of interaction and networking to dimensions not seen previously. While 50 years ago the innovation mainly took place within the neighbourhood, now it can be truly global. Face-to-face innovation has been supplemented by virtual and global places of innovation, where firms can interact, innovate and make business with different known and unknown actors, both formally and informally and using different levels of openness. Secondly, business offerings are nowadays increasingly complex. They may include several technologies — both hardware and software — accompanied with services. Market demand for complex and intelligent products and systems together with global competition has driven firms to search for external partners. In many cases it is no longer feasible and competitive for a firm to do the innovation work (or product development work) related to new business offering alone.

Any collaborative innovation action between two actors requires that the actors open and share their knowledge with each other in one way or another. Therefore, openness has become a technical and philosophical tenet which has a variety of definitions because works and processes cannot simply be described as open or closed (or proprietary). Instead there is a continuum that ranges from closed to open, the work's degree of openness being determined by the availability, accessibility and modifiability of the knowledge as an innovation outcome. A multiple of different models in terms of "collaborative", "democratized", or "open" innovation has been introduced to describe the variety of collaborative models of openness in innovation.[5] These models differ from each other in respect to the availability, accessibility and modifiability of the innovation outcome, forming a continuum of networked innovation from almost closed collaboration to full openness where the results are available and modifiable by all.

Networked innovation is a general expression that we are using in this book to cover all models of inter-organizational innovation as well as models where individuals can be actors of innovation.[6] The term "networked innovation" does not commit to the degree of openness in the innovation work. It only assumes that there is some kind of collaboration in innovation that goes over the boundaries of a firm (or another kind of organization) and, thus, there are external actors involved in innovation in one way or another. In some instances in the book we are speaking about open and networked innovation in order to underline openness in networked innovation.

Involvement of external actors opens up lots of new opportunities for a firm to create new business: the firm can utilize external knowledge or technology to create new offerings, and the firm can find external paths to commercialize its knowledge or technology. But like in a real bazaar, some actors succeed better in the Bazaar of Opportunities than others. Some actors are better prepared for finding the right partners for their innovation, negotiating with partners, creating successful models of collaboration and business, and managing the networked innovation through formal and informal methods. Firms must also manage additional risks when using external actors.

In this book, *Bazaar of Opportunities for New Business Development — Bridging Networked Innovation, Intellectual Property and Business*, we present basic models for open and networked innovation in firms and how they manage knowledge and IP in these relationships with external actors. We describe how firms' legal procedures should be adapted to networked innovation so that they do not only safeguard their own business but also encourage other contractual parties to innovate and create new business together. We also present how networked innovation should influence the IP management in firms, in the form of IP strategy that makes the firm prepared to be active in the Bazaar of Opportunities and in the way the firm valuates IP. The content of the book is based on a large multidisciplinary research project about firms' practices of knowledge and intellectual property management in inter-organizational innovation and new business development.

Collaboration, Open and Networked Innovation — Why?

Motivations for inter-organizational, collaborative, open, and networked innovation can be illustrated by examples given in Figs. 1.1, 1.2 and 1.3. In Fig. 1.1 the present knowledge of a firm is positioned in respect of the knowledge required for the planned future offering of the firm (where we have supposed that the offering has been described in such a detail that the knowledge required for the offering can be specified).[7] By the knowledge we mean here both explicit (i.e. codified) knowledge in the form of patents, copyrights, source codes, written documents, etc., and the tacit knowledge (i.e. know-how) that can be somewhat isolated and controlled by contracts, policies, norms, etc.[8] The knowledge can be related to technology, processes, services, business, markets, customers,

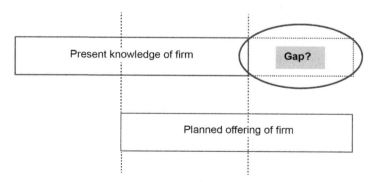

Fig. 1.1. Alignment of present knowledge of a firm in respect of the knowledge required for the realization of a firm's planned offering.

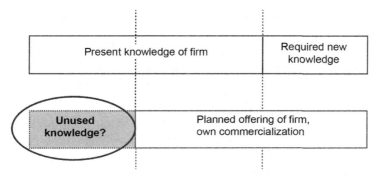

Fig. 1.2. Alignment of the present knowledge of a firm in respect of the knowledge to be used for the planned offering of the firm.

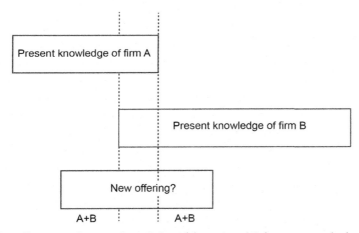

Fig. 1.3. Alignment of present knowledge of firms A and B in respect to the knowledge required for a potential new offering as an outcome of co-creation (joint innovation).

local business ecosystems, regulation, legislation, etc., covering all fields required for the running of a successful business.

In Fig. 1.1 the bars are to some extent overlapping, meaning that part of the knowledge required for the realization of the planned offering exists in the firm. However, in the upper-right corner of the figure there is a gap of knowledge meaning that not all the knowledge required for the realization of the planned offering exists in the firm. Now the question is, how can we fill the gap? Alternatives to fill the gap are: 1. Creation of the missing knowledge by in-house R&D; 2. Sourcing of the knowledge through a transaction from another actor (i.e. transaction of existing knowledge); 3. Co-creation of the missing knowledge with external actors (i.e. co-creation of new knowledge).

In-house R&D is the classical way of dealing with the problem. Sometimes it really is a good solution, but sometimes other alternatives could be better. Networking and knowledge acquisition through a transaction or co-creation of new knowledge are often more effective in time and costs than in-house R&D and lead to better solutions because "not all the smart people work for you".[9] Transaction of existing knowledge through buying, licensing, subcontracting, etc. is a good alternative when you know that there is another actor somewhere who already has the knowledge that you are missing and has an aligned interest with you, in the sense that you could agree on the conditions of transaction. In the past it was not easy to find such knowledge, but today the situation is different. Explicit knowledge is typically in an electronic form and there is a lot of information available on the internet in different kinds of databases which help in the search for knowledge.[10] Co-creation of new knowledge with an external actor is a good alternative when there is no existing knowledge available to fill the gap. In co-creation your own resources could be multiplied through networking.

Figure 1.2 sets up the question of unused knowledge in the bottom-left corner of the figure: what will the firm do with the unused knowledge? Most firms do nothing with the unused knowledge. But does that create value for the firm? Usually not. There are examples in which it is strategically reasonable to keep some part of a firm's knowledge unused in house and in this way create more "freedom of action" for the business of the firm,[11] but often one should consider making profit with the knowledge that the firm is not aiming to commercialize by itself. Then the alternatives are knowledge transaction (in this case we should speak about IP transaction) to another actor by selling or licensing the IP, or sharing the knowledge with an external actor and co-creating new business with her.

Innovations often arise at the interface between different pieces of existing knowledge, experience, culture, etc. Figure 1.3 illustrates the exploration of new knowledge and (later on) new business offering through opening and sharing of existing knowledge bases of Firm A and Firm B. A prerequisite for the co-creation is that the existing knowledge bases of the actors are supplementary and partly overlapping and that the interests of the actors are aligned so that conditions for an innovative dialogue are right. When successful, the result of co-creation is such that neither actor could have done that (easily) by him or herself. The commercialization of the offering could be done by Firm A, by Firm B, by a joint venture, or by a third party after an transaction of the joint innovation.

Collaboration, Open and Networked Innovation — What?

The aim of most firms is to create value and capture some portion of that value for itself. Creating and capturing value usually involves third parties both within the vertical value chain and from the value network of the firm, regardless of how the innovation has been arranged. In a so-called closed innovation model with inside R&D only, any innovation activities happen inside the boundaries of a firm and inter-organizational activities are transactions of products and services within the value chain or network. In an open model, the firm opens up its innovation activities and lets external ideas, knowledge, and technology flow in from the outside and lets internal knowledge and technology flow to the outside in a controlled way. Thus opening may happen both to the inbound direction of the value chain, which typically means external collaboration in the technical domain, and to the outbound direction, which typically means external collaboration in the market domain of a firm.

Networked innovation activities in the technical domain require different capabilities and skills from the firm than networked innovation activities in the market domain. In the technical domain (outside-in innovation activities) the firm acts as a customer for technical suppliers, regardless of the form of the customer–supplier relationship (principal-agency, equal partners, etc.). Much of the networked innovation activities in the technical domain are explorative in nature from the viewpoint of the firm in the role of customer. In the market domain (inside-out innovation activities) the firm acts as a supplier to its customers and end users, regardless of the form of the customer–supplier relationship. Much of a firm's networked innovation activities in the market domain are exploitative in their nature (i.e. exploitation of existing knowledge).[12] The firm must "wear different hats"[13] in outside-in and inside-out innovation, and changing the role (the hat) may not be easy. Many firms are good in one of these two cases but firms are rarely good in both.

Collaborative, open, and networked innovation is often considered to be R&D activity, but this is only true in part. If we are restricted in our consideration to R&D only, we miss the key point of open and networked innovation and the key point of the Bazaar of Opportunities, which is business, and business models[14] in particular. In the examples given in Figs. 1.1, 1.2 and 1.3, the search of knowledge for a new product or service is R&D, but all the other activity is related to business. Innovation can take place in the R&D domain, in the business model domain or in both of them. This is a fact which many people do not think about. Innovation which is confined to the R&D domain seldom leads to real success stories. Innovation in the business model domain (i.e. how the firm makes money), on the other hand, could easily improve the profit of the firm.[15] The best prognosis for success is when the innovation covers both the R&D and the business model.[16]

iTunes of Apple Inc.[17] is an excellent example of a real success story that covers innovation both in the R&D and in the business model domain. iTunes is also a good example of new business development with the use of networked innovation (or new business development using the Bazaar of Opportunities). The technical core of the iTunes media player computer program was not developed by Apple but by three men who distributed it using the name SoundJam MP[18] through a company called Casady & Greene. Apple became interested in the technology, purchased the rights to the SoundJam MP software from Casady & Greene as well as hiring the software developers of SoundJam MP. Then Apple added a new user interface and made some other changes to the features of the software and, finally, released it as iTunes. But that is just one part of the story. That is just about innovations that happened in the technical R&D domain. iTunes is not only a piece of media player software. It is also an internet store for various kinds of media (originally music). The iTunes internet store is where a radical business model innovation steps in. iTunes was not the first internet store for music. Earlier attempts tried to sell entire albums. There were also actors who distributed music without permission from the publishers, i.e. record companies. Apple looked at the business differently. They negotiated business deals with major record companies that allowed people to download songs for use on a limited number of devices, and started to sell individual songs instead of entire albums. The price of a song was adjusted to a level which was moderate for consumers but still gave satisfactory revenues for Apple as well as for the record companies. That was the second part of the story: the business model innovation. Together, the media player software and the internet store changed the business radically and became one of the most successful business stories of the last few decades.

As the example of iTunes showed, networked innovation offers lots of opportunities to innovate, not only in the R&D domain but also in the business model domain. Subcontracting is the classical way of doing collaboration in the value chain or network. In many situations, this is still a very good model of collaboration, but it is not a very innovative way of doing business under global competition. Different kinds of licensing models offer lots of alternatives to develop new models of innovation and business collaboration between the actors of the value network. Such models could also encourage the actors of the innovation network to focus their best efforts on the collaboration — not only in the short term but also in the long run. iTunes is a good example of a business offering that is made possible through a high number of actors in Apple's value network by using novel models of innovation and business collaboration both in technical and business domains. But the expansion of the innovation collaboration from the R&D domain to cover also the business model domain is far from easy. It requires a new kind of thinking, good capabilities for networking, business and contracting from all actors in question. As in a real bazaar, some actors succeed more than others in the Bazaar of Opportunities.

Collaboration, Open and Networked Innovation — How?

What then makes actors successful in the Bazaar of Opportunities? There is no single answer to that, but we may learn something by studying an oriental bazaar. To be successful, an actor must: understand his or her own role and interests as well as those of the opponent; know the value of the offering in question; be creative and skilful in negotiating and agreeing; understand the business model in question and what opportunities and limitations that will create, etc. In short, a successful actor in an oriental bazaar must be a multi-skilled person. The same applies to the Bazaar of Opportunities. One must be skilful in networked innovation, IP management, contracting, and business, and effectively bridge these capabilities together. Successful firms have managed to link these capabilities together and are working towards further integration of these capabilities.

In this book we will go through perspectives that are important for operating successfully in the "Bazaar of Opportunities for New Business Development". Chapter 2 "Open and Networked Innovation" defines the basic concepts of open and networked innovation, giving the basis for the remaining chapters of the book. It starts from the concept of open innovation, but quickly goes beyond that and expands the framework of the book to networked innovation systems and to networked innovation itself. A networked innovation system includes all inter-organizational relationships where the specific purpose is innovation for a potential or planned business offering. The networked innovation system — the Bazaar of Opportunities — is an active mart with several actors, including traders, dealers, and buyers. Chapter 2 also considers different levels of openness and barriers to innovate openly. Collaboration processes of firms involved in inter-organizational innovation have diverse forms, varying from formal to informal forms of collaboration and from open to closed forms of collaboration. The balance between different levels of openness and the ability to integrate closed and open innovation processes is one of the key success factors within the Bazaar of interconnected Opportunities.

Chapter 3 "Collaboration Models and Knowledge Management" bridges the concept of networked innovation with a knowledge-based approach of a firm. In this chapter we consider how the type of knowledge, the target of development, and the motivation of collaboration influence the choice of collaboration model. The models of collaboration (i.e. networked innovation) are divided into two categories: networks of knowledge transaction and networks of knowledge co-creation. This simple division is sufficient as long as the focus is on the management of organizational knowledge, for example in the sharing and protection of knowledge. Classical as well as novel forms of inter-organizational innovation are reviewed for both transaction and co-creation types of networked innovation. In addition to the forms of collaboration, business models and network roles of firms influence their motivation to collaborate in different phases of networked innovation (i.e. design, development, and offering phases of innovation). In Chapter 3, the different roles are reviewed and connected with the requirements of the knowledge management of a firm.

Networked innovation does not find solid protection from IP legislation, which is designed for protecting "closed" and proprietary innovation. Therefore, protection needs to be primarily built within private governance.[19] But IP management in networked innovation is not only about protection of knowledge. In networked innovation, controlled sharing of knowledge is as important a part of IP management as the protection of knowledge. Chapters 4 and 5 consider the management of IP from the legal points of view. Chapter 4 "IP in Networks" describes general principles of IP protection, and the extent to which they support practices of networked innovation. Licensing of existing IP as well as acquisition and use of existing IP as inputs of innovation are examples where IP legislation gives good support for networked innovation. Cases where IP is a result of collaboration, on the other hand, represent situations where the general principles of IP protection are not so well aligned with the practices and needs of networked innovation. Chapter 4 discusses aspects related to the cases where IP is a result of collaboration in more detail and what that means for the management of IP in networks.

Chapter 5 "Contract and IP Management in Networked Innovation" continues the discussion about IP management in networks. But instead of IP legislation, the focus is on IP management by private governance. In practice, contracts are the most important tool in arranging safeguarding in networked innovation. Besides safeguarding, contracts also have other functions such as co-ordination and control as well as preparing for contingencies. Good contracting policy requires contracting to be co-ordinated with respective collaboration models, business models and processes. Private actors can easily find models and examples of contracts for knowledge transaction from standard contracts of their industrial branch, but designers of contracts for co-creation networks usually lack such tools. Contracts also often lag behind the actual operation, and mechanisms of change are not included in the contract. In Chapter 5 we also show that trust is an important prerequisite for well-functioning private governance. In short, Chapter 5 discusses how to make contracting a tool that promotes co-operation in networked innovation.

Chapter 6 "IP Strategy and Collaboration" examines IP strategy of a firm in the context of networked innovation by going beyond the classical patent strategy approach of the firm. That is done in two ways. Firstly,

IP strategy is considered to cover knowledge management of a firm in a broader sense than just the knowledge that can be protected by patents and other formal rights defined in IP laws. Secondly, IP strategy is considered to cover not only the guidelines for the protection of knowledge that is important for a firm but also the guidelines for controlled sharing of the knowledge in order to support the firm's business. Accordingly, IP strategy is defined as a company's awareness about what knowledge is important for the firm and how it should be protected, managed or shared in order to support the business model and business strategy of the firm. Chapter 6 also discusses how IP strategy could support a firm's navigation in the Bazaar of Opportunities. An effective IP strategy helps to identify those technological or business areas where all of the critical knowledge needs to be kept in-house, those areas where IP can be subject to transactions in and out of the firm, and areas where open collaboration between suitable partners is the most beneficial mode of operation.

Network, IP, legal, and business management standpoints related to innovation and new business development are, in the extant literature, usually presented and discussed separately. In real business life, however, these standpoints are closely connected together. In Chapter 7 "Bridging Networked Innovation, Intellectual Property and Business" the standpoints are combined from three different perspectives: the business of system integration, IP valuation in the context of networked innovation, and openness of innovation in the Bazaar of Opportunities. System integration is about design, development, and offering of complex and intelligent products and systems that consists of "pieces" from several suppliers integrated together by an actor who can be called a system integrator. At the beginning of this chapter we said that in many cases it is not feasible and competitive for a firm to do the innovation work related to new business offering alone. Design and development of complex and intelligent products and systems is a very good example of when networked innovation is beneficial for firms. In the Bazaar of Opportunities, IP is a means of business. Accordingly, its valuation is an important, although difficult, part of business. The focus of IP valuation in Chapter 7 is not directly in the valuation of existing IP in a firm but in the addressing of issues that the actors in the Bazaar should be aware of and take into account when making any business deals related to IP, including, among other things, sharing the value of IP between the actors of innovation. The last perspective of the chapter deepens the discussion about the openness of open innovation started in Chapter 2.

Finally, Chapter 8 "When is Dealing in the Bazaar of Opportunities Beneficial?" gives concluding remarks for the book. This chapter, in line with the rest of the book, assumes that operating and dealing in the Bazaar may not always be beneficial for a firm. There must be a good motive in order to go into the Bazaar of Opportunities and preparations should be made before going there. The concluding chapter discusses when operation and dealing in the Bazaar is the most beneficial for an actor.

Research Behind the Book

The content of the book is based on a large research project about firms' practices of knowledge and IP management in inter-organizational innovation and new business development. The empirical material of the study was collected in two parallel ways: by an interview study about IP management in inter-organizational relationships (i.e. in inter-organizational innovation and new business development); and by active case working in innovative case companies. The research used qualitative data and multiple case study methodology[20] to assist in building the theory and conclusions reported in the book. The work had an interpretative orientation and aimed to understand the phenomena from the inside rather than the outside.

In the interview study 40 innovative organizations in the Netherlands and in Finland were studied using semi-structured theme interviews. The organizations represented different fields of industry and different firm sizes, bringing diversity to the empirical material and maximizing the variety in the data. The criterion for selection was that the organization was generally known to be innovative and was among the leading actors in its branch of industry. The list of the interviewed organizations is given in Appendix II. The interviews were conducted from February–October 2009. The interviewees were specifically senior corporate, R&D, business unit, or IP managers.

An interview usually began by enquiring into the company's business and its role and position in the business environment of the firm. The deeper inter-organizational relationships of the firm were then discussed, the main focus being on innovation and new business creation and offerings. Step by step, more specific questions related to knowledge and IP management practices within the firm, and in their inter-organizational relationships, were investigated. Questions were thematic, and included (among others): *"What kinds of collaboration practices are you currently using in your inter-organizational relationships (in innovation)?"*, *"How do you share and protect your knowledge in these relationships in the phases of exploitation and exploration?"*, *"How do you treat the outcome of the collaboration (IP, tacit knowledge)?"* and *"Do you perceive any barriers to innovating openly?"*. In some cases, the interviewees were also asked additional questions later on, in order to elucidate the company's practices and motives.

In the active case working approach, the authors took part in the actual process developed work of six firms in which the firms improved their capabilities in IP management in collaborative, open, and networked innovation. The case firms (Arcusys, Blancco, Medisize, Outotec, Sandvik, and Tamlink) included firms representing traditional and novel industries, manufacturing, and service business, as well as small, medium, and large enterprises. The case firms built up a consortium project for the development work where they shared their experiences and together searched for answers to issues of common interests such as *"How could you manage IP in joint development with multiple parties?"* and the subject of *"IP strategy of system integration"*. The consortium project started in Autumn 2008 and ended in Spring 2011. The consortium and its targets are reviewed in Appendix III in order to give more information about the research behind the book. Most of the ideas presented in this book have been field-tested in the case companies, and the origin of many ideas is in real business cases of the firms.

The book contains lots of direct quotations either from the interviewees of the interview study or from the experts at the case firms of the consortium project. To acknowledge the wishes of the managers and experts, these quotations will be presented anonymously because they reflect the current business practices of the firms.

The Term "Intellectual Property"

The interview study showed that almost all the included firms have innovation activities with other actors, mostly with their customers, suppliers, and research organizations. The detailed forms and practices of the collaboration, however, were very varied. The managers mentioned that the management of knowledge and IP is often challenging in these relationships.

One challenge identified in the interviews was related to the way in which companies understand the term "intellectual property" (IP) and use it in association with the firm's practices. In the words of one interviewee: *"At our firm we understand IP as intellectual property rights plus the know-how that can be covered by a NDA[21] and other agreements."* While this is just one (but nevertheless a representative) example, most managers said that know-how (i.e. tacit knowledge) plays an extremely important role in their innovation, and expressed their desire to isolate and control the know-how related to collaborative innovation. The managers interviewed typically attempt to achieve this through different contracts (NDAs, employee agreements, collaboration agreements, etc.) in conjunction with company policies. Some firms even use the term "intellectual property" in contracts with the broader meaning — not only as IP rights that are granted and protected by the IP laws.

The practice by firms of using the term IP in a very broad sense is understandable in three different ways. Firstly, knowledge plays an extremely important role in inter-organizational innovation in all its various forms. It is part of the firm's resources and represents capability in terms of the exchange of a special resource that makes a difference in a firm's performance. Legal protection of the tacit part of knowledge, however, is unclear. Only explicit, codified knowledge can have clear legal protection.[22] Secondly, collaborative, open, and networked innovation challenges the traditional conditions for the protection of IP in law. Patent law in particular tends to discourage open exchange and communication before patent filling, as a published and known idea will not be protected. Under this closed innovation model of IP law, firms need to control closely the exchange of innovative ideas. IP law also tends to discourage multiple patent and other claim holders because, although the IP law does regulate the question of co-inventors, co-creators, and co-owners, it does not regulate how these rights are co-ordinated or managed and in what hierarchy. To prevent disputes, proactive private ordering by contracts is necessary.[23] Thirdly, the very term "intellectual property" as a legal expression is not uncontested[24] and may include various patterns of human interaction.[25] Under national laws, IP law may include rights on patent, copyright, trademark, trade secrecy, rights in the topography of integrated circuits, industrial design rights, plant breeders' rights, publicity rights, and database rights, amongst others. Taking into account what is said above, it is easy to understand why firms would like to isolate and control the tacit knowledge related to inter-organizational innovation (in addition to the knowledge that can be formally protected by patents, copyrights and other formal methods of knowledge protection). Attempts to do that include contracts, company policies, and the use of the term "intellectual property" in contracts in a broad sense. Regardless of whether certain knowledge is protected as an IP right, firms contractually and behaviourally control and isolate the knowledge and other intangible resources related to innovation, and may view any controllable knowledge as the IP of the firm.

This practice, which may further differ from firm to firm, may cause misunderstandings and consequently problems in inter-organizational innovation. Thus it is crucial to align the practice of the firms and, to do so, all parties need to have one coherent understanding of the term. **In order to promote the forming of the coherent understanding in the context of collaborative, open, and networked innovation, we introduce a broad definition according to which the term "intellectual property" may include not only IP rights that are granted and protected by the laws, but also the knowledge and other intangible resources whose use may be controlled by contracts, policies, organizations and process routines and norms, both physically and technically.**

The broad definition of IP is actually one of the main conclusions of the study. We wanted to introduce it here in the first chapter because we will use this broad definition henceforth in the book. This broad definition reflects the interests and practices of firms in the context of networked innovation under the subject coverage of the book.

Methods of IP Protection

Control of IP (IP understood in the broad sense as defined above) is highly important in the Bazaar of Opportunities. As already said in this chapter, the control of IP in the Bazaar means not only the protection of IP but also controlled sharing of it with other specified actors in the Bazaar. Both in the protection and in the controlled sharing of IP, the motives should come from the business targets of firm and the practices should be aligned to support the business in question. Here in Chapter 1 we give an overview of common methods used for the protection of IP. These methods will be frequently referred to in the forthcoming chapters. The controlled sharing of IP will be discussed in more detail in the forthcoming chapters, especially in Chapter 6 "IP Strategy and Collaboration".

Approaches for protecting IP can, in general, be divided into three categories according to their formality: formal protection methods often called intellectual property rights (IPR), contractual protection methods, and informal protection methods.[26] Formal protection methods include patents, trademarks, utility models, rights to commercial names, and copyright. Formal methods require knowledge (IP) to be explicitly codified. In order to achieve the formal protection for the IP, one must go through a formal procedure defined in legislation.

Contractual protection methods include different types of contracts or contract clauses, such as confidentiality agreements, prohibition of competition clauses and recruitment freeze clauses in agreements, proprietary and access rights clauses in agreements, etc. Such agreements are aimed at two or more actors in the Bazaar of Opportunities. In addition to agreements that are used to formalize inter-organizational collaboration in the Bazaar, there are contracts, including aspects of IP protection, which are made between a firm and its employees. Such contracts or contract clauses may include issues related to employee invention, confidentiality, and prohibition of competition.

Informal protection methods attempt to prevent the loss of key knowledge (IP) or restrict undesirable access to sensitive information either inside the firm or in external relations. Secrecy is one of the main methods of informal IP protection. On the other hand, publishing can also be used as a method of IP protection: it prevents others from appropriating the knowledge, thus confirming the freedom of action for the firm. Product design may be distributed and supported with restricted access to information, through which the number of key persons that have a control over the whole innovation work can be limited to a few. The key persons are kept satisfied through human resources management. Client relationship management is an important form of IP protection when clients are involved in innovation. In addition to formal contracts, trust between the provider

Table 1.1.   Common methods for the protection of knowledge.

Formal protection methods	Contractual protection methods	Informal protection methods
— Patent	— Non-competition	— Secrecy
— Utility model	— Confidentiality	— Publishing
— Trademark	— Recruitment freeze	— Restricted access to information
— Design right	— Employee invention	— Client/supplier relationship management
— Copyright	— Proprietary and access rights	— Human Resources management
		— Distributed product design
		— Fast innovation rhythm

and client is needed in innovation in the Bazaar of Opportunities and active client relationship management supports the building and maintaining of the trust. The same applies in innovation relationships with suppliers. Supplier relationship management supports the building and maintaining of the trust needed for successful innovation. Fast innovation rhythm is a frequently used way to protect service business. Informal protection practices also help capture tacit knowledge and transform it into explicit knowledge, which can then be shared within the company or with external actors in a controlled manner. This will decrease the company's risks and dependence on individual employees.

An overview of typical methods for IP protection in business is given in Table 1.1 (modified from the work of Päällysaho and Kuusisto).[27] The emphasis of the table is on the methods that have an importance in the Bazaar of Opportunities.

Notes

1. The name of the book, *Bazaar of Opportunities for New Business Development*, was inspired by the oriental marketplace where customers and entrepreneurs from different parts of the world have traditionally met, interacted and made business with each other. We are also aware of the book *The Cathedral and the Bazaar* by Eric Raymond (1999) and the article "Neither Market nor Hierarchy nor Network: The Emergence of Bazaar Governance" (2006) by Benoit Demil and Xavier Lecocq, in which the authors compared the governance model of open source software communities to that of an oriental bazaar. Our perspective on the new models of innovation, however, is much broader than just open source communities. Accordingly, in our book we will go far beyond

the governance models to the actual networked business and innovation. It is due to the business and innovation aspects of traditional oriental marketplaces that we found some similarities between the bazaars and today's business ecosystems. These similarities, however, are not a subject of this study and should not be taken too rigorously. [Raymond, E. (1999). *The Cathedral and the Bazaar*, O'Reilly, Sebastapol, CA; Demil, B. and Lecocq, X. (2006). Neither Market nor Hierarchy nor Network: The Emergence of Bazaar Governance, *Organization Studies*, Vol. 27, No. 10, pp. 1447–1466.]

2. For more information see www.pgconnectdevelop.com (Accessed on 22 February 2012).

3. See, for example, the 'open source' section at http://en.wikipedia.org/wiki/IBM and the article by Douglas Heintzman titled 'An introduction to open computing, open standards, and open source' for more information. ["IBM", Wikipedia, http://en.wikipedia. org/wiki/IBM (Accessed at 22 February 2012.) Heintzman, D. (2003). An introduction to open computing, open standards, and open source, IBM, http://www.ibm.com/developerworks/rational/library/1303.html. (Accessed on 22 February 2012.)]

4. See the articles of DeBresson (1999) and Maxwell (2006) for detailed discussions about innovation, its openness, and networked character. [DeBresson, C. (1999). An Entrepreneur Cannot Innovate Alone; Networks of Enterprises Are Required, *DRUID Conference on Systems of Innovation*, Aalborg, Denmark; Maxwell, E. (2006). Open Standards, Open Source and Open Innovation. Harnessing the Benefits of Openness, *MIT Press*, Issue 3, pp. 119–176.]

5. By the collaborative model of innovation we refer to the work of C.A. Ellis *et al.* (1991), by democratized innovation to the work of E. von Hippel *Democratizing Innovation* (2005), and by open innovation to the work of H. Chesbrough (2003). [Ellis, C.A., Gibbs, S.J. and Rein, G.L. (1991). Groupware — Some issues and experiences, *Communications of the ACM*, Vol. 34, No. 1, pp. 38–58; von Hippel, E. (2005). *Democratizing Innovation*, MIT Press, Cambridge, MA; London; Chesbrough, H. (2003) *Open Innovation: The New Imperative for Creating and Profiting from Technology*, Harvard Business School Press, Boston.]

6. The expression "networked innovation" has its roots in the original articles of DeBresson (1999), Swan and Scarborough (2005), Maxwell (2006) and Valkokari *et al.* (2009) [DeBresson, C. (1999). An Entrepreneur Cannot Innovate Alone; Networks of Enterprises Are Required, *DRUID Conference on Systems of Innovation*, Aalborg, Denmark; Swan, J. and Scarborough, H. (2005). The Politics of Networked Innovation, *Human Relations*, Vol. 58, pp. 913–943; Maxwell, E. (2006) Open Standards, Open Source and Open Innovation. Harnessing the Benefits of Openness. *MIT Press*, Issue 3, pp. 119–176; Valkokari, K., Paasi, J., Luoma, T. and Lee, N. (2009). Beyond Open Innovation — Concept of Networked Innovation, *Proc. of the 2st ISPIM Innovation Symposium*, New York.]

7. The examples in Figs. 1.1 and 1.2 have been inspired by analogous examples of Henry Chesbrough in his book *Open Business Models* (2006) in which he illustrated the principles of open innovation by evaluating the alignment of a firm's technology with the patent coverage of the firm. [Chesbrough, H. (2006). *Open Business Models: How to Thrive in the New Innovation Landscape*, Harvard Business School Press, Boston.]

8. In this book the division of knowledge into explicit (codified) and tacit knowledge plays an important role. The division follows that introduced by M. Polanyi in the book *The*

Tacit Dimension (1966). Polanyi also addressed that explicit and tacit knowledge are not independent but always connected to each other. [Polanyi, M. (1966). *The Tacit Dimension*, Peter Smith, Gloucester, MA.]

9. "Not all the smart people work for you" is a slogan commonly used by open innovation consultants.

10. Information itself is just an ordered sequence of symbols, a message that has been received and opened. When the received and opened information is interpreted and understood in a specific context associated with the interpretation, the information may transform into knowledge.

11. Strategic use of knowledge will be discussed in more detail in Chapter 6.

12. Exploration of new knowledge and exploitation of existing knowledge, as introduced by J.G. March (1991) form another important pair in the theoretical framework of the book. [March, J.G. (1991). Exploration and Exploitation in Organizational Learning, *Organizational Science*, Vol. 2, pp. 427–440.]

13. Lance Newey (2010) used this expression when describing the skills needed for successful open innovation. [Newey, L. (2010). Wearing Different Hats: How Absorptive Capacity Differs in Open Innovation, *International Journal of Innovation Management*, Vol. 14, pp. 703–731.]

14. The meaning of most firms is to create value and capture some portion of that value for itself. The way the firms are doing that (i.e. to transform the innovation input to economic output) is described by the business model of a firm. [Chesbrough, H., Rosenboom, R. (2002). The Role of the Business Model in Capturing Value from Innovation: Evidence from Xerox Corporation's Technology Spin-off Companies, *Industrial and Corporate Change*, Vol. 11, pp. 529–555.]

15. According to the study of The Doblin Group, Presentation to the Institute of Design Strategy Conference, May 2005.

16. The book *Blue Ocean Strategy* by W. Chan Kim and Renée Mauborgne (2005) contains several examples of success stories based on the innovation that took place both in the R&D and business model domains. [Kim, W.C. and Mauborgne, R. (2005). *Blue Ocean Strategy — How to Create Uncontested Market Space and Make the Competition Irrelevant*, Harvard Business School Press, Boston.]

17. For more information about the development of iTunes, see for example Wikipedia and the references therein ["ITunes", Wikipedia, http://en.wikipedia.org/wiki/ITune (Accessed on 22 February 2012.)]

18. See the Wikipedia article on SoundJam MP ["SoundJam MP", Wikipedia, http://en.wikipedia.org/wiki/SoundJam_MP (Accessed on 22 February 2012.)]

19. Private governance means rules and principles agreed between companies or in the field of business without court interference. Private governance includes contracts and disputes settled either with negotiations within business parties or by using mediation or arbitration outside the national court. The term "private ordering" is a synonym of private governance.

20. The case study method is nicely described in the two articles by K. Eisenhardt (1989) and Eisenhardt and Graebner (2007). [Eisenhardt, K. (1989). Building Theories from Case Study Research, *Academy of Management Review*, Vol. 14, pp. 532–550; Eisenhardt, K. and Graebner M. (2007). Theory Building from Cases: Opportunities and Challenges, *Academy of Management Journal*, Vol. 50, pp. 25–32.]

21. i.e. a Non-Disclosure Agreement.
22. See the article by D.J. Teece (1998) for a discussion about the forms of knowledge and their value for a company. [Teece, D.J. (1998). Capturing Value from Knowledge Assets: The New Economy, Markets for Know-how, and Intangible Assets, *California Management Review*, Vol. 40, pp. 55–79.]
23. More detailed discussion about intellectual property rights in open innovation is given in the paper by Lee, Nystén-Haarala and Huhtilainen (2010). [Lee, N., Nystén-Haarala, S. and Huhtilainen, L. (2010). Interfacing Intellectual Property Rights and Open Innovation, *Open Innovation Research Seminar*, Kouvola, http://stratnet.jalusta.com/files/download/LUTResearchReport225-TorkkeliEdit.-FrontiersofOpenInnovation.pdf (Accessed at 22 February 2012.)]
24. [Gordon, W. (2003). 'Intellectual Property', in Cane, P. and Tushnet, M. (eds), *Oxford Handbook of Legal Studies*, Oxford University Press, pp. 617–646.]
25. Article 2 of the Convention that established the World Intellectual Property Organization (WIPO) shows that the term "intellectual property" may include any rights resulting from intellectual activity in the industrial, scientific, literary, or artistic field.
26. The division of methods used for knowledge protection in business into three distinct categories according to the formality of the method was used by Päällysaho and Kuusisto in their report for Tekes — the Finnish Funding Agency for Technology and Innovation (2006). [Päällysaho, S. and Kuusisto J. (2006). Intellectual Property Protection in the Service Business (trans), *Tekes Technology Report*, Helsinki. The report was later on translated into English and can be downloaded from http://www.iccwbo.org/uploadedFiles/ICC/policy/intellectual_property/pages/IP%20protection%20in%20service%20sector.pdf (Accessed on 22 February 2012.)]
27. The table is a modified version of that of Päällysaho and Kuusisto, *ibid.*, where we have included in only those methods of knowledge (IP) protection that have a special importance when dealing in the Bazaar of Opportunities. The original table of Päällysaho and Kuusisto included several (informal) methods that have an importance only in an intra-firm context.

Chapter 2

Open and Networked Innovation

Most of the readers may have heard *ad nauseam* how in the present business environment fast-changing global competition requires firms and other network actors to look for new models to innovate. Uncertainty, complex products, distributed knowledge as well as social media have been listed as the main factors why firms cannot be innovative and competitive alone. Furthermore, Open Innovation has formed the latest popular fad, although most of the ideas behind the concept are not new.[1] The Open Innovation literature argues that the future belongs to those who do the best job of integrating the best of their internal ideas and knowledge with the best external ideas and knowledge. In the words of Henry Chesbrough: "*open innovation is the use of purposive inflows and outflows of knowledge to accelerate internal innovation, and expand the markets for external use of innovation, respectively. [This paradigm] assumes that companies can and should use external ideas as well as internal ideas, and internal and external paths to market, as they look to advance their technology.*"[2]

Anyhow, it seems that from a crossing of business, intellectual property, and networked innovation perspectives, the Open Innovation concept may have reached new audiences (e.g. CEOs of technology-intensive companies).[3] This is something that the innovation, network, and knowledge management literature failed to reach for so many years, although research could support firms in finding new collaborative ways to continue their business development and innovativeness in a networked business environment. Designing and orchestrating a global network of knowledge is the basis for a brighter future for all actors within the Bazaar of Opportunities.

Due to the growing complexity of products, services, and required knowledge, a combination system approach is needed in order to be successful.[4] Furthermore, as pointed out in the above quotation from Chesbrough, utilization of Open Innovation necessitates *purposive inflows and outflows of knowledge*, e.g. a strategic approach to decisions and choices within the Bazaar of Opportunities is important. The question "why are we open or closed?" should be the starting point when utilizing Open Innovation. In the Bazaar of Opportunities it is important to raise questions like: how open should we be?, to whom are we open?, and on which issues are we open? The discussion about these questions is started in this chapter, which also opens up what the Bazaar of Opportunities is all about and lays a basis for the forthcoming chapters of the book. Challenges of innovation as a dynamic process and its systemic nature are discussed first, in order to go beyond the traditional thinking of IP management and bridge it to business development within a networked innovation system, e.g. the Bazaar of Opportunities.

Challenges of Innovation

Innovation itself is multidimensional and has more definitions than you could count. Innovation is an idea, a new technology (or combination of technologies), a process, a change, a development, a learning process, and a dynamic capability. Thereby, innovation has several forms: value innovation, incremental innovation, radical innovation, disruptive innovation, and open innovation. In this book we define innovation as **a new idea that can be commercialized and is significantly better than an earlier solution. The innovation can be related to products, services, technologies, business and organizational models, operational processes, or operational methods.**[5] Furthermore, we want to highlight that innovation is typically "more than one idea" and connect the innovation management to business development and renewal.[6] Both the exploration of new ideas and exploitation of present knowledge in order to commercialize an innovation require firms to integrate different knowledge sources and network actors to their dynamic networked innovation process (see Fig. 2.4). Still, the tools and processes successfully used for the management of incremental innovation development exploiting current lines of business may not give much help in the opposite case of knowledge exploration.[7] Because of multiple uncertainties of radical innovations, companies need several approaches in order to navigate successfully within the Bazaar of Opportunities.

In the example of Apple's iTunes given in Chapter 1, the innovation took place both in technology and business model domains.[8] The example underlines that the future competitive edge can be found from business model and management innovations.[9] As in an oriental bazaar, in the Bazaar of Opportunities you must have a clear idea of your offerings and their value to your customers in order to be successful and innovative. This requires a broad view about all the actors in the Bazaar as well as their interests and targets. In a business landscape, the development of business model and management of innovations requires an understanding of the *networked innovation system* and the mechanisms within this system. This networked innovation system includes all inter-organizational relationships where the specific — and in most cases shared — purpose is on innovation as defined already in Chapter 1.

From the business development point of view, the innovation process starts from fuzzy front-end and ends ups with commercialization of innovation outcome (see also the innovation funnel in Fig. 2.1). The innovation itself is a cyclic and iterative process where feed-forward and

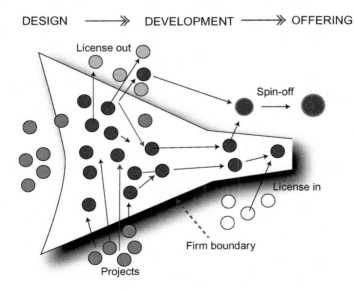

Fig. 2.1.   The innovation funnel.

feedback mechanisms are necessary. Furthermore, it is important to notice that innovation can start, and new business opportunities can emerge, anywhere. Ninety-nine per cent of invention is perspiration and only one per cent inspiration,[10] and the innovation of the process is not linear.

A knowledge-based innovation can no longer be attributed to one network actor. Innovation is almost always a cumulative and unending process, with every innovator "standing on the shoulders of giants".[11] In other words, almost every innovation process is a follow-on from previous innovations. The problem with formal IP protection methods and patent law is that they do not consider this networked and dynamic innovation system sufficiently. The IP protection focuses on protecting the rights of the innovator first and thereby it fails to facilitate the follow-up and systemic innovations, which are the most typical forms of commercialized innovations. Thus, new methods and models for knowledge sharing and protection are needed. Common methods for protection of knowledge are presented in Chapter 1, Table 1.1. IP protection is discussed in greater detail in Chapters 4 and 6.

The process of innovation is always uncertain and the winners in the Bazaar of Opportunities are the actors who can turn this uncertain risk into an opportunity. The players who understand the different forms of inter-organizational innovation are also able to manage the uncertainty better, while they are better aware about the choices and decisions of others and their influence on the game as whole. They are open to new opportunities and understand their role — but, concurrently, they are able to close their unique knowledge and strengthen their competitive edge. With the following example about the New Factory in Tampere, Finland[12] we aim to describe how the game is about to change and what kind of new collaboration models have already been tested in practice.

When thinking about a path of innovation through the innovation funnel — from an idea, through design and development to a running business (see Fig. 2.1) — it will go through several phases and each of them may have a different model of inter-organizational innovation and practices of openness.

This simplified picture[13] of ideas that freely "fly in" and "fly out" through the innovation funnel ignores the mechanisms and company-level or inter-organizational processes required to transfer or share knowledge and to turn an idea or new knowledge into an innovation and a commercial product. There are plenty of different models of inter-organizational as well as internal models of co-operation that enable the transfer of ideas. The example below offers interesting viewpoints about a novel innovation platform and how collaboration models may change through the innovation process.

Case Example: The New Factory in Tampere

The New Factory is an open innovation platform, a community open to all members of the surrounding environment: companies, universities, professionals, students, financiers, etc. It is operated by an innovation mediator, Hermia Ltd. The New Factory has three innovation apparatuses: Demola, Protomo, and Suuntaamo. In Demola, multidisciplinary teams of university students in collaboration with companies produce demonstrations of new products, services and social practices. In Protomo, diverse teams of professionals and spin-off entrepreneurs develop product and service prototypes and business concepts. Suuntaamo is an open community for affecting the development of novel products and services and the living city environment through brainstorming of concepts and testing of demos. Here we will take a closer look at Demola and Protomo where the main difference is that Demola is for students and Protomo for professionals — but otherwise they are pretty similar.

Demola and Protomo serve two needs. In the first instance there are lots of good ideas of business at local companies that do not proceed in the company because they do not fit with the business model of the company. In the case of a technological idea, the company may patent the technology and then either sell or license out the patent. But there are lots of ideas that are not patentable (such as most ideas and concepts related to new services, etc.). In the second instance there are students and professionals who are interested in becoming entrepreneurs but who have not yet discovered a good enough business idea and who would be happy to receive external support in building up a firm. For them Demola and Protomo offer an opportunity to find such an idea and to develop a prototype and spin-off business idea of a product or service in co-operation with potential clients without an immediate entrepreneur risk.

As a fictitious example,[14] let us consider an idea for a software application that reminds elderly people to take medicine, which runs on a mobile phone. The idea was created in the local research center of the Nokia Corporation in Tampere; however, it was not suitable for Nokia's business model of development and commercialization. Regardless, such an application would support the device and service platform of Nokia, therefore it would be in the company's interest for the idea to be commercialized by someone else. Nokia gave the idea to Demola, who put together a project team for the idea. The team developed the idea into an innovation, found an opportunity to establish a firm, and commercialized the innovation through Nokia's mobile service platform. In Finland there is a long-standing practice in which companies give problems to university students to solve as part of their studies. Students get credit points while the company retains all IP related to the results. What is new in the Demola as well as Protomo concepts is that, while the company gives the idea to Demola, it also transfers the rights to possible results to Demola, which passes it forward to the actual project team. The New Factory has simple but clear formal processes and contracts to do that. So the team will get all IP related to the results that they have created. The company behind the original idea, however, may retain the right to purchase a license for the results with a commercial price or become an owner of the new firm with a limited ownership. In this fictitious example, the project team could create their own firm to commercialize their work because they gained the IP of the Demola project. Nokia benefits from the collaboration by receiving a new application that is commercialized through Nokia's platforms.

The Demola or Protomo process starts with a transaction of an idea (IP) from a company to Demola or Protomo. Then the work continues by using the innovation mediator platform for an open and co-creational model of networked innovation. If this step is successful, the enriched IP will be transferred to a new firm and the open and networked innovation process will turn into a closed development of new business. The Demola/Protomo operator, Hermia Ltd, has a type of non-profit business model and receives public support to cover its expenses. The fact that the project team will get the IP has made Demola and Protomo very attractive innovation apparatuses for students, professionals, and companies searching paths to gain value for their unused ideas. The New Factory with its Demola and Protomo apparatuses has produced several spin-off companies in a short time.

The above description of the New Factory is a good example of novel networked innovation. It creates an interactive innovation platform where different actors of the innovation network will work together for joint purposes. Consequently, all actors have an intrinsic motivation to collaborate, which means that they all win and will therefore be motivated to work harder for innovation. This has required the establishment of a new business model for the New Factory apparatuses where, when compared to a classical transaction of ideas, there is a new network actor in the process, namely an innovation inter-mediator that co-ordinates the process.

Although the innovation platform itself is open to everyone, the innovation process within certain ideas is closed, e.g. there is a defined working group, where actors know each other and share the risks and benefits. Next we will deepen the discussion about differences between closed and open innovation models.

From Closed to Open Innovation

The term Open Innovation is still new or confusing to companies — and also to researchers. In our recent interview study[15] a representative of a large global company described Open Innovation as *"a buzzword"* and another interviewee described it as *"a suggestion box"*. One of the interviewees compared Open Innovation to fishing: *"...Open innovation is constant fishing for ideas"*, which is quite compatible with Chesbrough's ideas about openness to external knowledge sources.[16] This viewpoint might also be connected to the phenomenon that companies from the industry in which this interviewee was working are typical industrious users of innovation inter-mediator platforms.[17] Many of the interviewed companies were equating "open" with "public" and this was named as a typical barrier to more open innovation.

Another misunderstanding was to confuse "open" with "free". The reality is, of course, quite different and is focussed on the utilization of external knowledge sources rather than spare money. Similarly, free software, freeware, and open source software are often confused as being the same, although they have different meanings.[18] According to one interviewee, the collaborative and networked innovation, or even the search for ideas, is costly: *"How much does it cost to bring people together, formulate contracts, facilitate sessions, collect and filter ideas? What are the ways to do open innovation and what does it cost in reality?*" In order to illustrate the difference between free, open, and closed innovation activities we will distinguish between different levels of openness in innovation later on in this chapter (Table 2.4).

It is important to consider the concept of Open Innovation as work-in-progress and understand that closed and open innovation models are theoretical extremes within the continuum of networked innovation.[19] There is no "one size fits all" solution available to these questions, although the hype around the term Open Innovation has generated such feeling. Within the Bazaar of Opportunities, each actor is in a unique position and must choose if and when it makes sense to tap into distributed sources of innovation. As pointed out already in Chapter 1, there are always alternative ways to innovate and these different ways are suitable for different situations — e.g. both the closed and open innovation models have strengths and weaknesses (Table 2.1). In reality, however, scarcely any company has ever been able to manage and organize its R&D or business development in complete isolation without input from key customers, suppliers, and contexts of use. All inter-organizational innovation relationships conform to Chesbrough's definition and it is more reasonable to divide the extreme ends of networked innovation system, e.g. closed and open innovation models, based on actors involved. Within the closed innovation process only known and previously

Table 2.1.   Differences between open and closed innovation models.

Closed innovation	Open innovation
— Only known and defined actors are involved in the innovation process (static relationships and joint identity)	— Both actors and knowledge resources may change (dynamic relationships and different knowledge bases)
— Competitive edge is based on owning the IP (technology); competition can be restricted by protection of IP	— Competitive edge is created through intangible assets (like services)
— Enables deep, continuous learning and co-creation of knowledge	— Radical innovations through dynamic and open collaboration
— Challenges related to radical innovations, knowledge exploration (lock-in to existing knowledge, path-dependency).	— Challenges related to knowledge sharing and creation (missing trust, shared interests and transparency between actors).

defined actors are involved, which is in contrast to open innovation, where actors may change dynamically throughout the innovation process and even unknown actors may take part. From the viewpoint of organizational boundaries, the most closed innovation equates to an internal innovation process of one company, although in such cases there might be collaboration between different business units or organizational functions.

Closed innovation is typically based on tight relationships with well-known actors, which enables deep and continuous learning between actors. This continuous collaboration may lead to locking into existing relationships and knowledge. Conversely, open innovation, which is based on dynamic relationships, is more likely to create radical innovations. Nevertheless, uncertainty and risks are substantially higher.

Next we will go through the earlier discussion related to inter-organizational innovation models, e.g. semi-closed and open models of innovation between two or more actors. There are several partly over-lapping concepts for inter-organizational innovation relationships, their operation models, relationships, and the actors involved. Based on their approach, the concepts emphasize either the *vertical relationships* with customers[20] and suppliers[21] or *horizontal relationships* and alliances even with competitors.[22] Naturally, customers are an important source of knowledge of the needs, requirements, wants, and ideas crucial for developing new offerings that meet market demand. In addition to direct supply in the form of products or resources, there is a range of intangible knowledge such as reputation, network connections and experiences, which is important to business development. In horizontal relationships consultants, universities, research centres, other companies, innovation inter-mediators, and funding agencies act as an important source of knowledge for developments such as information, technology, and finance innovation processes. In such co-operation settings the similarity between the knowledge bases as well as network positions has a significant influence on the possibilities and willingness to share or transfer knowledge.

The focus of customer–supplier relationships is typically (and by definition) on the supply of *existing* products. This leads thinking to incremental innovation and co-configuration offering. In customer–supplier collaboration, the vertical relationship often guides the actors to a one-way mindset of actions, where the customer is a major player and a supplier of a subject of actions. In such relationships, the feedback loops and bidirectional interaction are also often missing. For smaller supplier companies especially, the claim for and the protection of their rights in relationships with larger customers is typically inconvenient, as pointed out by the representative of a smaller supplier company: "*Large customers want to own all the results — they don't even give up the rights to utilize the solution in other industry sectors very easily.*" In contrast, horizontal alliances may counteract the equality between the actors, and thereby elide the need for vision and mechanisms for decision making and management of the operations. For example, one interviewee described how the industry association focuses mainly on the common good: "*When the joint assets cannot be directly connected to business benefits of involved actors, this leads to compromises and choosing supporting activities, like advertising campaigns, industry promotion, and education.*"

Recently, the emergence of social media has increased the interests of companies to involve more horizontal models like the user-communities to their innovation and R&D processes. In B-to-C (business-to-consumer) markets the utilization of social media and user-communities is already quite typical, although the companies could benefit more from clearer connection to strategic targets.[23] It is especially true in the leisure equipment industry, where participation of user innovators is typical; the virtual developer community of the toy manufacturer Lego is a well-known example of this type of user-led innovation. On its online user-community, Lego involves consumers through chat facilities, virtual games, competitions, and a free design tool. With the Lego Digital Designer (LDD) users can design their own 3-D models and share them with others. The users are also able to purchase their own designs and also put their designs on sale. Users are rewarded in accordance with their interests: if the other users buy your design, Lego will pay you in Lego bricks. In B-to-B (business-to-business) markets the opportunities may be more limited. In the words of one interviewee, a representative of an industrial company, "*Such developer communities can play a role in the development of consumer products, but only our industry partners are able to take part in the development of our products.*"

All the above concepts emphasize one direction of co-operation, and often ignore the importance of understanding the networked innovation system itself, e.g. how interaction, relationships and processes between the actors should be supported. In addition to involving actors, inter-organizational innovation models can also be distinguished based on their operation model. The terms "collaboration" and "co-operation" have often been used as synonyms,[24] although it is useful to draw a distinction between them.[25] In co-operations, partners split the work, solve sub-tasks individually and then assemble the partial results into the final output (through transaction of knowledge), while in collaboration (knowledge co-creation) partners do the work together.[26] The different collaborative concepts that highlight the social capital[27] and trust between the actors, like open source projects,[28] communities of practice,[29] crowd-sourcing[30] and peer-to-peer production,[31] have emerged as new models within the open and networked innovation environment. They all point out the importance of shared interests and voluntariness of collaboration between actors. In these models at least some of the actors are typically individuals; they do not consist purely of companies.

The result of this is the argument that the approach of co-creation between multiple partners is partly missing from the literature of Open Innovation, although according to our interview study it is quite general in firms' practices.[32] As one of the interviewees pointed out: "*...open innovation is all about sharing...*". From the information gathered in these interviews, it became apparent that most typical inter-organizational innovation relationships were based either on bilateral contracts between customers, suppliers, and innovators or on multilateral consortium agreements between firms and other actors, like research institutes and innovation inter-mediators. Still, especially in the case of co-creation, the companies prefer the semi-open or closed collaboration models where they know all the participants (see Table 2.1). In that way they decrease the risk of knowledge leaks, although consequently they might lose opportunities for more radical innovations through new knowledge combinations. Then again, companies' attitudes towards co-operation or collaboration can vary a lot depending on their earlier experiences, resources and strategic thinking. In Fig. 2.2 we represent the continuum of networked innovation and how the above-mentioned concepts settle themselves on it.

Starting with in-house innovation, the left side of Fig. 2.2 describes those innovation models that are clearly specified and relatively closed

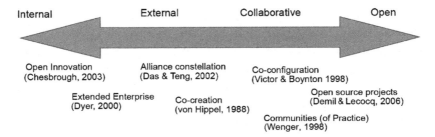

Fig. 2.2.   The continuum of networked innovation.

systems of innovation. As a rather opposite position, the right side of the figure illustrates open systems of innovation, where partners can be dynamically changing or even unknown. These open systems of innovation require radical changes in existing value systems and in the creation of new value activities. Moreover, they are characterized by uncertainties related to value activities and the actors' roles, business models, and commitment. Between the polar opposites are external and collaborative systems of innovation. Within external systems of innovation specified actors, like suppliers, are participating in a process controlled by the core company. Typically these innovation models are based on co-operation rather than collaboration. Extended enterprise concepts and alliances are typical examples of these external models of innovation, which quite often are based on bilateral relationships between the actors like a customer and a supplier or a developer.

Collaborative systems of innovation, where the outcome of innovation is co-produced by involved actors, are more dynamic and multilateral models. These innovation models differ from each other according to forms of joint processing, participating rules, and ownership of results. Levels of openness describe the differences between the models and will be gathered later in this chapter. Different multilateral development or research consortiums as well as open source communities and innovation inter-mediators platforms are examples of collaborative systems of innovation.

In practice, associations, social networks as well as research consortiums are typical examples of networked innovation models, where purpose is related to knowledge exploration, learning, and a search for new ideas. In other words, the actors are wandering through the bazaar without a shopping list, in order to catch interesting titbits and look for new possibilities. Closed business networks, strategic alliances and joint ventures as well as peer-production and communities are typically networked innovation models with the specific shared vision about targets of the collaboration; in the oriental bazaar, this translates to certain traders deciding to co-operate in order to gain better or new business opportunities.

Within the latter examples, e.g. the communities, the shared target might be connected with learning at an individual level, but in the others the connection with business targets of actors is more obvious. A representative of KIBS[33] company, which assumes the role of innovation inter-mediator, supporting the innovation transfer from research to business, stated: *"In order to have a successful project the key is to construct a group in which the interests are appropriately balanced."* In terms of openness these models also differ from each other, e.g. in communities the participation is more open, based on personal motivation of actors, and because there are no gate-keepers unknown actors may also take part in the collaboration, while in the other forms the companies typically insist on limiting the participation.

Networked Innovation Systems

As described above, a networked innovation system — the Bazaar of Opportunities — is an active mart with several traders, dealers, and buyers. In this book we focus on inter-organizational relationships where the specific purpose is innovation. By this definition we distinguish the networked innovation from collaboration and networking in general, although we point out that at the fuzzy front-end this purpose might be informal or undefined and the focus of collaboration or co-operation is quite broad. This definition equates also with a distinction between the intentionally created strategic networks and macro-level networks of organizations[34] and Chesbrough's original definition about Open Innovation as *purposive flows of knowledge*. Still, according to the innovation phase the purpose might vary from knowledge exploration to exploitation[35] and thereby we consider different networked innovation models through the innovation funnel. For the above described different inter-organizational innovation processes, we use the definition that Swan and Scarborough have proposed for networked innovation: *"Networked innovation occurs through relationships that are negotiated in an on-going communicative process, and which relies on neither market nor hierarchical mechanisms of control.*"[36] Similarly, from the viewpoint of organizational boundaries, networks are also defined as a hybrid model of organizing between hierarchies and markets.[37]

Furthermore, we define networked innovation to have the following characteristics:

(1) the specific shared vision about targets of the collaboration,
(2) the collaboration process has several levels of openness and it is seldom open for everyone, although multiple actors are involved in the innovation,
(3) the collaboration covers both the knowledge transfer (co-operation) and the co-creation activity between actors,
(4) there is a contract either written or otherwise formed between the involved actors, and
(5) the co-ordination is based on both control-governance and self-organization.

In contrast with the definition from Swan and Scarborough but similarly with the broader concepts of collaboration and co-operation, we consider all contractual inter-organizational innovation relationships belonging to models of networked innovation. Therefore, our definition includes, similarly to Swan and Scarborough, closed strategic business networks, joint ventures, and alliances, as well as more open models like communities, consortiums, and associations with more fuzzy targets — but then again, in these situations there is also a written or unstated agreement between the actors. Within this broader definition we highlight the importance of loosely coupled[38] networks and the fact that all these collaborative arrangements need to be connected to strategic knowledge management and business targets of a firm. Thus, we do not include all informal, haphazard interactions to networked innovation models as with contractual relationships we highlight that actors have agreed on co-operation in one way or other. Chapter 3 bridges the networked innovation concept with the knowledge-based approach of a firm and discusses the collaboration models and motivations to collaborate in more detail.

Due to its network position a firm typically has experiences from one collaboration type or certain collaboration partners, and thereby it has difficulties in managing several concurrent innovation models. For example, the R&D manager of a contract manufacturer described how strategic considerations about new partners and directions of collaboration may help the company to change its network position: *"Our typical innovation partners are the large customers, although the collaboration with them is often unidirectional and the customers indicate their will to own all rights regarding the process innovations. On the other hand, I have been thinking, how small start-up companies from the same industry sector could be interesting innovation and development partners. Through the collaboration with start-ups we would be able to take part in product development earlier and influence to the manufacturability of products."* In addition to better manufacturablity of the products the R&D manager envisaged that new business opportunities could be found through these collaboration relationships. He stated: *"If we are able to choose the winning start-up companies, which have or will in future have co-operation relationships with our main customers, we could also change our negotiation position to larger customers and strengthen our position at the commercialization phase."* Still, in such cases the payback period of networking investment is quite long and thereby firms are seldom able to intentionally develop such inter-organizational innovation relationships.

The above-described constant search for new opportunities also requires high frequency and range of possible interactions with several innovation partners and resources of firms are limited. Thus, the role of innovation inter-mediators, e.g. actors, which speeds up the quest for possible solutions to a customer's problems by drawing on broader sources of ideas and by helping inventors find firms interested in their inventions,[39] has been growing. In addition to online innovation platforms, other innovation intermediaries[40] such as consultants, research institutions, and technology parks offer companies new tools and mechanisms to navigate in the Bazaar of Opportunities. Moreover, our intention is especially to emphasize the ongoing communication, negotiation and contracting process, e.g. the interaction and the type of relationships between the actors. In the following chapters we consider the role of contracts in management of dynamic networked innovation, IP and knowledge, and thereby concepts of incomplete and evolving contracts are explored in Chapter 5. With these concepts we aim to highlight the supporting role of the contracting process as a device of mutually beneficial collaboration, not a document locked in a safe-box for potential court procedures.

Characteristics of Networked Innovation Systems

The innovation funnel (see Fig. 2.1) describes the linear innovation process starting from an idea, a problem, or a target at the fuzzy front-end going through the decisions, and ending up at a commercial solution. In practice multiple actors are involved in this innovation process, and they might have different ideas, problems, and targets — or at least they might all have different viewpoints of the same object. Furthermore, they make different decisions and finally end up at several solutions related to the object of innovation. As in the oriental bazaar, it is also important to remember that within the innovation funnel the relationship we have with one actor is connected to our relationship, and the relationship of our partners, with other actors. All these relationships are developed and co-evolve in connection with each other and the environment, e.g. the Bazaar itself. Together the interconnected relationships form the networked innovation system and business environment where the targets and the decisions of one actor always reflect those of other actors and the environment.[41]

Figure 2.3 presents how characteristics of networked innovation reflect the actor and the relationship level elements. At the network actor level

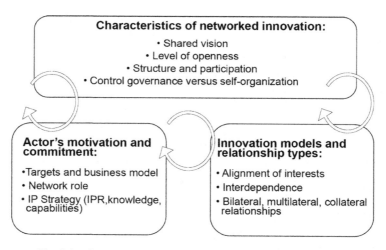

Fig. 2.3.   Characteristics and elements of networked innovation.

motivation and commitment to networked innovation is conducted from the actor's business targets, network role and IP Strategy (including both IPR and knowledge). These actor level elements are then connected to innovation models and relationships types. Thus, alignment of interests (e.g. actors' targets and business models) and interdependence (e.g. the network roles and IP of actors) have an influence on the ongoing negotiation and contracting process between the actors.

The next section, 'Management of Networked Innovation', goes through how the actor level elements should be considered. The type of relationships also has an influence on the functioning and processes within an innovation marketplace. Still, there is an intense debate[42] in network literature as to whether the tight relationships or loose relationships are more beneficial for innovativeness (Table 2.2). Our argument is that they are both needed for different purposes. Co-operation and collaboration within closed networks and tight relationships generate trust and facilitates learning and the exchange of tacit knowledge between actors. On the other hand, more "open", loosely coupled networks with many weak ties[43] and structural holes[44] may have more advantages due to the fact that network actors can build relationships with multiple unconnected actors and explore the brokerage opportunities.

Table 2.2. Typical characteristics of tight and loose relationships.

Tight relationships	Loose relationships
— Continuous or long-term term relationships (for instance customer–supplier relationships)	— More occasional or one-time relationships
— Trust and shared norms facilitate exchange of tacit knowledge and learning between actors	— Experiences that are too different, knowledge bases and missing "joint language" hinder knowledge exchange and learning
— Shared experiences and knowledge base form lock-ins and path-dependency	— Higher degree of weak ties and structural holes between actors increases diversity of viewpoints and knowledge
— Continuous co-operation and collaboration on several levels increases the complexity of relationships	— Occasional co-operation and collaboration moderate finding right parties

Besides the formal observable business relationships it is important to notice that underneath there are informal relationships between the actors[45] — and these social networks and interconnections may be even more of an efficient way to find new solutions and fill structural holes within a networked innovation process. Therefore, the strategic considerations are needed in order to also utilize these informal relationships between individuals. If informal social interconnections of employees are identified as an important source of new knowledge, the IP strategy of a company should clarify to its employees how and with whom these connections could and should be configured. Still, according to our interview study, most of the inter-organizational innovation relationships are still based on bilateral contractual relationships, although more than two actors are involved in the innovation process. Multilateral or collateral relationships and contracts[46] are more typically utilized in research than in R&D projects.

Management of Networked Innovation

Management of networked innovation is challenging and not so well understood. As described above, the main reason for that comes from the dynamics of networked innovation: objectives, actors and their roles — as well as relationships between the actors — may change depending on a network's development phases with respect to technology life cycle and innovation development process (Fig. 2.4).

In our framework illustrated in Fig. 2.4 the object of innovation is divided into two main dimensions: knowledge exploitation and exploration. The innovation process is simplified to consist of three phases: design, development and offering. The design phase is often called the fuzzy front-end and thereby it includes opportunity identification and analysis, as well as idea generation, enrichment and selection. The development phase starts from idea selection, and turns through concept development and research to development of new products. Finally, the offering phase connects to commercialization and business development. Respectively, knowledge exploration is linked to the fuzzy front-end of the innovation process, while knowledge exploitation is related to more concrete objects, e.g. development and offering phases.

The network actors can be organizations, organizational units, other groups of people, or even individuals. Still, the main focus of our book

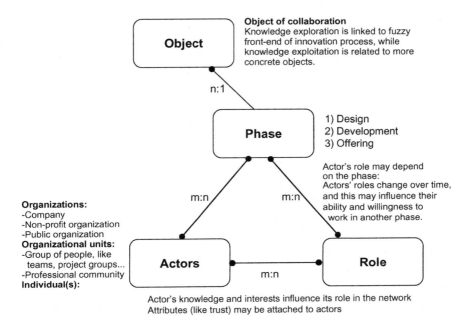

Fig. 2.4.   Dynamics of networked innovation process.

is on innovation relationships between organizations and the relationships between the individuals are not gathered in detail. Thus, network actors have to integrate internal and external interests at several levels of organization. The role of network actors may change according to the innovation phase, and this may influence their ability or willingness to collaborate. Dynamics of inter-organizational innovation occur when interdependent but independent network actors co-produce the innovation outcome. These innovation operations can therefore be expected to be nested and interacting. Consequently, progress within the innovation process may also require the reshaping of the network and transition from one phase to another always challenges the network.

Network dynamics and timing pose challenges to management, e.g. network actors can be at different phases of the innovation process. For instance, one of the network actors might consider the objective to be the exploration of new knowledge and future business opportunities, while others operate within the present business model and expect that the benefits will be realized faster. As the example below points out, the role and the network position of the firm are critical factors in the selection of suitable methods for innovation network development as well as knowledge or IP management.

A simple business case describes the dynamics of the innovation process between two companies (a developer and a customer). Together they were involved in a software solution (resource planning tool) development project for several months. As well as the solution development, related processes of the customer company were also re-engineered during the project. Later on, as already agreed at the beginning, the developer commercialized the solution and started to sell the solution to its customers. For the developer it was easier to turn its mindset from the development to the offering phase because it had several customer relationships related to the developed solution. Thus, the customer company, which was involved in the development process, became used to a tighter relationship than other customers and thereby formed some misconceptions about how the collaboration would continue, e.g. it expected that the employees of the developer would also participate in its implementation process as deeply as in development phase. In the words of the customer company: "*When moving away from the development stage there was a small torque within the contract negotiations about the service content related to solution at the offering phase.*" Still, both of the actors described the co-development process as successful — and pointed out how different network positions but aligning business operations within the same industrial sector enabled a win–win situation and learning between actors. The representative of the developer pointed out: "*Collaborative development of the solution was essential within our networked business environment — we did not have enough knowledge about user needs ourselves. On the other hand, we have shared a lot of our own expertise with the customer company and helped them to calculate the benefits to their customers.*" This example also highlights how within the same business case concurrently explicit IP (the solution) and tacit knowledge (know-how about industry sector and user needs of solution) was transferred and created between companies. The actors have a clear agreement about rights related to the explicit IP (the developed solution), but issues related to background information were at a quite general level. Still, both of the involved actors pointed out how the co-created tacit knowledge was valuable to them and they would not have been able to create it by themselves.

It is also important to realize that the elements of networked innovation are actors — like firms — that make their own decisions. Because an actor is a subject that makes its own decisions, it has an internal structure, own operation models and itself forms a sub-system of a networked innovation system. These decisions and operations of sub-systems cause emergent changes to their business environment and innovation networks. One of the interviewed managers representing a pioneer company in the field of Open Innovation, described how it is important to understand relationships behind the open innovation: *"If you engage in open innovation it's much more about these other players...what are their strategies? If we do this, what will they do — try to figure that out up front. It only makes sense if you really know the different players. If you do not know the player, however, it has no value. Because then you start dreaming."* The knowledge bases, the capabilities and experiences of actors, also have an influence on their operations and activity within networked innovation. Even the tacit knowledge at individual level has an important influence on a firm's capability to utilize the networked innovation. For example, one interviewee mentioned: *"You need people that are open to innovation, people that have been in the job for a couple of years that understand the business, that understand the technology, and then they can make the link."* The organizational capabilities related to collaboration, team working, and communication are required in order to participate in networked innovation processes. Such networking capabilities support creating and maintaining mutually beneficial innovation models and resultant trust between co-operation partners. Chapter 5 considers networking and contracting capabilities required for networked innovation in more detail.

At the relationship and collaboration level the management of networked innovation is all about balancing the different interests and the collaboration models. As pointed out already in Chapter 1 in our book the networked innovation is defined as a hybrid form of organizing, having elements from both hierarchies and markets. In other words, the network level co-ordination is based on both control-governance and self-organization. The balance between control governance and self-organization is different within different models of networked innovation. The continuum of networked innovation (Fig. 2.2) also presents this polarization; closed and external models of innovation are more tightly controlled, while collaborative and open models of innovation are based on self-organization developed by social capital, like shared norms and trust, between actors. Still, the collaborative and open models of innovation also have, either written or unstated, rules about co-operation as well as rights and responsibilities of actors.

Similarly to the innovation process itself, the networks involved in innovation are dynamic, evolving and emergent. Ring and Van de Ven proposed already in the 1990s a cyclical model of network formation, encompassing four distinctive activities taking place amongst networks partners — negotiations, commitments, executions, and assessments — each playing generative roles in the development of further network relations.[47] The contribution of their processual view is particularly valuable to deepening the understanding about the balance between control and self-organization within the management of networked innovation. It highlights the ways in which network partners adapt and re-evaluate their roles and commitment, as a response to decisions and acts of each other. The original process framework of Ring and Van de Ven focuses on formal, legal, and informal processes between the actors and therefore it forms an important base to our approach to management of networked innovation. Still, our intention is to also connect the knowledge and IP management perspectives to network formation and management as will be presented in Chapter 3. In Fig. 2.5 we describe the main steps towards collaborative, networked innovation and the tasks related to management of networked innovation, e.g. designing and orchestrating a global network of knowledge and the related business opportunities. Moreover, Chapters 4 and 5 focus especially on the legal aspect, e.g. the contracting process, within networked innovation, whereas formal and informal collaboration between the actors are gathered through the book.

As pointed out in the above quotation of the interviewee from the Open Innovation pioneer company, the choices and decisions of innovation partners can be perceived only when decision makers have an understanding about development agenda and strategic targets of partners. During all steps toward networked innovation (Fig. 2.5), a firm has to deal with explicit and tacit knowledge needs, the search for competencies, and the use of available intellectual property. Chapter 3 will further link these steps towards networked innovation to strategic knowledge management of a firm

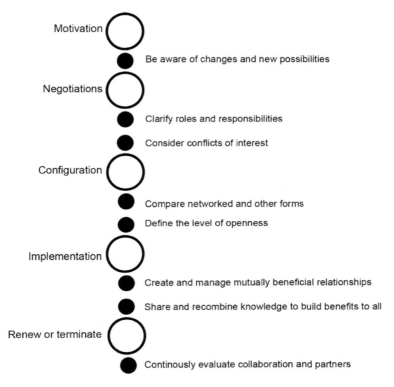

Fig. 2.5. Steps toward networked innovation.

and the decisions made within. (See particularly the discussion related to Fig. 3.1.)

Firstly, in order to foresee the development path of networked innovation it is critical to understand the targets and motivation of each involved actor. Furthermore, actors should be aware of changes and emerging new opportunities within the Bazaar of Opportunities. These considerations about motivation factors enable actors to answer questions like: "Why should we open the innovation process?" and "How open should we be?" Or when looking at the joint process from the viewpoint of other actors: "Why should they be open?" and "What are their interests and motivations to co-operate and give their best efforts?"

Secondly, through negotiations actors must clarify the roles and the responsibilities and consider conflicts of interest. Consequently, the involved actors search the answer to the questions: "To whom are we open?" and "On which issues we are open?" Based on the negotiations and contracting, the actors are able to, thirdly, configure an appropriate form of networked innovation and commit to it. Anyhow, actors have to anticipate comparisons between networked and other forms of innovation, create relationships in a mutually beneficial manner, and define the level of openness within their relationships. This could be done through answering the questions again from the viewpoints of other involved actors: "Who are they are willing to collaborate with?" and "Which issues are they prepared to share?"

Fourthly, the conscious and transparent steps toward networked innovation enable actors to share and recombine knowledge to build unique intellectual properties for all network actors at implementation and execution. Still, all involved actors should continuously evaluate collaboration and partners, in order to decide whether to renew or terminate the co-operation.

It is important to evaluate the targets and relationships regularly, while firms are sold and bought and their strategies change. Within the Bazaar of Opportunities an exit strategy is also needed. Firms and entrepreneurs might find themselves in situations whereby they have invested heavily in developing and building their businesses, but have failed to devote the necessary attention and effort to planning adequately for how they might capture value from the business. In other words, the traders in the oriental bazaar have been so keen on developing their stand and offerings that they have not thought over the possible changes in the bazaar or the possible influences on the demand of their products. Typically, the consideration of exit strategies often occurs at the least propitious times, such as when they are actually needed. Therefore, scenarios about the development paths of networked innovation and its actors should be identified beforehand in order to form an exit strategy and to consider the post-contractual situations.

No firms are in a position to manage the whole networked innovation system. However, every firm is able to manage its own position and role within the networked innovation environment. This requires only systematic and strategic analyses of the innovation environment, its actors and their targets as described by the former example about strategic consideration of the contract manufacturer. Based on these analyses the firm is able to make more conscious decisions, take calculated risks and leap at emerging opportunities. Naturally, the strategic analyses of innovation and business environment are challenging and time-consuming, thereby they require more open dialogue with innovation partners — especially with new partners with whom it might be hard to find a common language. Still, when you think about the oriental bazaar, you can easily understand how important it is to go through other shopping arcades regularly and discuss with other trading partners in order to keep in touch with the forthcoming changes. There again, you also know that in the oriental bazaar some of the sellers come from different cultures and have different approaches to bargaining as well as to contracting.

Openness of Innovation (Process)

Figure 2.2 described the continuum of networked innovation. In the literature of inter-organizational innovation, openness has already been given a variety of different meanings.[48] Firstly, the openness in innovation may refer to innovation activities and forms. It may also refer to the number of external sources of innovation, or to the flow of knowledge. Fourthly, openness may be related to innovation process and to innovation outcome which could be closed (proprietary) or open (available to others). As already pointed out the inter-organization innovation process has several levels of openness. Furthermore, the innovation process is seldom open for everyone, although multiple actors are involved in the innovation. Anyhow, the innovation process, e.g. the acts of accessing, acquiring, accumulating and generating knowledge, is changing. That change demands a rethinking of core principles related to the openness of innovation.

The coin always has two sides so the management of networked innovation process deals with a balance between openness towards new possibilities and closed development with specific targets. To guarantee the appropriate levels of IP protection and innovativeness, the network actors negotiate during the contracting process about what is open or shared and how open it is — and to whom. Respectively, strategic meaning of knowledge described by IP strategy is an important factor when deciding between the levels of openness and methods of IP protection. IP strategy formation is examined in Chapter 6.

The levels of openness within the innovation process can be determined by the availability, accessibility and responsiveness of the outcome.[49] Within the context of networked innovation we define availability as openness of input knowledge (both explicit and tacit) inside the network, while within this model the innovation process and its output are closed. Within this framework we consider input to gather both know-how and background information relevant to the subject of collaboration. Accessibility refers to openness of both input and process, e.g. agreement about co-development of knowledge between the network members. Work's responsiveness defines the potential for modifying it based on contributions from others. In our framework the broad responsiveness corresponds to modifiability, which refers to more transparent co-creation process, in which network members can take part in each other's development work.

In Table 2.3 we have summarized the levels of openness. In contrast with the criteria defined above — availability, accessibility and modifiability — closed, typically bilateral and public models of innovation, form the opposite end levels. "**Closed**" refers to an internal innovation process of a firm, where external knowledge or IP can be bought — or internal knowledge or IP sold within a frame of bilateral contracts. Innovation in the restricted levels of openness, namely in the levels "**available**" and "**usable**", calls for discussions between the actors, and discussions with restricted openness can be done only with known actors (the actors can be previously unknown but they become known during the work). "**Modifiable**" is the level of full openness but, in order to make a difference between situations where the openness applies only within a closed relationship or consortium and where the work is public (i.e. modifiable by all), there should be a separate level of openness for fully open innovation works with open access. Thus, "**public**" refers to the most open models of innovation, where both the input and the output are open, modifiable and exploitable to all participants. Participation is open but typically controlled, e.g. the innovation process might include unknown actors.

The presented levels of openness describe model situations.[50] In practice, innovation projects may include elements (input, process, output) from more than one characteristic level of openness, and the boundaries between neighbouring levels may not be unambiguous. However, if a project contains an element that differs more than one level from the basic characteristic of openness of the project, one may expect some kind of problems to appear either during or after the project work, e.g. collaboration or co-operation.

Table 2.3.   Levels of innovation openness.

Name of level	Closed	Available	Usable	Modifiable	Public
Key characteristics	IP transaction within closed, bilateral agreements	Collaborative models of innovation within bilateral or multilateral relationships			Public innovation processes within open networks
Input for innovation	Own R&D and sourced knowledge	Shared (readable) during the development work	Freely utilized within the consortium partners during the development work	Input is the object of co-development and freely modifiable by consortium members	Public (open and modifiable and exploitable by all)
Innovation process	Closed development	Closed own development, opened to network members based on own decision	Co-development between some or all members, network members have right to observe each others development work	Results of co-development work will be shared, network members take part to each others development work	Participation open but typically controlled (might include unknown actors)
Innovation outcome	Proprietary own IP and confidentiality	Proprietary own IP	Ownership and utilization of IP agreed between the network members	Joint IP (ownership and rights to utilize)	Public
Transparency	Non-transparent		Translucent		Transparent

Within the contracting process the input is typically guarded with clauses concerning protection and sharing of background information. On the other hand, as will be discussed in Chapter 4, the output of the joint-innovation process can be divided into "foreground" and "side ground" knowledge based on its relationship with the main activities of collaboration. In many cases the side ground knowledge might be even more relevant than the foreground, e.g. the interaction between parties creates new insights. Still, it is also more risky and harder to manage. The above scenario of the joint-development process of software solution between the developer and the customer is a good example of such a situation.

Here the customer company considered this side ground knowledge — the understanding of their customer's business — to be particularly valuable.

In order to better understand the differences between the levels it might be more appropriate to consider transparency[51] instead of openness. At the closed end the innovation process is non-transparent — neither input nor outcome knowledge is shared between the actors. Availability, accessibility and modifiability are all partly translucent innovation models. At the availability level the input knowledge is transparent, while the innovation process and output knowledge are non-transparent. At the availability level the openness means making an innovation process welcome input knowledge from a wide set of innovation makers. At the accessibility level the input knowledge is transparent, the innovation process is translucent, but the output knowledge is non-transparent. At the accessibility level openness stands for making input and process accessible to others. At the modifiability level the input knowledge, the innovation process, and the output are transparent to the involved network actors. At the modifiability level the openness is all about making an innovation process capable of debating distinct points of view and making the decisions related to the process transparent to involved actors. When transparency is present, knowledge flow must be reciprocal, e.g. both outside-in and inside-out innovation actions exist between the network actors. At the public end the innovation process is transparent, both the input and the output knowledge is shared between the involved actors. At the public level openness signifies making an innovation process available, even to unknown partners, and outcomes accessible to others as well. This kind of openness increases the viewpoints and through serendipity it enables the actors to find new innovative solutions.

It is important to recognize that transparency, e.g. openness, also has risks and costs that self-interested participants can, and will, seek to avoid in networked innovation environments. The levels of openness must be considered strategically and adjacently with a contracting process. One interviewee described how contracting about openness must ensure balance with sharing the results: "... *it of course depends on how much the input is from each company. There's always a balance of course, when one brings in a lot and the other less then you have to see how you can arrange it so that the one who brings in the most will get the most out of it.*" Within translucent innovation models there are several nuances of openness in particular that are defined by the agreements.

Chapter 5 of this book describes in detail how contracts are utilized as a means of private governance to agree on the level of openness within networked innovation. However, in a B-to-B context the motivations and the business purposes of the parties are the key questions within the negotiation and contracting process, while in a B-to-C context different personal intrinsic motivation factors — like enjoyment, peer recognition, or intellectual challenges — also have an influence and should be understood. Transparency of the innovation process between the involved actors typically increases social capital and trust between the actors, although these things may not exist at the beginning of collaboration. So, the evolving contracts might support business and innovation processes in order to reach the mutually beneficial collaboration models. In addition, while thinking about the contract as an evolving means of collaboration, the involved actors are able to bake the cake before sharing it. In other words, the actors can concentrate on the actual development work instead of contract negotiations.

At the public innovation models the contracts can also be supported by informal industry-specific rules of the game[52] or more specified rules of a community. Industry-specific rules and dominant logic have formed during the years, and they might also hinder the emergence of new innovative solutions. The community-specific rules are set by the whole community, its core actors or innovation inter-mediators, who are responsible for the facilitation process. The openness of innovation process and how it influences the dealing in the Bazaar of Opportunities will be discussed in more detail in Chapter 7.

Conclusions — Why Innovate Openly?

Why would a firm want its innovation operations to be transparent to others if they gain strategic advantages from cagey secrecy? Neither the question nor the answer is simple. The starting point for decision making about whether to utilize in-house development, sourcing of external knowledge or co-creation of knowledge is the motivation related to business opportunities. For a small or a big company the motivation factors are probably different, while their resources, knowledge bases and network positions are different. The motivation to innovate openly should be clearly connected with the strategic approach to knowledge. As in any business development case the motivation can be (i) either efficiency of present business process, e.g. cost reduction or (ii) search for new ideas, e.g. increasing the diversity of viewpoints and ideas. "Why" is the key word in the question in order to decide about openness of innovation and figure out possible collaboration models. As described in this chapter there are several models of more open and networked innovation.

In addition to the "why" in the above question, it is important also to consider the "if" sentence and the elements of strategic advantage and its sustainability. As pointed out, for instance by the concept of dynamic capabilities[53] in a fast-changing business environment, firms must continuously evaluate their competitive edge. Our empirical analyses already bring out that companies' thinking about their competitive edge — e.g. possibilities to open the innovation process — is changing. Therefore, the variety of networked innovation models has increased. The future competitive edge could be formed by the ability to integrate closed and open innovation processes within the Bazaar of interconnected Opportunities. Still, the right strategic choices to innovate more openly can make the firm a key player within networked innovation systems and help it to find its blue ocean.

To sum up the contents of this chapter, every actor is able to manage its own position and role within networked innovation system. This requires only systematic and strategic analyses of innovation environment, its actors and their targets. In the next chapter we consider the different networked innovation models in more detail and bridge the concept with a knowledge-based approach of a firm in order to research the motivation and opportunities.

Notes

1. Trott and Hartmann (2009) present a critical review of the Open Innovation concept and point out that most of the principles on which Open Innovation was founded existed long before the term for this new model was actually coined. According to them broad attention and intense debate around the concept can be based on its simplicity (it is appealing because it is simple and retains the linear notion of science to the marketplace). [Trott, P. and Hartmann, D. (2009). Why 'Open Innovation' is Old Wine in New Bottles, *International Journal of Innovation Management*, Vol. 13, pp. 715–736.]

2. [Chesbrough, H. (2006) 'Open Innovation: A Paradigm for Understanding Industrial Innovation', in Chesbrough, H., Vanhaverberke, W. and West, J. (eds), *Open Innovation: Researching a New Paradigm*, Oxford University Press, Boston, pp. 1–12.]

3. Huizingh (2011) has given reasons for what he thinks has made Chesbrough's works so attractive. Firstly, Chesbrough assigned a single term to a collection of developments. Secondly, the timing was good and coincided with several business management trends and the explosion of the internet. [Huizingh, E. (2011). Open Innovation: State of the Art and Future Perspectives, *Technovation*, Vol. 31, pp. 2–9.]

4. For instance with the concept of business ecosystem some authors have highlighted the need for systemic thinking. The concept of ecosystem has its origins in Natural Science (where Maturana and Varela introduced the term autopoiesis (self-creating) to describe the dynamic nature of living systems), and Moore (1996) and Iansiti and Levien (2004) are the well-known authors and initiators within business management literature. The Business Ecosystem approach points out the co-evolution of firms and their networked environment. [Maturana, H. & Varela, F. (1980). *Autopoiesis and Cognition: the Realization of the Living*, D. Reidel Publishing Company, Holland, Moore, J.F. (1996). *The Death of Competition. Leadership and Strategy in the Age of Business Ecosystems.* Harper Business, New York; Iansiti, M. and Levien, R. (2004). *The Keystone Advantage. What the New Dynamics of Business Ecosystems Mean for Strategy, Innovation, and Sustainability*, Harvard Business School Press, Boston.]

5. The definition is modified from Paasi and Valkokari (2010). [Paasi, J. and Valkokari, P. (eds) (2010). *Elucidating the Fuzzy Front End — Experiences from the INNORISK Project*, VTT Publications 743, Espoo.]

6. [Apilo, T. (2010). *A Model for Corporate Renewal. Requirements for Innovation Management*, VTT Publications 750, Espoo.]

7. [Paasi, J. and Valkokari, P. (eds) (2010). *Elucidating the Fuzzy Front End — Experiences from the INNORISK Project*, VTT Publications 743, Espoo.]

8. iTunes is an example of a huge global success that rarely occurs. However, on a smaller scale there are lots of (local) success stories that are based on smaller or larger innovations both in technical and business model domains. Typically we just do not hear about these success stories, because many companies, especially in the field of service business, are just happy to be successful locally, without any interest in expansion of the business onto national or global levels that would bring their cases publicity and a wider audience. Still, to be successful in local markets the firm usually needs to have some competitive advantage brought by innovation. And in local markets, one should not underestimate business model innovations as the key factor for competitive advantage.

9. [Hamel, G. (2007). *The Future of Management*, Harvard Business School Press, Boston.]

10. Stated originally by Thomas Edison: "Genius is one percent inspiration, ninety-nine percent perspiration". According to Wikipedia this was a spoken statement (c. 1903); published in Harper's Monthly (September 1932).

11. According to Wikipedia this famous western metaphor was first recorded in the twelfth century and attributed to Bernard of Chartres. Anyhow, it was famously uttered by seventeenth-century scientist Isaac Newton ["Standing on the shoulders of giants", Wikipedia, http://en.wikipedia.org/wiki/Standing_on_the_shoulders_of_giants (Accessed on 20 February 2012.)]

12. For more details see www.uusitehdas.fi, www.protomo.fi and www.demola.fi.

13. Chesbrough (2003) visualized the Open Innovation as a funnel which enables the run of ideas along the innovation process from the fuzzy front-end to commercial products in markets. [Chesbrough, H. (2003). *Open Innovation: The New Imperative for Creating and Profiting from Technology*, Harvard Business School Press, Boston.]

14. The example idea is fictitious although the names in the example are real and the case itself is such that it could have taken place.

15. [Luoma, T., Paasi, J. and Valkokari, K. (2010). Intellectual Property in Inter-organizational Relationships — Findings from an Interview Study, *International Journal of Innovation Management*, Vol. 14, pp. 399–414.]

16. Chesbrough (2003) highlighted that, because "not all the best people are not working for you", companies need to be enriched by new external knowledge outside the company. [Chesbrough, H. (2003). *Open Innovation: The New Imperative for Creating and Profiting from Technology*, Harvard Business School Press, Boston.]

17. One factor behind the phenomenon is that within these sectors problem description and solution can be more easily codified.

18. Free software, which may or may not be distributed free of charge, is distinct from freeware which, by definition, does not require payment for use. On the other hand, open source software can be utilized according to different licencing terms.

19. [Valkokari, K., Paasi, J., Luoma, T. and Lee, N. (2009) Beyond Open Innovation — Concept of Networked Innovation, in *Proc. of the 2nd ISPIM Innovation Symposium*, New York.]

20. A pioneer in approach that emphasizes lead-customer involvement in new product development is Eric von Hippel (1988). He emphasized how the challenge in strategic thinking is to find innovative ways of *co-creating value with customers*, a technique for finding unique competitive advantage. Von Hippel (2005) has covered the user-centric innovation also in his book *Democratizing Innovation*. In accordance with the principles of open source this book can be downloaded from the web under a "Creative Commons license". On the other hand, Victor and Boynton (1998) provide a useful historical framework for a reintegration of organization, work, and learning. They identify five types of work in the history of industrial production: craft, mass production, process enhancement, mass customization, and co-configuration. Multiple collaborating producers that need to operate in networks within or between organizations; mutual learning from interactions between the parties involved in the configuration actions. [von Hippel, E. (1988). *On the Sources of Innovation*, Oxford University Press; von Hippel, E. (2005). *Democratizing Innovation*, MIT Press,

Boston; Victor, B. and Boynton, A.C. (1998). *Invented Here: Maximizing Your Organization's Internal Growth and Profitability*, Harvard Business Press, Boston.]

21. Dyer (2000) point out how competitive advantage is jointly created and shared among a *team of enterprises working together in intimate, trust-based relationships* to develop, produce and deliver complex products. Supplier involvement and co-design are other key concepts related to an extended enterprise approach. [Dyer, J.H. (2000). *Collaborative Advantage: Winning Through Extended Enterprise Supplier Networks*, Oxford University Press.]

22. According to Das and Teng (2002) alliance constellations differ from simple bilateral, dyadic alliances because they are a "collection of several alliances" among players in a certain industry. Strategic alliances are inter-firm cooperative arrangements between two firms, aimed at achieving the strategic objectives of the partners. [Das, T. K. and Teng, B. (2002). Alliance Constellations: A Social Exchange Perspective, *Academy of Management Review*, Vol. 27, pp. 445–456.]

23. [Antikainen, M. (2011). *Facilitating Customer Involvement in Collaborative Online Innovation Communities*, VTT Publications 760, Espoo.]

24. Originally proposed by Ellis *et al.* (1991), 3Cs implicating communication, coordination and cooperation. In both the cooperative and coordinative business networks participants are *independent organizations*, who come together for a specific purpose. In a collaborative network the participants are *interdependent* and co-creation occurs in several levels of network organizations. [Ellis, C.A., Gibbs, S.J. and Rein, G.L. (1991). Groupware — Some Issues and Experiences, *Communications of the ACM*, Vol. 34, pp. 38–58.]

25. [Antikainen, M. (2011). *Facilitating Customer Involvement in Collaborative Online Innovation Communities*, VTT Publications 760, Espoo.]

26. [Dillenbourg, P. (1999). 'What Do You Mean by Collaborative Learning?', in Dillenbourgh, P. (ed.), *Collaborative-learning: Cognitive and Computational Approaches*, Elsevier, Oxford, pp. 1–19.]

27. The term "social capital" initially appeared in community studies. Nahapiet and Goshal (1998) suggest that in the context of exploration of the role of social capital in the creation of intellectual capital, it is useful to consider the social capital in terms of three clusters: the structural, the relational, and the cognitive dimensions of social capital. [Nahapiet, J. and Goshal, S. (1998). Social Capital, Intellectual Capital and the Organizational Advantage, *Academy of Management Review*, Vol. 23, pp. 242–266.]

28. Demil and Lecocq (2006) propose how open source projects illustrate a new more open governance structure that they label "bazaar governance". They distinguished bazaar governance from other networking models with three criteria: anonymity, absence of partner selection process and no requisite long-term engagement. Firstly, a bazaar is made up of anonymous agents who do not know each other. Secondly, a major difference between a network and a bazaar concerns the selection of members. In the bazaar, membership is open (Lee and Cole, 2003), because nobody can prohibit access to an open source community and no one can appropriate property rights over the open source product, resulting in a principle of non-excludability even though a small number of well-known agents can emerge. The third main criterion that distinguishes a bazaar from a network relates to the different timeframes of actor relations. Where a network calls for long-term engagement to minimize opportunism, the bazaar does not presuppose any

long-term engagement or strong ties among actors. [Demil, B. and Lecocq, X. (2006). Neither Market nor Hierarchy nor Network: The Emergence of Bazaar Governance, *Organization Studies*, Vol. 27, pp. 1447–1466.] [Lee, G.K. and Cole, R.E. (2003). From a Firm-based to a Community-based Model of Knowledge Creation: The Case of the Linux Kernel Development, *Organization Science*, Vol. 14, pp. 633–649.]

29. Wenger (2007) defines *communities of practice* as groups of people who share a concern or a passion for something they do and learn how to do it better as they interact regularly. According to him, communities of practice have three critical elements: a domain, a community, and a practice. Firstly, a community of practice has an identity defined by a shared domain of interest. Membership therefore implies a commitment to the domain, and therefore a shared competence that distinguishes members from other people. Secondly, in pursuing their interest in their domain, members engage in collaboration — e.g. they have joint activities and discussions, help each other, share information — and thereby form a community. Thirdly, members of a community of practice are practitioners. They develop a shared repertoire of resources: experiences, stories, tools, ways of addressing recurring problems — in short a shared practice. [Wenger, E. (2007). *Communities of Practice. A Brief Introduction*, http://www.ewenger.com/theory/ (Accessed on 22 February 2012.)]

30. The concept of *crowdsourcing* is defined as an act a company or institution taking a function once performed by employees and outsourcing it to an undefined (and generally large) network of people in the form of an open call (Howe, 2006). [Howe, J. (2006). The Rise of Crowdsourcing, *Wired*, Vol. 14, pp. 176–183.]

31. Bauwens (2009) defines (1) *"peer to peer" production* as a relational dynamic that emerges through distributed networks. Distributed (2) networks are networks in which the structure is such that agents and nodes can take independent action and maintain relationships "on their own", i.e. through voluntary self-aggregation and "without prior permission". It is important to look at such a network from the point of view of the human: what matters is not the purity of the structure of the distributed network, (3) but whether or not, "in the last analysis", such self-aggregation is made possible. [Bauwens, M. (2009). Class and Capital in Peer Production, *Capital & Class*, Vol. 33, No. 1, pp. 121–141. Also available online at http://www.thefreelibrary.com/.]

32. [Luoma, T., Paasi, J. and Valkokari, K. (2010). Intellectual Property in Inter-organizational Relationships — Findings from an Interview Study, *International Journal of Innovation Management*, Vol. 14, pp. 399–414.]

33. Knowledge Intensive Business Service (KIBS).

34. Möller and Rajala (2007) define strategic nets as intentionally created network organizations. Within their theoretical framework three ideal types — current business nets trying primarily to achieve efficiency gains through demand-supply co-ordination, business renewal nets looking for local business process improvements by incremental innovation and change, and emerging new business nets seeking to create more effective technological applications and business concepts by means of radical innovation and business system change — are distinguished as strategic net types. [Möller, K. and Rajala, A. (2007). Rise of Strategic Nets — New Modes of Value Creation, *Industrial Marketing Management*, Vol. 36, pp. 895–908.]

35. [March, J.G. (1991). Exploration and Exploitation in Organizational Learning, *Organization Science*, Vol. 2, pp. 427–440.]

36. Swan and Scarborough (2005) refer to Phillips *et al.* (2000) and Hardy *et al.* (2003) for former definitions. [Swan, J. and Scarborough, H. (2005). The Politics of Networked Innovation, *Human Relations*, Vol. 58, pp. 913–943; Phillips, N., Lawrence, T.B. and Hardy, C. (2000). Inter-organizational Collaboration and the Dynamics of Institutional Fields, *Journal of Management Studies*, Vol. 37, pp. 23–43; Hardy, C., Phillips, N. and Lawrence, T.B. (2003). Resources, Knowledge and Influence: The Organizational Effects of Inter-organizational Collaboration, *Journal of Management Studies*, Vol. 40, pp. 321–347.]

37. Similarly, networks are typically defined as hybrid-organizations between markets and hierarchies. Markets are characterized by competitive relationships and suppliers, while the price is the central criteria. On the other hand, hierarchies refer to firms, where controlled relationship, authority, clear structure and decision model are the key characteristics.

38. The interpretation of loosely coupled systems was first proposed by Orton and Weick (1990). According to them, the extent of coupling across organizational subunits is determined by their degree of responsiveness and distinctiveness: If there is neither responsiveness nor distinctiveness, the system is not really a system and it can be defined as a non-coupled system. If there is responsiveness without distinctiveness, the system is tightly coupled. If there is distinctiveness without responsiveness, the system is decoupled. If there is both distinctiveness and responsiveness, the system is loosely coupled. [Orton, J.D. and Weick, K.E. (1990). Loosely Coupled Systems: A Reconceptualization, *Academy of Management Review*, Vol. 15, pp. 203–223.]

39. [Chesbrough, H. (2006). 'Open Innovation: A new Paradigm for Understanding Industrial Innovation', in Chesbrough, H. Vanhaverbeke, W. and West, J. (eds), *Open Innovation: Researching a New Paradigm*, Oxford University Press. pp. 1–14.]

40. Lopez and Vanhaverbeke (2010) divide the roles of innovation inter-mediators into: Innovation consultants, Innovation traders, Innovation Incubator and Innovation mediator. Furthermore, they suggest that innovation intermediary functions might be grouped under three general headings: (1) connection, (2) collaboration and support and (3) provision of technological services. [Lopez, H. and Vanhaverbeke, W. (2010). Connecting Open and Closed Innovation Markets: A Typology Intermediaries, in *DIME conference organizing for networked innovation*, http://emma.polimi.it/emma/events/ dimeconference/attachments/henry%20lopezvega.pdf (Accessed 25 November 2009).]

41. [Valkokari, K. (2009). *Yhteisten tavoitteiden ja jaetun näkemyksen muodostuminen kolmessa erityyppisessä verkostossa*, VTT Publications 715, Espoo]

42. Valkokari, 2009 (*ibid.*) and Valkokari *et al.* 2009. [Valkokari, K., Paasi, J., Luoma, T. and Lee, N. (2009) Beyond Open Innovation — Concept of Networked Innovation, in *Proc. of the 2nd ISPIM Innovation Symposium*, New York.]

43. Originally, Granovetter (1973) considered "strength of weak" ties in inter-personal relationships. Later on, the concept of weak ties has also been utilized at an inter-organizational level. [Granovetter, M.S. (1973). The Strength of Weak Ties, *The American Journal of Sociology*, Vol. 78, pp. 1360–1380.]

44. Since Burt's (1992) configuration of a concept based on sociological theory the study of structural holes spans the fields of sociology, economics, and computer science. According to Burt (1992, 2004) actors, who occupy bridging positions between groups in a network are at a "higher risk of having good ideas". Also, within strategic and

innovation network formation the concept has been utilized to define possibilities to new connections between actors. [Burt, R.S. (1992). *Structural Holes: The Social Structure of Competition*, Harvard University Press, Boston; Burt, R.S. (2004). Structural Holes and Good Ideas, *American Journal of Sociology*, Vol. 110, pp. 349–399.]

45. Moliterno and Mahony (2010) highlight that organizations are multilevel systems. According to them network theory of the organization should therefore be multilevel in its scope, considering how networks at one level of the organizational system influence networks at higher and/or lower levels. [Moliterno, T.P. and Mahony, D.M. (2011). Network Theory of Organization: A Multilevel Approach, *Journal of Management*, Vol. 37, No. 2, pp. 443–467.]

46. Bader (2006) described different collaborative contractual settings as bilateral (one-to-one), multilateral (one-to-many) and collateral (many-to-many) [Bader, M.A. (2006). *Intellectual Property Management in R&D Collaborations: The Case of the Service Industry Sector*, Physica-Verlag, Heidelberg.]

47. [Ring, P.S. and van de Ven, A.H. (1994). Development Processes of Co-operative Inter-organizational Relationships, *The Academy of Management Review*, Vol. 19, pp. 90–118.]

48. [Paasi, J., Valkokari, K., Erkkilä, J., Hakulinen, J., Kirveskoski, K. and Räsänen, V. (2011). Levels of Openness in Open Innovation, *Proceedings of 2011 ISPIM Conference*, Hamburg.]

49. In his article Maxwell (2006) points out that due to the increasing penetration of information and communications technology, availability of digital information has been growing exponentially. According to him the open model of value creation rests on several assumptions: (1) creative acts take place for a variety of reasons; (2) the value of a creative work can be increased by sharing the work and allowing, even encouraging, more potential innovators to contribute to its development; and (3) economic value can be enhanced by such sharing. [Maxwell, E. (2006). Open Standards, Open Source and Open Innovation. Harnessing the Benefits of Openness, *MIT Press*, Issue 3, pp. 119–176.]

50. The model for the levels of openness is configured and tested with two case companies and presented in our paper Paasi *et al.* (2011). The model for the levels of openness in open innovation is based on a very theoretical (and nearly mathematical) approach towards the openness, despite the fact that it has its roots in the extant literature of open innovation — 2X2 framework presented by Huizingh (2011) and three levels presented by Maxwell (2006). Still, the boundaries between two neighbouring levels of openness are not so clear in practice than in a simple theoretical model. [Paasi, J., Valkokari, K., Erkkilä, J., Hakulinen, J., Kirveskoski, K. and Räsänen, V. (2011). Levels of Openness in Open Innovation, *Proceedings of 2011 ISPIM Conference*, Hamburg; Huizingh, E. (2011). Open Innovation: State of the Art and Future Perspectives, *Technovation*, Vol. 31, pp. 2–9; Maxwell, E. (2006). Open Standards, Open Source and Open Innovation. Harnessing the Benefits of Openness, *MIT Press*, Issue 3, pp. 119–176.]

51. Lamming *et al.* (2001) have applied the metaphor of how much light (information) can shine through a mineral (the space between two organizations — the relationship). In their work, the concept of transparency is argued to be an element of a relationship instead of part of a property of a system. Thus, different degrees of transparency may be present in a buyer–supplier relationship. Instead of being completely transparent,

relationships may be translucent in some respects, information may be only partially shared or opaque, or information may not be shared at all. Also, Hultman and Axelsson (2007) have explored and extended the concept of transparency in marketing management research. They outlined four types of transparency and extended them by adding three related facets. Their findings indicated that increased transparency in buyer–supplier relationships brings about not only positive, but also some negative effects. [Lamming, R.C., Caldwell, N.D., Harrison, D.A. and Phillips, W. (2001). Transparency in Supply Relationships: Concept and Practice, *Journal of Supply Chain Management*, Vol. 37, pp. 4–10; Hultman, J. and Axelsson, B. (2007). Towards a Typology of Transparency for Marketing Management Research, *Industrial Marketing Management*, Vol. 36, Issue 5, pp. 627–635.]

52. Dominant logic of the industry describes the shared insights about success factors and rules within the industry (Lane *et al.*, 2001). When firms have similar operational priorities or dominant logics knowledge transfer or co-creation is easier for them. Dominant logic is thereby connected to absorptive capacity of firm. Cohen and Levinthal (1990) define absorptive capacity as the firm's ability to learn from external knowledge through processes of knowledge identification, assimilation and exploitation. [Lane, J., Salk, J.E. and Lyles, M.A. (2001). Absorptive Capacity, Learning, and Performance in International Joint Ventures, *Strategic Management Journal*, Vol. 22, pp. 1139–1161; Cohen, M. and Levinthal, D.A. (1990). Absorptive Capacity: A New Perspective on Learning and Innovation, *Administrative Science Quarterly*, Vol. 35, pp. 128–152.]

53. Teece *et al.* (1997) define dynamic capability more broadly as "the firm's ability to integrate, build and re-configure internal and external competencies to address rapidly changing environments". [Teece D.J., Pisano, G. and Shuen, A. (1997) Dynamic Capabilities and Strategic Management, *Strategic Management Journal*, Vol. 18, pp. 509–533.]

Chapter 3

Collaboration Models and Knowledge Management

Within the Bazaar of Opportunities firms' possibilities and motivation for business development and innovation is always connected to both external and internal factors. Networked innovation environments are one-of-a-kind from every actor's viewpoint. Each firm also has its own set of knowledge, part of which might be protected with intellectual property rights (IPR). One of the typical problems — likely to be familiar to all readers — is that the value of potential knowledge or IPR seems to be extremely hard, if not impossible, to estimate with any reasonable accuracy. Notwithstanding the inherent challenges in valuing long-term research or development projects with payoffs directed well into the future, the perceived problems in knowledge management and valuation may also partly reflect the fact that the broader objectives for different knowledge are not adequately defined in a company's strategy. The key questions in the valuation of innovation initiatives should always be: "What do we hope to gain from this effort?" and "How does that support our present and future business development targets?" Chapter 6 goes through these key questions related to IP strategy and valuation within networked innovation. In this chapter we will reflect on how the knowledge type, the development targets and motivation influence the choice of collaboration models.

In order to study the motivation of network actors and its influences to the choice of collaboration models, this chapter bridges the concept of networked innovation with strategic knowledge management. A strategic approach to knowledge management[1] is needed in order to describe what a firm knows and must know about its present networked business environment and competitive position. In order to be successful in the Bazaar of Opportunities the strategic considerations about the future competitive edge form an important groundwork. However, our intention is to highlight the fact that you must consider both the internal factors as well as external drivers in order to define the game, the players, your own position and possibilities to set the rules of the game within the Bazaar of Opportunities.

Strategic Dimensions of Knowledge

The IP strategy of a firm points out the importance of orientation towards understanding what knowledge is strategic and why — as discussed in more detail within Chapter 6. Most of the managers recognize the multidimensionality of knowledge and are familiar with a well-known division between the explicit and tacit dimensions of knowledge, which was originally made by Polanyi in the 1960s.[2] Still, knowledge management in firms often focuses on explicit knowledge and IPR. Explicit knowledge has been or can be articulated, codified, and stored in certain media. Therefore, it can be more easily transmitted to others. The concept of tacit knowledge refers to knowledge that cannot be codified and is difficult to communicate to the rest of the organization. Furthermore, tacit organizational knowledge is often embedded in complex organizational routines and developed from experiences. This tacit component of organizational knowledge is also connected to an organization's capabilities, e.g. its abilities to utilize its knowledge to perform its actions and gain potential competitive advantages. Still, regarding the knowledge as well as capabilities is more important to examine the connectivity and contradictions between them than analyse independent capabilities. Moreover, external connections to customers, partners, suppliers, and investors are important for the success of organizations; the knowledge of their perceptions forms an important part of the assessment of an organization's capability. Thus, understanding of the conditions of knowing is closely connected to the tacit dimension of knowledge. That makes it challenging to transfer tacit knowledge from one place to another, i.e. across the borders of a team, a firm, or an industry.

According to our broad definition as presented in the introduction the term IP includes both the IPR and partly tacit dimension of knowledge or other intangible resources.[3] Still, a strategic approach to organizational

Table 3.1.   Strategic knowledge dimensions.[4]

Knowledge type	Present core-competences	Unique knowledge	Innovative, future knowledge
Strategic meaning	Minimum scope and level to be competitive (differentiation is limited)	Unique knowledge of particular firm and its partners	Orientation to the future business models

knowledge emphasizes that firms must intentionally analyse their knowledge base and its importance to business development, competitive advantages, and innovativeness. Hence, the strategic dimensions of knowledge as presented in Table 3.1 describe the connection between the firm's strategic position and its knowledge base. A firm's knowledge position within the networked systems of innovation defines that firm's competitive position related to customers, partners and competitors.

Firstly, the knowledge and core-competences based on present IP form the basic level of knowing within an industry and a value chain. This kind of knowledge is also connected to dominant logic industry, the knowledge that is assumed to be "worth knowing" within an industry.[5] Competitors also have most of this knowledge and thereby the differentiation is limited and this knowledge does not offer a competitive edge to a firm. In other words, this is the knowledge an actor should at the very least have in order to act in the Bazaar. Secondly, in order to be competitive firms and networks need other relevant — often tacit — knowledge to form a unique knowledge base and differentiate themselves from competitors. The tacit form of knowledge tends more easily to be unique and difficult to imitate,[6] and thereby it can form a more sustainable competitive edge. The key ingredients of such unique knowledge are connected to organizational capabilities and processes, like networking and contracting capabilities or learning ability – and the related processes like networking process. With this unique knowledge an actor sticks out from the crowd in the Bazaar. Thirdly, a strategic approach to knowledge management highlights how the future-oriented, innovative knowledge enables organizations to focus on a search for new knowledge and business opportunities. This future orientation means that an actor is having discussions and bargaining with several other actors within the Bazaar all the time.

The concept of networked innovation brings out that it is important to understand how the innovative, future knowledge is constructed through the choices and decisions made by the actors within the present value networks and innovation systems as pointed out in Chapter 2. This innovative knowledge related to future business opportunities and competitive advantages enables a firm to change the rules of the game itself, although it cannot be owned or protected by single firms as the present core-competences based on the IPR. As one of the interviewees pointed out, the firm's speed of innovation process and its position as a forerunner enables it to utilize more open innovation: *"You do open innovation if you can run faster than the others. So if you stay on top of the game yourselves then that is OK."* The starting point is to picture the present and future value networks — when you are able to understand the networked innovation system you can more easily orchestrate it.

The strategic knowledge environment of an industry can be viewed as the sum of interactions and operations of individual firms within the networked system of innovation, e.g. the Bazaar of Opportunities. These interactions and operations are based on knowledge strategies of firms. Where the strategic knowledge base is strong, the firms can focus on enabling knowledge sharing and distribution, and ensuring that learning is focused on maintaining a strong competitive knowledge-position. In other words, you and your partners have a good position within the Bazaar and can strengthen your position by intentional collaboration with other actors. Where opportunities abound, firms can focus on exploiting the firm's knowledge platform by deriving new products or services from or by locating new markets for its knowledge. Where weaknesses exist, firms must focus on acquiring knowledge, for example through training, recruiting, or alliances and networks.[7] In other words, you need new knowledge and partners to develop your business in the Bazaar, but due to a weak knowledge position you are not able to set the rules of co-operation.

Knowledge Sharing and Protection

In order to form their own unique knowledge base and competitive advantages, firms must consider internal factors as well as external drivers within the networked environment. Furthermore, firms must have a balance between knowledge sharing and protection. However, knowledge sharing and protection is connected to a firm's opportunities and willingness to collaborate. The strategic knowledge dimension influences appropriateness of knowledge sharing and protection methods within innovation activities. The summary of protection methods is presented in Chapter 1 (see Table 1.1). The methods for protecting knowledge have been divided into three categories according to their formality: formal protection methods often called intellectual property rights (IPR), contractual (semi-formal) protection methods, and informal protection methods.[8]

Present knowledge and core-competences can most probably be protected by formal protection methods, like patents, copyrights, and design rights. Thus, in this case when external actors are required firms typically choose closed collaboration models (see Table 2.1 about levels of openness). A firm's unique knowledge base, and its tacit components in particular, is typically protected by semi-formal contractual or informal methods. Accordingly, the future-oriented innovative knowledge is also typically protected by informal methods, like trust and loyalty building among personnel and partners. Furthermore, the openness of collaboration should be defined as non-transparent by agreements, if there is a risk to knowledge leaps. One of the interviewees pointed out the importance of understanding and protecting the unique knowledge base in order to sustain a competitive edge: *"The only thing is, which I always point out at the beginning of the co-operation, that you have to figure out first, is what is absolutely core (unique) to you — something that you will never share."*

In the present networked business environment firms are not able to construct this knowledge alone and, therefore, networking and contracting capabilities are required in order to define the right level of openness. With the informal protection methods and intentional knowledge sharing, a firm always has opportunities to influence the evolution of its environment. It is important to discover that knowledge sharing and publishing can also be used as a method of influencing environment or knowledge protection. Knowledge sharing or publishing prevent others from appropriating the knowledge, thus confirming the freedom of action for the firm. Publishing can also be used to prevent other companies from claiming patents in the same area. A representative of a large system provider described how publishing is a typical way to protect solutions which cannot be formally protected by patents: "*...everyday decisions are made to ensure that something is published in order to shorten the R&D time and to prevent others from applying for a patent...*" In addition, large firms also utilize opening their innovations to strengthen their position and construct their brand. For example, quite recently the largest seller of athletic footwear and athletic apparel in the world, Nike, announced its commitment to open innovation and sustainability, e.g. how it shares an "Environmental Apparel Design Tool" with other companies and designers.[9] This sharing of a design tool probably supported Nike's positive image and leading position in the Bazaar. However, it had very little, if any, direct impacts on Nike's return on investment and its actual business model.

Innovative firms with the best learning and absorbing capability (i.e. the ability to recognize the value of new external information, assimilate it and apply it to commercial ends)[10] will however benefit most from the Bazaar of Opportunities. Still, quite often the firms are missing the systemic management and control especially with future oriented knowledge and its protection or sharing. Knowledge and future-focused organizations seek opportunities to maximize their innovativeness through co-operation or collaboration among actors of the Bazaar in order to create knowledge synergies and new business opportunities. For the future competitive edge it is also important to identify the structural holes and white spots within the networked innovation. In other words, the actors in the Bazaar must constantly consider if there are missing links between them and other actors — or free space for new selling counters between the arcades.

The key is to re-think the Bazaar, the connections between actors, and your own offerings and position within the Bazaar. You must also be able to raise the questions related to missing knowledge on a regular basis, e.g.: "*What don't we know?*" and "*What should we know?*" Furthermore, you must consider who you are not collaborating with but should be, in order to find new opportunities and sense the changes within the networked innovation environment.

Strategizing Networked Innovation

Within networked and distributed innovation environments, firms must constantly look for and decide between different co-operation or collaboration models in order to gain required IP and knowledge. The basic elements of

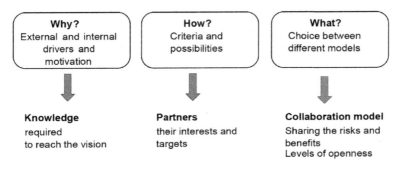

Fig. 3.1.   Elements of the decision-making process.

the decision-making process are described in Fig. 3.1. As in the general decision-making process, the basic elements and related key questions are:

(1) analyses about motivation and drivers, e.g. **why?**,
(2) scenarios about possibilities and criteria, e.g. **how?** and
(3) negotiation of collaboration models, e.g. **what?**

In practice, these elements of the internal decision-making process are also connected to the steps towards collaboration within a networked innovation system (see Fig. 2.5).

A firm's IP strategy should form the guidelines to decision making between different collaboration models, so while it is linked to a firm's network role and the business model it clarifies the motivations for collaboration. This strategic link between business model and IP management is considered in more detail later in this chapter. The motivation behind the knowledge acquiring, accessing, and collaboration could be in:

- searching of new knowledge or for new business opportunities,
- improving operational efficiency of R&D,
- commercialization of innovation,
- participating in industrial standardization,
- influencing the business environment and choices of other actors (for instance to increase own technology diffusion, market share or brand value), or
- interactive learning with no direct commercial targets (associations, forums, benchmarking of best practices, etc.).

Innovation is also closely connected to the organization's ability[11] to sense the emerging opportunities, to see the coming-into-being of the new and to pro-actively address the rapidly changing environment. However, a firm's current position and its history define its possible development paths.[12] In other words, a seller in the oriental bazaar cannot easily change its offering or place of sale overnight — it takes time to look for other possibilities, familiarize with new customers, competitors, and complementary products. Based on the analyses of external drivers and internal factors a firm should be able to form a vision for the future and turn it into a credible development agenda. The IP strategy of a firm is an important guideline for these analyses and decisions. The analyses of required IP, knowledge and their type (well-documented, explicit knowledge or IPR versus tacit knowledge) influences the collaboration model, whether the IP is easily transferred or co-creation required in order to manage the tacit knowledge. Secondly, the firm has to define the criteria and the possibilities to access and acquire the required knowledge, e.g. external knowledge sources and collaboration with partners. This also assumes picturing the network and defining the firm's negotiation position, targets, and interests of possible partners and connections between them.

Furthermore, the success in innovation process requires an ability to communicate the development agenda and the strategic targets to other members of networked innovation as described also in Chapter 2 (see Fig. 2.5). Both the internal and external communication and discussions are typically needed in order to find and commit the right actors to take part in the development work. Quite often Not Invented Here (NIH) syndrome[13] hinders the crossing of boundaries even inside the organization. Therefore, more systematic and transparent co-ordination between knowledge sources and actors within the Bazaar of Opportunities enables crossing the borders and NIH syndrome both inside and outside the organizations. This requires a strategic approach to knowledge management and a clear development agenda. Furthermore, implementation of the development agenda within networked innovation necessitates co-operation and collaboration between actors — and this is based on negotiations between the targets of given network actors and the targets of the network itself. Selection of collaboration model is always an iterative process between the firm and other network actors — and thereby it overlaps with the contracting process (see also Chapter 5) as well as networking steps (Fig. 2.5). Understanding why collaboration is required by us and by partners enables the parties to agree also about the targets, the activities and the contracts related to collaboration settings, e.g. how they should be designed and managed.

Alternative Collaboration Models

Different knowledge must be managed differently and thereby the phase of innovation process has an influence on required collaboration models. When studying collaborative practices in inter-organizational innovation,[14] it was found that these practices generally involved either the **co-creation of new knowledge** (knowledge exploration) or **transactions involving existing knowledge** (exploitation of an earlier innovation outcome). In this book networked innovation relationships have been divided into two categories: the transaction networks and the co-creation networks,[15] according to the intrinsic role of knowledge in these relationships (Table 3.2). In other words, the actors within the Bazaar of Opportunities have relationships with each other that are either based on a single deal, or instead target jointly generated returns.

As described in Chapter 2, the structure of the network can be divided into: vertical customer–supplier co-operation; horizontal collaboration with more equal partners; or multidimensional collaboration consisting of both vertical and horizontal interaction. However, in both transaction and co-creation networks there could be either two or more actors involved.

Table 3.2.   Characteristic differences between co-creation and transaction networks.

	Transaction networks	Co-creation networks
Target of collaboration	Exploitation of existing knowledge	Exploration of new knowledge
Challenges of relationship and network orchestration	Participation interests according to appropriate business models	Participation and commitment based on shared interests
Nature of knowledge	Explicit knowledge, IP managed by formal methods (patents, etc.)	Tacit knowledge during co-creation, possible explicit background IP, explicit outcome knowledge

Furthermore, this division of collaboration models is connected also to typical dimensions of business development targets of firms, e.g. firms are seeking either efficiency of present IP and business or innovativeness and new business opportunities. Still, firms must also be able to combine different closed and open models of innovation.

As the focus of this book is on management — e.g. sharing and protection — of organizational knowledge the division between two types of knowledge is utilized in spite of multidimensionality of knowledge. In transaction networks (existing) knowledge is acquired by a transaction. The direction of a transaction may be: (1) from outside to in, when a company is acquiring explicit knowledge from another actor, or (2) from inside to out, when a company is selling, licensing or donating their own generated explicit knowledge to another actor. In co-creation networks the intention is to create new knowledge together with (an)other actor(s). Interaction and shared processes between the actors are required to create or transfer tacit knowledge. This knowledge can be related either to the present business model and the competitive position of firms, e.g. a firm's unique knowledge base, or to future business opportunities, e.g. innovative, future knowledge. Often a prerequisite for this kind of collaboration is a somehow limited access to the existing knowledge of each other as described in Chapter 2 (different levels of openness, see Table 2.3). The direction of co-creation can be considered based on the initiator's network position and sharing of innovation outcomes.

Also the interest of an actor to participate in collaboration differs in these two types and this challenges relationship and network orchestration. In the transaction networks present business models of actors must be appropriate, while in co-creation network participation and commitment is based on shared interest and vision for the future. The motivation factors and requirements of actors based on their network role are considered later in this chapter (see the section about network actors and their roles). The challenge of a network co-ordinator is to understand the business models and the interests of other actors involved in the innovation network and to align the network orchestration actions along with the business models and the interests.

The degree of interdependence between the actors is typically higher in the co-creation networks than in the transaction networks, e.g. the outcome of the co-creation network is dependent on the incentives of all participants. Furthermore, the degree of control by an individual firm is lower in the co-creation networks. The organizational members' ability to transfer knowledge from outside-in as well as inside-out or co-create knowledge with other organizations is tied also to the degree to which knowledge is independent or dependent.[16] It is concerned with whether knowledge is a standalone component that can be transferred without a strong awareness of the larger system — or conversely, whether it is an element of a set of interrelated components. In the latter case, co-creation is required in order to generate new knowledge and business opportunities.

Transaction Networks

In the knowledge transaction networks the focus is on the existing IP and the new business is built on that, and thereby inter-organizational innovation is based on co-operation, not on collaboration. Transactions of knowledge may take place in either open or closed relationships (Fig. 3.2). As defined in Chapter 2 (see Tables 2.1 and 2.2 about different networked innovation models), in open models of the transaction network the other end of action can be indefinable, e.g. public domain, or an open source community, where typically some of the actors are unknown. In innovation relationships within the public domain it is still important to define connections and influences related to publishing, disclosing, or abandonment of IP. Furthermore, the other end of public domain or a community can have several different operation models. The firm's opportunities, as well as interests, to influence these models vary significantly. In closed transaction networks the other end of IP transfer is known and thereby a firm can precisely define with whom

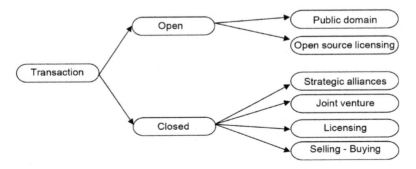

Fig. 3.2. Classification of transaction network types.

it is playing and more easily analyse the elements of decision making (as defined in Fig. 3.1). Furthermore, through the negotiation and contracting with other actors you end up with a certain level of openness, co-operation and collaboration. Based on their levels of openness, organization models and legal structure closed transaction networks can be defined as strategic alliances, joint ventures, licensing, or selling–buying relationships.

In the closed type of transaction network the relationships are most typically dyadic between a customer (buyer) and a supplier (seller). These bilateral relationships between the customer and the supplier can be either occasional or continuous depending on the business models and the interests of actors. Each of the transaction type has a myriad of operation models, even a bilateral selling or buying relationship can vary depending on targets, subject, time frame, price ruling, responsibilities, rights, etc. For example, depending on the subject of transaction (e.g. what is transacted) the selling or buying relationship can be defined as consulting (transaction of existing knowledge), franchising (transaction of rights to utilize certain concepts), or contracting for specialized capacity or work assignment (transaction of results, like documents, designs, etc.).

In order to choose the most appropriate collaboration model, you must consider your own targets and criteria carefully. For example, one of the interviewees — a representative of a system provider — described how they have formal processes in order to integrate open source code to their own software solutions: *"OS software must be clearly in the black-box and independent from other source code. We insert clauses and make sure we have a clear structure all the time, so if anyone wants to see the source code, we are able to show it to them. So for us the main point isn't that the co-operation is open, so everyone else can easily join in development which we can benefit from. Actually, for us the point is that one of our experts recognized that this is a really good package, something we do not need to develop ourselves, which is operationally very good and already tested."*

Within a networked business environment the importance of other collaboration models than traditional, bilateral selling–buying relationship is growing. Both strategic alliances and joint ventures consider joining of forces, capabilities, or resources, in order to reach a shared target. Joint venture means that a two or more network actors create a legally independent company together, while strategic alliances stand for co-operation between actors for a specified or indefinite period. Besides, there are two main types of strategic alliances: (1) equity alliance is an alliance in which two or more actors own different percentages of the company they have formed; and (2) non-equity alliance is an alliance in which two or more actors develop a contractual-relationship.

The challenge related to transaction networks orchestration can often be stated as a contract design problem,[17] e.g. how contracting about rights and responsibilities and the alignment of interest between actors can be done in a mutually beneficial way. One alternative to diminish the unwanted effects from too detailed or too superficial agreements is to contract for the outcomes (the desired result of the contracted work) rather than the actor's behaviour (the work itself). On the other hand, flexible contracting may offer tools to solve these challenging situations. Chapter 5 will focus on the contracting process and contract design in more detail. Anyhow, the contract design is more complex within strategic alliances and joint ventures than selling or buying individual IP, while the former models often include characteristics from co-creation, e.g. all the results of innovation incentives are not known beforehand.

The intellectual property ownership structures agreed by the contracts in selling or buying can be seen as a way to align the interests of the firms. When the IP resulting from the work is transferred from the seller to the buyer, the seller often sees the further development of that IP is not in its interests. As a CEO stated: *"If the customer does not give us the rights to use the developed software on the other solutions, we don't put our best employees to the development work"*. On the other hand, when part of the IP that belongs to the developed innovation is retained by the seller, also the future development of the knowledge is easier.[18] Such a situation may potentially transform the relationship from being purely transactional into a co-creation type of relationship. Accordingly, it requires that the actors also align the future business development targets and might lead to a more risky situation.

Co-creation Networks

The co-creation networks are characterized by nested and interconnected relationships. Explicit background IP may lie at the core of the co-creation initiation, but tacit knowledge plays a highly important role in the actual

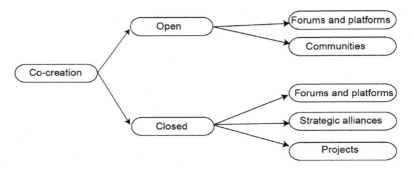

Fig. 3.3.   Classification of co-creation network types.

co-creation. Similarly to the transaction networks the co-creation networks can also be classified at a high level into two types depending on whether all actors of the network are known or not (Fig. 3.3). This division of closed and open collaboration models has a strong impact on individual actor's possibilities to influence the negotiations and the agreement on collaboration forms and rules. Besides, an actor's position related to others has an effect on its possibilities to set the rules of the game.

In general, within the co-creation network the collaboration is largely based on shared interests and trust between partners. Open co-creation models, e.g. where unknown actors are involved, can be divided into forums, platforms and communities. Further, based on the maintainer these can be distinguished between business forums or platforms (company as a maintainer) or communities (individuals as maintainers). The maintainer who offers the platform or facilitates the collaboration between actors is typically also able to have most influence on the targets, focus areas, and rules of collaboration. Still, within the most open and even public forms, like open discussion forums and communities around them, the existence of shared interest or joint targets is limited. For instance, in open discussion forums of hobbyists the participants share interests and enthusiasm for a certain hobby — but each of the actors has their own targets related to their development within the hobby.

As pointed out already in Chapter 2, within the context of B-to-C, firms already utilize different online forums in order to increase users' involvement in their new product development. Still, some of the firms have realized how companies' own online communities may not be the most suitable platforms to understand the needs and requirements of users (consumers).[19] In company-based forums users might focus on discussing faults of current products whereas in another forum they may share their new ideas. So, instead of companies' forums the most relevant comments about users' expectations can be found elsewhere. Since needs and preferences are fluid and malleable, several iterations of exploration and development are usually needed before companies and their customers arrive at mutual understanding or further on new offerings.

Thus, within the community-based innovation models sharing of both the interests and the norms of collaboration is made transparent by participation not directly by formal agreements. Typically, also within the community-based innovation models there is a core group, which is in charge of operations and forms the rules of the community. Open source communities are the most well-known models of collaborative peer-to-peer production (e.g. the innovation process that is performed together). In co-operation with the open source community the firm's position within the community influences its chances of negotiating about licensing terms,[20] e.g. rights to utilize, protect, or share IP outside and inside the community.

Still, in B-to-B collaboration business user communities — or even discussion forums — are rare and co-creation is typically emphasized to closed networks with known partners. The closed co-creation models can be classified as forums and platforms, strategic alliances, and projects. They differ from each other based on an initiator, a focus, and a structure of collaboration. Informal collaboration within different forums typically precedes the more intentional and defined collaboration within research or R&D alliances and projects. In other words, the actors of the oriental bazaar first familiarize themselves with each other in a market day or fair — they may meet up by chance or somebody may introduce themselves to each other. And later on, if the actors find shared interests they form a closed co-operation arrangement to reach the shared targets through co-creation.

The experience, however, has shown that, if the actors are used to the transaction type relationships and the closed operational model, any more open models of collaboration and innovation may be challenging in practice. One interviewee said that "*despite a shared interest in the beginning to innovate openly and co-create new offerings, it is very easy to go back to entrenched routines and attitudes as the process goes on"*. As we all know, changes can take time and learning away from customary operation models. Furthermore, the industry tradition leads firms to act in a certain way, for example formal protection methods can be an industry standard as a representative of a system provider explains: *"Yes, ownership of IPR is important to us, it is partly on the grounds that it is important to many of our customers, so we are in that sense a part of our customers IPR chain."*

While the results of collaboration are seldom known at the beginning, semi-formal knowledge of protection methods (see Table 1.1) such as contracts and confidentiality agreements are important within co-creation networks. Still, a legal counsel of a global technology industry company described how the network orchestration is more challenging within the co-creation network: *"Heterogeneous interests with respect to the collaboration model make the coordinating of the network challenging. Often it is hard to agree, even inside the company, about the criteria of knowledge sharing and levels of openness within collaboration."* Thus, regardless of the shared interests and trust between the partners, also a formal contract describing the rights and obligations of the parties is required. Similarly, contracts can be utilized in order to extend the root of the collaboration from the initial personal relationships to a company level as highlighted by one of the interviewees: *". . . you have to make sure, that from the personal relationship,* [trust] *goes into a, let's say, a company relationship. And therefore, we need agreements to secure that."* Contracting process and the role of flexible co-ordination aspects in the contracts of the co-creation networks will be covered in more detail in Chapter 5.

To avoid suboptimal performance of the network arising from the potentially opportunistic behaviour of an individual network actor in the co-creation network and the associated free-riding problem, the jointly-agreed innovation incentive mechanisms need to be designed so that each company is encouraged to utilize their best knowledge in the collaboration rather than keeping that information private.[21] As will be pointed out in Chapter 5, evolving contracts and contracting process may support this by making norms of collaboration visible, and thereby it is important to notice that trust and contracts are not opposite to each other. In some cases unwillingness to make contracts may even suggest that participators do not find collaboration interesting or strategically important.

The Business Model as a Navigator within the Bazaar of Opportunities

While developing the present offering or looking for new business opportunities within the Bazaar of Opportunities firms must constantly make choices between possible knowledge sources, collaboration partners and models. Open Innovation literature highlights the importance of a business model[22] and thereby the business model can be seen as a frame for these decisions and a tool to communicate and negotiate about the targets of collaboration both inside and outside of a firm (Fig. 3.4).[23] A business model describes how a firm creates, delivers, and captures value. Briefly, it defines the offering (what), customers (to whom), value network (how) and earning logic (how much). Within the collaboration earning logic also defines how the risks and the benefits of collaboration are shared between the involved actors. Typically, the sharing mechanism can be based on a lump-sum payment, licensing, or a sum tied to revenues.

The business model is connected to a firm's IP strategy and it also describes a firm's role and position within the present business environment and the networked innovation system. The business model is often illustrated as a link between business strategy and operations and processes — and similarly, in Chapter 6, IP Strategy, IP practices and IP actions are

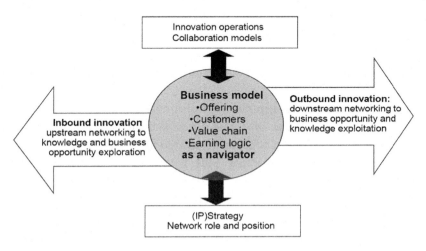

Fig. 3.4. Business model as a navigator.

(see Fig. 6.1) defined as the three levels linked together. Together they all define boundary conditions to a firm's innovation operations[24] and frame the decision related to collaboration models. In other words, a seller may communicate its bargaining principles to a buyer through its business model, e.g. what is included in the sales, to whom the offering is done, how and with whom the offering is produced and how the compensation should be made. In addition, in its own organization the seller co-ordinates the offering through the business models with the IP strategy and the network role as well as the internal targets, like for example the intention to strengthen its network position. Finally, the decision and choices made by actors become visible to other actors within the Bazaar by their (joint) innovation operations.

In the outbound innovation operations, e.g. from inside a firm to out, the business model frames the knowledge creation, exploitation, and utilization in order to commercialize new opportunities and develop present business operations. In the Bazaar of Opportunities new models of collaboration and openness within the outbound innovation may support a firm to strengthen its position and gain legitimacy from the external environment. In addition firms can influence other stakeholders, foster incremental innovation, or improve diffusion of its solutions. On the other hand, openness within inbound — e.g. from outside a firm to inside — innovation might help a firm to gain access to a wide array of ideas, new resources and knowledge. The main challenges of inbound innovation operations are linked to evaluation and decision making between many alternatives and possible partners. Therefore, the business model can help to funnel the relevant knowledge sources and innovation partners in inbound innovation operations.

While the Bazaar of Opportunities is fully booked with ideas, opportunities, knowledge — and at the same time risks and dead-ends — a firm needs a navigator and its business model can be utilized as a tool to understand and communicate the motivation factors. Still, within the development of new business opportunities the flexibility of a company's current business model is also essential. The words of one interviewee explain why: "*...because* [senior management] *have to understand that there's a shift in the business model, and we need open innovation to help us to make that shift. Open* *innovation itself should create a completely new, different business model. And that needs to be communicated as well, and the consequences for us have to be fully understood.*" As pointed out the successful transformation of a business model requires deep understanding about networked business environment, so that the actor is able to change its position, re-structure the competition, and thereby renew the rules of the game.

In both the transaction networks and the co-creation networks contracts describe the rights and responsibilities of network actors and thereby they define how well the relationship is aligned and how it support the business models of involved actors. Furthermore, firms can utilize networked innovation better when they understand their partner's business models, e.g. their motivation to collaborate and transfer or share knowledge. For example a business model might explain how product and service companies have totally different approaches to IP protection as pointed out by one of interviewees: "*. . . Do you want to focus and bother yourself too much with IP discussions, and in that way, cause conflict, and disrupt the possibility of relationships? We are a service company trying to work together with a product company — when two product companies are working together, IP relations are easier, more so than the service and the product company work-ing together. Cos that's a completely different ballgame.*" As described in the above quotation the importance of tacit knowledge explains why service developers often must operate in co-creation networks with customers.[25] Furthermore, as pointed out already in Chapter 2 (see Table 2.1 about differences between open and closed innovation models) semi-open and collaborative are more suitable to such cases when competitive advantage is not based on owning the IPR. Increase of service business has also challenged contracting and new ways, like performance based contracting, are required. In the near future, designing and managing the knowledge that bundles products and services together to create new ways to satisfy customers seems as though it will be a common approach for success in the Bazaar of Opportunities. Thus, companies should open their innovation process in a proper manner to involve other actors to collaborate, customize, and extend the offering. One example of this kind of ongoing progress and related structural changes is the growing number of system suppliers and integrators within the manufacturing industry.

Network Actors and their Roles: How the Sum is More than its Parts

This last section goes through the different roles of network actors and connects them with the requirements of an actor's IP strategy. A firm's possibilities to control negotiation and contracting processes are dependent on its network position, role and business model. The vertical upstream business partner is a supplier, while the vertical downstream business partner is a customer or belongs to other interest groups. This difference has implications for the control that the actor can exercise, for the nature of dependence in the relationship, and for the firm's ability to make changes in processes and systems in the interface. The suppliers and customers have different capabilities as well as interests to contribute to innovation process or business development — and the alignment of interests may have quite easily been understood based on their business models. Anyhow, the relationships between suppliers and customers are typically long-lasting and this relational embeddedness denotes strong ties and trust between the actors (see Tables 2.1 and 2.2 in Chapter 2). That directs the actors to improve the prevailing dominant design and value network, and thereby the incremental innovations are more typical than radical.

Within horizontal relationships actors, who have similar positions in value networks, operate together. Because of similar experiences, network positions and knowledge bases, the competitors could easily learn from each other and generate incremental innovations or broader solutions for customers. Still, firms typically are not willing to collaborate with competitors. Naturally this kind of co-opetative — e.g. concurrent competition and co-operation — relationships require careful considerations about knowledge protection and sharing. On the other hand, the horizontal relationships over industry branches, that bridge knowledge gaps and structural holes between the collaborators, are the most likely to generate radical innovations and new business opportunities.

In order to support the formation of successful collaboration, network actors must have clearly defined but different roles. Table 3.3 summarizes the different network roles (business models) and their influence of motivation factors for inter-organizational innovation. In accordance with the elements of the decision-making process (the Fig. 3.1) the input column is connected to a "why" question. It describes the actor's

Table 3.3. Actors of networked innovation: their roles and characteristic interests (related to IP management).

Role	Input: value and background knowledge	Responsibilities	Confidentiality	Motivation	Output: IP ownership and rights
End customer/User	Knowledge about requirements, relevant processes and value networks	Describe the needs and requirements (define a pilot case)	Business and technology solutions	"First mover advantage" Rights to use the product or service	Rights to utilize the results (knowledge) in other similar cases
Product/service company	Knowledge about business solution and customer needs, network connections	Develop, commercialize, offer products/ services/ technology	Business and technology solutions	New approaches, solutions, knowledge about end user needs	Rights to utilize solution/ technology to offer products or services (in core areas IP ownership)
Subcontractor Contract manufacturer	Easily purchased and specified product/solution	Offer products/services (transaction)		Sales and references	Rights to offer products to other customers
Supplier/System Supplier	Product/solution connected to offering, complementary resources	Provide and develop (customize) product/service (co-creation)	Business and technology solutions and processes	New approaches, solutions, knowledge about customer and end user needs	Rights to utilize the technology/ solution to offer products or services in other business areas

(*Continued*)

Table 3.3. (*Continued*)

Role	Input: value and background knowledge	Responsibilities	Confidentiality	Motivation	Output: IP ownership and rights
System Integrator	Networking and integration competencies and position (close relationships to customer)	Integrate the products/services of several actors to customer solution	Customized business solutions and processes	New approaches, solutions, knowledge	Rights to offer the solution to other customers
Research partner	Research experience, knowledge about methods and tools	Create new solutions based on the research work	Theoretical frameworks, solutions and research networks	Funding to research, practical cases, business understanding	Intent to own IP in core research areas, utilize the results in further research projects
Innovator	Knowledge related to innovative solution	Offer innovative solutions and IP rights	Customized business solutions	Transaction of IP by selling, licensing, joint-venture, employment	IP ownership in order to offer IP to other customers (licensing agreements)
Co-ordinator Inter-mediator	Knowledge related to networked innovation and research projects	Co-ordinate collaboration and integrate solutions	Business solutions and research networks	Compensation about co-ordination work	No interest to own IP rights, interested to offer the co-ordination capacity to other actors

value to collaboration and its relevant background information. Secondly, responsibilities, confidentiality and motivation define the "how" question. Finally, the output column specifies the answers to the "what" question. It describes the actor's interests to IP ownership and rights related joint-results. Network roles cover the whole value network from the end customer to subcontractors, as well as innovators, inter-mediators, and technology developers. Naturally, the described roles are theoretical simplifications and in practice firms have several concurrent roles in different value networks.

End customer and user's involvement to innovation is a hot topic — especially in B-to-C markets.[26] In B-to-B settings the end user's interests in participating in innovation work could be found from "the first mover advantage" or search of new future-oriented knowledge about the industry. On the other hand, end customers as network's leading companies could target to have an influence in the surrounding business ecosystem. Based on their interests in some cases the rights to use the product or service can be important motivation factors, while in some cases the tacit knowledge shared within collaboration is the most desired benefit.

On the supplier side, product companies, different suppliers from sub-contractors to system integrators, have based on the business model different approaches to knowledge sharing and protection in networked innovation. While the knowledge of product design, architecture and manufacturing is vital, protection of explicit IP is important to the supplier side company, in order to capture its share of the business. In the case of system suppliers and system integrators tacit knowledge and the collaboration process itself might create higher value. As pointed out earlier, the growing importance of knowledge as a competitive advantage has also changed the role of suppliers towards knowledge-based business models.

Once again, when studying the interests and motivation factors of other actors within the business ecosystem, e.g. research partners, innovator and inter-mediators, they all have different viewpoints of the Bazaar of Opportunities. Funding for research, in one way or another, is essential to research institutions, while additional interest in practical cases and deeper business understanding may lead research institutions to closer co-operation with companies. Furthermore, research institutions are keen on utilizing the results in further research projects or within teaching and in their core research areas — and at least some research institutions are intent to own

IPR. The innovator typically targets the transaction of their IP (either tacit knowledge or IPR) by selling, licensing, joint venture, or employment. Typically, in licensing agreements innovators insist on having IP ownership in order to offer IP to other customers. In many cases IP evaluation is naturally hard and thereby different mind-sets of small innovator (even one individual) and larger companies can hinder the collaboration. For instance, the innovator might have spent years with the idea and sees it rather ready to markers, whereas a larger company has a broader view of the business ecosystem and based on that it evaluates that the commercialization phase will be harder. In such cases some kind of innovation inter-mediators can offer their knowledge-based services. In general, a business model of inter-mediator is to get compensation about their co-ordination work, and thereby it does not have interest in owning IP rights.

Conclusions: How to Utilize Networked and Open Innovation

How could you most successfully benefit from networked innovation? A key to collaboration is the understanding of business models, network positions, and roles of partners, e.g. to answer the question: "Why should they bother and commit to the joint innovation process?" The sum is more than its parts only if the interests of actors are aligned and the knowledge bases are both different and similar enough. Because learning is based on the current knowledge, there must also be similarities in knowledge bases, and on the other hand new knowledge can be generated only if there are differences, structural holes, and white spots between the knowledge bases. Therefore, the assets should be complementary and transaction or co-creation of IP is possible.

Within the strategic approach to knowledge management and novel thinking about competitive edge the companies are even able to collaborate with competitors as a representative of a large European industrial group explains in the following quotation: "*So, therefore we sometimes are looking for a competitor who we could develop a product with, so that we have a multi-source possibility for our customers. That's one option. The other option is that we have a competitor that has certain know-how and we have different know-how and we combine them, so you can come up with new products. For instance, one competitor has good knowledge of application technologies, how to use a product (in the market) whereas the others have a good knowledge of the processes needed to make that product. To combine that know-how can bring…it can create a product which is easily put on the market. And we now have two, maybe three ways, in which we now co-operate with competitors, and where, let's say, in the pre-competitive area, IP is less of an issue than it is in the other areas."* In order to be successful in the Bazaar of Opportunities you do need this kind of strategic approach to your uniqueness, e.g. distinctive competences, and future-oriented innovative knowledge.

To sum up the contents of this chapter, we divided collaboration models of networked innovation into two types: the transaction networks and the co-creation networks. In the transaction networks (existing) knowledge is acquired through a transaction, while in the co-creation networks new knowledge is generated jointly by the participants. This division is connected also to the typical dimensions of business development targets of firms, e.g. firms are seeking either efficiency of present IP and business or innovativeness and new business opportunities.

Notes

1. There is wide agreement among organization theorists that "knowledge" is one of the most (if not the most) important assets of an organization. Still, in both theorizing and practise the construct of "knowledge" has several meanings, concepts and dimensions. For example skills, resources, capabilities, and competencies are concepts utilized within resources based view to a firm. Still, scholars differ in their understanding and application of these concepts. Likewise within knowledge based view there are several concepts of knowledge, organizational knowing and learning. Anyhow, organizational knowledge is predominantly a result of social construction, and for knowledge to exist, members of organization have to agree that it exists.

2. Polanyi (1966) pointed out the multidimensionality of knowledge; according to him explicit and tacit dimensions are always connected to each other. In innovation literature, such accumulated know-how, e.g. tacit knowledge, is also referred to as architectural knowledge, i.e. knowledge developed and enacted in innovation processes by aligning heterogeneous business and technical elements (Henderson and Clark, 1990). Other popular taxonomies distinguish between general and situated context-specific knowledge, and individual and collective knowledge. [Polanyi, M. (1966). *The Tacit Dimension*, Peter Smith. Gloucester, MA; Henderson, R.M. and Clark, K.B. (1990). Architectural Innovation: The Reconfiguration of Existing Product Technologies and the Failure of Established Firms, *Administrative Science Quarterly*, Vol. 35, pp. 9–30.]

3. As defined in Chapter 1: the term IP includes not only IP rights that are granted and protected by law, but also the knowledge and other intangible resources whose use may be controlled by contracts, policies, organization and process routines and norms, both physically and technically.

4. Modified from Zack, 1999. [Zack, M.H. (1999). Developing a Knowledge Strategy, *California Management Review*, Vol. 41, pp. 125–145.]

5. According to Teece *et al.* (1997) the degree to which a core competence is distinctive depends on how well endowed the firm is relative to its competitors and on how difficult it is for competitors to replicate its competences. [Teece, D.J., Pisano, G. and Shuen, A. (1997). Dynamic Capabilities and Strategic Management, *Strategic Management Journal*, Vol. 18, pp. 509–533.]

6. Teece (2008) utilized the term distinctive competences from the competences that provide the competitive edge to a firm. [Teece D.J. (2008). 'Firm Capabilities and Economic Development', in Teece, D.J. (ed.), *Technological Know-How, Organizational Capabilities and Strategic Management: Business Strategy and Enterprise Development in Competitive Environments*, University of California, World Scientific, pp. 175–198.]

7. [Zack, M.H. (1999). Developing a Knowledge Strategy, *California Management Review*, Vol. 41, pp. 125–145.]

8. Formal protection methods include patents, trademarks, utility models, rights to commercial names, copyrights. Contractual/semi-formal protection methods include different types of contracts, such as confidentiality agreements, prohibition of competition clauses in agreements, proprietary and access rights clauses in agreements. [PRO INNO Europe 2007, http://www.proinno-europe.eu (Accessed on 23 February 2012.)]

9. According to Nike's announcement the Environmental Apparel Design Tool was designed and built by it over seven years with a six million dollar investment. The software-based tool helps designers to make real time choices that decrease the environmental impacts of their work. [Nike, http://www.textileweb.com/article.mvc/Nike-Furthers-Its-Commitment-To-Open-0001 (Accessed 19 January 2011)]. Nike, Inc.'s principal business activity is the design, development, and worldwide marketing of high quality footwear, apparel, equipment, and accessory products. NIKE is the largest seller of athletic footwear and athletic apparel in the world.

10. A firm's absorptive capacity was originally highlighted by Cohen and Levinthal (1990) and since then it has been studied on multiple levels (individual, group, firm, and national level). Still, from the viewpoint of networked innovation the concept can be criticized as a somewhat restricted approach, e.g. it does not consider the motivation factors related to the other participants of innovation process. [Cohen, W.M. and Levinthal, D.A. (1990). Absorptive Capacity: A New Perspective on Learning and Innovation, *Administrative Science Quarterly*, Vol. 35, pp. 128–152.]

11. This organization's mystic ability of renewal, innovativeness, and future-orientation has several overlapping descriptions. Originally, Cohen and Levinthal (1990) highlight the critical importance of absorptive capacity to the innovative and learning capabilities of firms. Furthermore, Teece *et al.* (1997) define dynamic capability more broadly as "the firm's ability to integrate, build and re-configure internal and external competencies to address rapidly changing environments". [Cohen and Levinthal *ibid.*; Teece, D.J.,

Pisano, G. and Shuen, A. (1997). Dynamic Capabilities and Strategic Management, *Strategic Management Journal*, Vol. 18, pp. 509–533.]

12. The notion of path dependencies recognizes that "history matters". Thus a firm's previous investments, knowledge and its history constrain its future behaviour and possible development paths.

13. Not Invented Here (NIH) is a term used to describe persistent social, corporate, or institutional culture that avoids using or buying already existing products, research, or knowledge because of their external origins.

14. [Paasi, J., Luoma, T., Valkokari. K. and Lee, N. (2010). Knowledge and Intellectual Property Management in Customer-supplier Relationships, *International Journal of Innovation Management*, Vol. 14, pp. 1–26.]

15. In our study, we have utilized the distinction between the two dimensions of organizational knowing identified by earlier knowledge-based literature (Grant and Baden-Fuller, 2004), while similar conflicting dimensions are also recognized in the business development of firms. Firstly, there are activities that increase an organization's innovativeness and stock of knowledge — what March (1991) refers to as "exploration" and Spender (1992) calls "knowledge generation". Secondly, there are activities that deploy existing knowledge to efficiently create value — what March (1991) refers to as "exploitation" and Spender (1992) calls "knowledge application". In the next section we review the literature of networks and alliances and summarize how earlier typologies have described the differences between knowledge exploration and exploitation. [Grant, R.M. and Baden-Fuller, C.A. (2004). Knowledge Accessing Theory of Strategic Alliances, *Journal of Management Studies*, Vol. 41, pp. 61–84; March, J.G. (1991). Exploration and Exploitation in Organizational Learning, *Organization Science*, Vol. 2, pp. 427–440; Spender, J.-C. (1992). Limits to Learning from the West: How Western Management Advice may Prove Limited in Eastern Europe, *The International Executive*, Vol. 34, pp. 389–410.]

16. [Hansen, M.T. (1999). The Search-transfer Problem: The Role of Weak Ties in Sharing Knowledge Across Organization Subunits, *Administrative Science Quarterly*, Vol. 44, pp. 82–111.]

17. This kind of problem is studied extensively in the principal-agent literature (for a review, see Eisenhardt, 1989), where a contract is made between the principal (customer) and the agent (supplier) about work to be done by the agent on behalf of the principal. However, the information asymmetry, that the principal can not completely observe the quality of the agents work, gives rise to moral hazard and adverse selection. [Eisenhardt, K.M. (1989). Agency Theory: An Assessment and Review, *Academy of Management Review*, Vol. 14, pp. 57–74.]

18. [Leiponen, A. (2008). Control of Intellectual Assets in Client Relationships: Implications for Innovation, *Strategic Management Journal*, Vol. 29, pp. 1371–1394.]

19. [Kaarela, I., Koivisto, T. and Valkokari, K. (2011). Strategizing for Open Innovation, *Proceedings of ISPIM Conference*, Hamburg.]

20. According to Watson *et al.* (2008) dual licensing is as an example of second-generation open source (OSSg2), within this kind of operation actors integrate open and closed co-creation models in order to receive revenues from both traditional license fees and open source offerings. For example, Nokia's dual-licensing strategy for Qt actually includes three distinct licensing options. The first option is commercial; the user pays a

licensing fee and receives a high degree of freedom. The next two options align with two versions of GNU licenses (Schreuders *et al.*, 2011). [Watson, R.T., Boudreau, M.-C. York, P.T., Greiner, M.E. and Wynn, D. (2008). The Business of Open Source: Tracking the Changing Competitive Conditions of the Software Industry, *Communications of the ACM*, Vol. 51, pp. 41–46; Schreuders, J., Low, A., Esprit, K. and Nerva, J. (2011). Nokia's Hybrid Business Model for Qt, *Open Source Business Resource*, pp. 31–36.]

21. [Jarimo, T. (2008). *Innovation Incentives and the Design of Value Networks*. D.Sc. Thesis. Helsinki University of Technology, Espoo.]

22. Chesbrough (2006) defines a firms business model open when the part of the innovation actions that supports the value creation, value delivery and value capturing of the organization takes place outside the borders of the organization, i.e. the organization applies open innovation. This model, and its opposite (the closed business model), has been criticized for being too theoretical. According to paradigms of network literature "no company is an island" originally pointed out by Håkansson and Snehota (1989), e.g. firms and their business operations are always connected to and evolve with business environment. Dahlander and Gann (2010) re-conceptualized the idea of openness and with the division of peculiar and non-peculiar (in-direct) benefits of innovation within their literature review they indicated two inbound processes (sourcing and acquiring) and two outbound processes (revealing and selling). [Chesbrough, H. (2006). 'Open Innovation: A New Paradigm for Understanding Industrial Innovation', in Chesbrough H, Vanhaverbeke, W. and West, J. (eds), *Open Innovation: Researching a New Paradigm*, Oxford University Press, pp. 1–14; Håkansson, H. and Snehota, I. (1989). No Business is an Island, *Scandinavian Journal of Management*, Vol. 5, pp. 187–200; Dahlander, L. and Gann, D.M. (2010). How Open is Innovation?, *Research Policy*, Vol. 30, pp. 699–709.]

23. The picture is modified from Koivisto, 2011. [Koivisto, T. (2011). 'Avoin innovointi, yritys ja luomisverkostot', in Ahonen, M., Koivisto, T., Mikkonen, T., Tuomisto, M., Vadén, T., Vainio, N. and Valkokari, K. (eds), *Rajoja ylittävä innovointi*, Tampere University Press, pp. 32–76.]

24. According to Ostenwalder *et al.* (2005) the difference between strategy and business models is unclear. Some authors use the terms "strategy" and "business model" interchangeably. In contrast, others understand the business model as an abstraction of a firm's strategy that may potentially apply to many firms. The latter definition has similarities also with network role, which also apply to many firms but each of them has an own strategy to execute that business model and differentiate from others. In our work we have utilized the latter definition and thereby highlighted how business model can be consider as a tool to communicate firm's strategic targets both internally and externally. [Ostenwalder, A., Pigneur, Y. and Tucci, C.L. (2005). Clarifying Business Models: Origins, Present, and Future of the Concept, *Communications of the AIS*, Vol. 16, Article 1; Magretta, J. (2002). Why Business Models Matter, *Harvard Business Review*, Vol. 80, pp. 86–92.]

25. [Chesbrough, H. (2011). *Open Services Innovation — Rethinking Your Business to Grow and Compete in a New Era*, Jossey-Bass, San Francisco.]

26. Eric von Hippel (1986) is the well-known pioneer within the discussion about lead-user involvement. One of the latest examples of a book related to this issue is

written by Bhalla (2011). [von Hippel, E. (1986). Lead Users: A Source of Novel Product Concepts, *Management Science*, Vol. 32, pp. 791–805; Bhalla, G. (2011). *Collaboration and Co-creation — New Platforms for Marketing and Innovation*, Springerlink, New York.]

Chapter 4

IP in Networks

IP management in the Bazaar of Opportunities is about protection of knowledge that is important for a firm's business and about controlled sharing of knowledge with other, often selected, actors in the Bazaar in order to support the business targets of the firm. In Chapters 4 and 5 we focus on the IP management in open and networked innovation from legal perspectives. Chapter 4 "IP in Networks" considers the subject from the standpoint of IP law and Chapter 5 "Contract and IP Management in Networked Innovation" is from the standpoint of private ordering.

IP Protection and IP Management

Knowledge is intangible. Unlike tangible goods, knowledge is difficult to control physically. Once produced and disclosed, it is difficult to control how it gets distributed further. This aspect of knowledge makes it non-excludable, as it makes it difficult to exclude others once created. At the same time, knowledge is what economists call non-rival goods.[1] If one consumes one unit of a tangible resource, others may no longer consume it. In contrast, two or more people may use the knowledge at the same time, as consumption of the knowledge by one person does not make the knowledge unavailable for others. For the society, the more knowledge that is used, the better it is. As a result, knowledge production suffers from a public good problem with positive externalities. It is costly to produce, but once produced it is difficult to exclude others from the benefits. When a private utility of non-disclosure and non-production is greater than the cost of production, the producer of knowledge will not disclose or produce the knowledge. In its most natural state, the producers of knowledge, without any means of excluding others from making use of the fruits of their labour, would either keep the knowledge secret or would choose not to produce the knowledge at all. Thus the knowledge production suffers from inefficiency.

The system of intellectual property law addresses this dilemma by providing exclusive rights. Industrial property rights (patents, design, and trademark that require registration) and copyright provide legally constructed control over the uses of intangible. The law sanctions unauthorized uses of the knowledge covered by these rights and grants exclusive rights. Intellectual property law gives inventors and creators legal means to control the use of knowledge that is subject to the protection of intellectual property. Thus, IP makes it possible for the knowledge, separated from the tangible goods, to be the object of market-based transaction. By providing exclusive rights, IP law encourages not only the disclosure of the intangible knowledge but also provides incentives to produce and invest in the production of intellectual goods. With the legal protection of exclusion, IP allows inventors and creators to recoup the cost of the inventive and creative inputs and also to use it as a means of financing their inventive and creative efforts and further commercialization of products using inventions and creation.[2]

IP law grants rights to the inventors and authors. Initial entitlement for IP is attributed to the natural persons under most countries' law. As corporate inventors or corporate creators are not commonly recognized in intellectual property law, firms who own IP are often the assignee of rights, who acquire the rights either based on separate transfer agreements or through employment agreement. For protecting an employee-inventor, there is often legislation that ensures the inventor a fair compensation for the commercialized innovation. Legislation on employee invention may also protect the employer obliging the employee to offer the invention made for his employer, who has provided the environment enabling the invention. In all these situations, firms also make agreements with the inventor. Firms may then use the IP through commercialization in the sense of producing tangible innovative products based on the inventive idea and created works.

Increase of networked innovation challenges IP laws. To a degree, IP law already regulates network innovation through joint ownership arrangement. However, there are many aspects of open innovation that fit poorly with the standards in IP law. Utilizing resources and capabilities which are outside the boundaries of a firm generate multiple claim holders who have heterogeneous interests on the rights, and the use of the innovation.[3]

Moreover, where there is no clear legal protection of IP, confidentiality is relied on. For this reason, confidentiality has traditionally been used as a method for protecting on-going innovations whose protection under IP law is uncertain. Most countries' laws protects confidentiality and often legislation sanctions disclosure of business and commercial secrets.

As the protection through confidential information does not require the information to meet the formal threshold of required in IP law, protection of commercially valuable information with confidentiality is broad. IP in its broadest sense may be protected as a commercial secret by both law and contracts. In practice, firms tend to apply the concept of IP in a broader sense covering both IP protected by law and IP, such as know-how, which can be protected by contracts or other, more or less informal, ways as we have already discussed in Chapter 1 (Table 1.1.) In this book we apply the broader practical concept of IP instead of only legally protected IP (see the section "The Term 'Intellectual Property'" in Chapter 1).

In open and networked innovation, however, sharing and communication, which IP law does not deal with, is crucial among multiple claim holders. To introduce openness, a decision as to when and what to strategically disclose has to be made.[4] IP management in networked collaboration is thus mostly about co-ordination and communication inside the network and less about protection of IP from leaking out of the network. In this chapter we discuss how to protect IP in a broader sense and how to share information in a controlled way. Firstly we discuss transaction networks with already existing IP and then move to co-creation.

Existing IP — Licensing as a Means of Trading IPs

In IP law, if knowledge cannot be transferred and is inherently personal, it cannot be called an object of "property". In this sense, what is called an IP in law needs to be always transferable. This excludes the knowledge that is embedded in the human resources, which cannot be transferred as such. As an object of property, IP can be bought and sold and the ownership may change. In addition to the classic buying and selling, IP is a right of exclusion and the rights holders may grant a license, a permission to use the underlying knowledge. As the law requires the users of intangible knowledge to seek permission from IP rights holder, users need a license from the rights holder to use the knowledge if they are subject to IP, even if they may have developed the technology themselves. This is particularly true in the case of patented inventions where there is no independent invention defence, which is true in most countries.

Typically licenses are applied in transaction networks in closed co-operation. The differences between transaction and co-creation types of networks are described in Figs. 3.2 and 3.3 in Chapter 3. Thus, licensing is the most typical method provided under IP law as a means to access underlying knowledge — i.e. technology and know-how. At the same time, licensing may simply mean the IP owner's promise not to sue the users of a technology who are already practising and using the knowledge. In the latter, licensing itself does not provide access, but rather provides a clearance over the use of particular technology.

Innovation networks and platforms reflect these two different functions of licensing and IP. Some networks and platforms are created and formed to access and develop certain innovative ideas and technology while others are formed simply as a way to trade existing IPs and form network of clearance. In a business to business innovation context, when firms know clearly which technology, knowledge, and IP that they need to use, firms may need to buy patents and other IP covering the technology or license in the technology. Likewise, firms may sell IP or license them out. Firms may collaborate by allowing other firms to license their IPs as well as by licensing in other collaboration partner's technology, and may form transaction networks. In certain cases, licensing networks are simply used to preserve freedom of operation or to avoid litigation, rather than to acquire access to the underlying knowledge. In networks, firms may also barter their IP through cross-licenses and form licensing platforms to avoid litigations. This is particularly the case where there is numerous IP in electronics and telecommunication industries, where complex and comprehensive licensing platforms are formed as a kind of IP clearing house.

Licensing agreements are often also governed by mandatory law limiting the use of available contractual terms. Often statutory limitations concern disproportionate payments with the value of the technology, or limitations for the transferee to use alternative technology or develop the licensed technology, or exemptions of the transferor for any liability resulting from any defect. Importantly, fairness of licensing contracts and competition are subject to competition regulations.

As most modern state contract laws incorporate freedom of contract, the terms of licenses and the types of licenses (exclusive or non-exclusive) as well as formats vary. While ideally a tailor-made contract suitable for each object of transaction, reflecting the nature of knowledge, would be beneficial for the parties to the contract, in practice model contracts and templates with boilerplate clauses are often used. As licenses are becoming more pervasive, and may need to address a group of actors at the same time, there are various attempts either by industry associations, or by individual firms themselves, to standardize the terms or to draft model licensing agreement to serve as template.

In addition to ordinary licenses, there are community drafted licenses. Perhaps the most widely known licenses of these kinds are the GNU General Public License (GPL), which forms the basis of open source code software licenses,[5] and Creative Commons (CC) license, used in the context of copyright licenses. In both of these community based licenses, a certain ideology and a norm base code of conduct are enshrined explicitly as terms of licenses in which the licensee agrees to follow certain rules of conduct. For example, as open source code licenses set rules on applying and developing "free" information in the open source community, it requires the codes developed to be contributed back to the community.

While not all aspects of the codes are to be openly shared, most new developments based on the shared codes of others need to be contributed back to the community. Despite the obvious shortcoming of the terms that they cannot control all aspects of their products, open source based products are nowadays widely offered. Firms view them as a faster and cheaper way to acquire new technological ideas, on which they can build their own solutions to market. Software is often developed from different sources, which are partly open source. The mix of open source codes with own codes for commercial products creates particular challenges. A manager in an IT company complained in the interview: "... *I know from the legal departments, it is almost impossible to protect yourself if you're talking about software. Because you just add something to it and then it's extremely hard to prove that we have stolen something from another party or* [if it is] *the other way around. So we usually don't protect this."*

In the context of open source and information technology, the existing IP protection seems archaic. This is because the technology seems to develop fast and the rights surrounding the technology become highly fragmented. IP adds uncertainty to the technology and the uncertainty raises the risks. When it is nearly impossible to know who has the rights to the different parts of technology, IP prevents innovation rather than promotes it, and firms strategically leverage or block rivals' technological developments with IP.

In contrast, licensing agreements may promote collaboration. A network of co-operation and co-creation may be formed based on license agreements. Such contracts should however contain more than simply a grant of license, and include various collaborative tools for sharing both costs and profits of technological development. As noticed by one interviewee, licensing in technology may promote collaborative innovation: *"We licensed in certain technology, because we thought that was really the best way of moving forward, and in the same deal we arranged how the companies would actually divide the benefit. And I think, to me that is a modern example of how you do innovation, because you really derive a lot of strength from your partner, but you also bring very good things to the table. Together you are really more powerful than any of the individual partners would have been."*

Contingencies may, however, rise up and change the circumstances so that the original rules of sharing may not seem fair any more. At an extreme, licensees may sometimes face the changed owner of IP who may no longer wish to grant the licenses and who may not even be subject to the terms of contract. To prepare for these contingencies and changed circumstances, networked innovation therefore requires flexibility and trust from all the participants and calls for a mechanism of deciding on contingencies.

Rules on Acquisition and Use of IP as Inputs

Joint rules of collaboration should be discussed before disclosing information or knowledge. A framework contract may set the rules of collaboration to prevent the abuse. A framework contract with clear stating of the aims of collaboration and the treatment of background information and knowledge (including IP) would avoid misunderstandings at the outset. Dishonesty, however, cannot always be prevented and the contract also cannot prevent the defection of another collaborator.

The discussions should also cover how the rules can be implemented. One possibility for implementation is through the creation of a governing entity to manage co-creation and collaborative innovation, with an administrative process such as invention reporting, to monitor inputs and outputs. An interviewee described his own experience of setting up a managing entity with a university-industry research collaboration: *"This is connected with something which may actualize perhaps after ten years or maybe happen somewhere else. And there were four universities. Then there is this administrative organ, which in a way runs the whole research work. And then we have three companies ... Then we research something inside this network. Apparently not co-operating terribly much. Then an invention is born which is then reported. And then for a while we will see what it is about and then we will send a report to everybody that such an invention exists. So that you are welcome to inform everybody in case you want to participate in filing the patent and getting the rights. Then they file the patent and when there are two of them they split all the bills and send us half of the bill. In addition we may also pay them a certain sum of money early."* The process of reporting allows collaborators to be aware of others' intent. At the same time it also allows selective disclosure. If there is an entity that oversees the process, this may promote efficiency in co-ordination, if there are conflicting claims.

Co-creation and collaborative innovation also need to set rules on the use of IP brought into the network, created during the collaboration, and after the collaboration. These are best advised to be agreed in advance with contracts. A contract or clauses on the background is typically on the use of the information and knowledge brought into the collaboration. The term "background" in contracts can contain previous IP of the participants, and other documented or not-documented knowledge and information. As background information would be subject to a set of access rules, participating firms must carefully decide what to include as background information. Separately, firms need to agree on the rules on the use of IP and information resulting from the collaboration as "foreground" (if it is directly related to the main activities of collaboration) and "side ground" information and knowledge (if it is related yet not part of the core activities of the collation). Additionally, as firms will engage in other businesses than collaborative innovation, they would also generate their own IP outside of, and unrelated to, the collaboration. Thus their own or separate IP is also often found in the contracts. Differing degrees of confidentiality and exclusivity, as well as access to all IP, need to be considered, from the beginning, during and even after the project is completed. As summed up by one interviewee: *"So background information is treated separately from foreground information, which is shared if it's developed by more parties. And confidentiality on the results of the project are quite common in our agreements."*

When all this advice is taken into consideration, the resulting contract document could be complex, verbose and detailed. However, while firms try to protect themselves from opportunism with contracts, sanctions based on the breach of contract and threat of litigation do not always promote collaboration. Similarly, detailed rules on knowledge used in the collaboration may prove to be meaningless if the collaborators do not clearly understand the rules as well as which knowledge would be subject to which rules. Rules need to be clearly understood and there should be sufficient motivation for co-operation. Collaboration always needs motivation for future benefits. Trust can be built on sharing the potential benefits, and potential to generate values through continued collaboration, not on the threat of legal sanctions which may terminate the collaboration arrangement. The role of trust in written contracts and in the absence of a formal contract is discussed in Chapter 5.

Both our and other empirical findings show that a change of attitude is needed in favour of settling and discussing rules of conduct, since without clear rules of conduct and management structures, open communication will be a naive illusion of collaboration. Additionally, models for rules of use of IP and management structures for networked innovation are needed. Experience will increase knowledge in setting rules of conduct and spread best practices.

IP as a Result of Collaboration

When firms know the type of knowledge and technology necessary for a particular product's development and innovation, IP is seen more as an object of transaction. In contrast, when firms need to develop technology either alone or with other specified or unspecified number of external collaborators, IP is both an input to the process of innovation as well as an outcome of the collaboration. While there are some rules in the IP law as to who may be entitled to a right, but how the rights may be shared, and co-owned over a collaborative outcome are not regulated in detail. Thus it is important to agree on the main rules of governing or sharing the costs and beneficial outcome of the input.

Free-riding is a risk that discourages joint production or collaborative innovation. As noted by one of our interviewees, claims for IP may block the collaboration: "*Yeah, we have a lot of co-operation, but that is not easy if you have the IP thing in there. Very often it blocks things.*" The quick phase of innovation sometimes leads to an inevitable mixture of collaborative inputs and ends up with IP claims over each input. Our interviewee notes that in the innovation stage, "*I prefer everyone* [to generate] *their own IP. Don't try to blend it or have workshops...*" In other words, if IP acquisition is considered, truly innovative co-creation or collaboration would not happen as each collaborator may be less forward in contributing their share as they worry that other parties may free ride and even claim IP over their idea.

Rules on sharing IP which results from collaborative input need to discourage free riding. One solution is to entrust one of the collaborators or even a third-party association with the task of managing and claiming rights. Often one of the parties may claim rights for the co-created innovation. It may be agreed that one of the parties, usually the one who invests most and has the resources may acquire the right and maintain the rights, while others may get some compensation or benefit. A joint ownership of patents as well as copyrights is possible in the IP law of many countries. Conditions on how joint owners of an IP may exercise their ownership might differ. As a result most firms are reluctant to opt for joint ownership. Earlier studies recommend it as a second best option that should be avoided and alternative arrangements should be sought.[6] Our interviews support this view as firms adopt the policies against joint ownership, even if it would cost less. Joint ownership of patents seems to be assessed as a potential source of disputes. One manager noted that: "*... our central management is fairly sensitive to these joint, intellectual properties, property rights. And so, it's really ... because we are always investing, almost always investing* [more] *... we* *also claim all the rights. So it is really difficult to find a* [modus] *for sharing that, in practice."*

A more neutral sentiment was noted in another interview with a representative of a research organization: *"Joint ownership . . . we have had that, too, yes . . . Usually it happens in a consortium that the consortium has the priority right, and that also goes according to financial shares and if there are very different shares of financing. If the consortium is not willing, then we can — and this has been included (in the contract) — that we can freely sell it to others. The consortium first considers if it is to be commercialized. Most often there is in the consortium somebody who wants to commercialize."* The different sentiment may be caused by the presence of a consortium. A consortium may oversee the use of jointly owned IP, and co-ordinate the interests of joint owners.

In other words, while joint ownership may seem a natural choice to share IP over the outcome of collaboration, concern for free riding and co-ordination of the joint owners present a particular challenge in practice. Furthermore, decisions on licensing or selling the patent in changed circumstances may be more difficult to make when the rights are jointly owned. The main issue may not be the absence of trust on other partners, but ease of decision making when circumstances change in the future. In the words of one interviewee: *"We don't favour joint patenting, and that is not only because of increased bureaucracy it entails. It's what the management of joint patents through the life cycle of the patent involves. Twenty years is a long time and a lot can happen. There can be changes in the interests and ownerships of the firms. And that can make things very complicated."* According to our case and interview studies, the ownership of IP related to joint innovation was usually allocated to one of the partners and then licensed to others. When there is joint ownership, the decision has usually been thought over, calculated, and aligned with the business model, as reflected in the reply of the interviewee on joint ownership of a patent: *"But then of course we did some scaling up and when we made the contract we also translated that background knowledge into monetary units, and that was part of the calculation. Well we had also sums that moved, but, on the other hand, it was also taken care of in the royalty calculations . . ."*

The rules of patentability may cause unwanted surprises for joint innovations. Patent applications are evaluated in terms of the subject matter, novelty, inventive steps (non-obviousness) and industrial applicability (utility) in most countries.[7] Among these rules, for example, requirement of novelty may present hurdles for collaboration. The invention should be novel and not known to others. In a networked innovation inventive ideas may become known within the network prior to patent filing. Perhaps there may be cases where a collaborator in the network may want to contest novelty to prevent the patent being issued to one of the co-innovators. In this respect, networked innovation is contradictory to the principles of patentability rules which assume that there would be one inventor/inventing entity who would contribute to the inventive process. In countries, such as the US, where there is a general grace period for novelty preserving it within a given period, there is a certain reprieve to this, but as European countries do not have such general grace period, disclosure made in the collaborative network may destroy novelty.

Losing novelty may be prevented by non-disclosure agreements (NDAs). However, as NDAs prevent free flow of information, networked innovation is rarely truly open in industry sectors where patents are important and information should be kept confidential. In many traditional industry sectors, patents are still important and constitute a valuable tool for technological development of the industry. On the other hand, some industry sectors develop so fast that the patenting cycle cannot keep up and new technology has to be taken into use as soon as possible. It may also be beneficial to spread the information as fast as possible to get new improvements and generate network effects. In computer technology and services, for example, the patenting cycle seems to slow and even hinder technological development. Networked and open innovation, therefore, seems a practical and viable means of innovating in those sectors. In this regard, the decision to adopt an open and collaborative approach to IP needs to reflect not only the individual firm's business model, but also the strategy of rivals and norms of the industry.

Co-creation and collaborative innovation always includes risks, because the "open" environment may be misused. A classic prisoner's dilemma is most manifested in this situation and as openness makes it easy for the collaborator to leave the network, one bad experience alone or self-interest may make parties defect rather than collaborate. This was noted by a R&D manager interviewee: "*We did it in good faith within a R&D project, which*

*was large with several partners including one of our clients. We had the
idea that if we do something, we will get a product and so on, and so we did
and with a lot of trouble as well . . . When it was ready, the representatives of
that client company told us that they had, by the way, patented the solution
already before the project and thank you for the development work, but
you cannot apply that anywhere else. And it was such, businesswise, such a
really small thing, but still . . . exceptional. Quite often we confront this, but
not with clients . . . But that is what happened quite recently. It was quite
nasty . . ."*

The interviewee identifies two of the core aspects of the risks involved
with co-creation and collaborative innovation: that the outcome of the
result is uncertain, and parties to co-creation and collaboration may have
heterogeneous interests and motivation for participation. To ensure and to
motivate collaborative input, it is important to have norms or regulations
which clearly instruct collaborators in the network on what to expect and
how to behave over the outcome. As IP law does not regulate how parties
in the network should behave, this falls squarely in the domain of private
ordering.

Dynamic Innovation and Static IP Law

As a theory on innovation paradigm, a networked innovation or open innovation influences the incentive theory. Incentive theory, which is touched
upon in the beginning of this chapter, explains the need for IP protection
in law to arise as the law needs to provide incentive for production of
valuable intangible knowledge. Open innovation as an innovation paradigm
advocates that it is not the IP that provides incentives for the inventors and
creators, but in a commercial context it is the opportunities of the market
for knowledge goods which drive the inventors and creators to innovate.
Within the Bazaar of Opportunities the focus shifts from IP protection to
the market and business models, and it challenges the assumption that IP
protection provides incentives to invent and create.

The innovation process is always dynamic and fluid. In networked
and open innovation both participants and forms of network co-operation
are heterogeneous and dynamic. Often there are different kinds of firms
involved; they can be subcontractors or competitors, small firms and big

corporations, universities and research institutes, consulting firms and so on (see Table 3.3 in Chapter 3). The motivations are not always aligned and the interests vary. For example, university researchers want to perform research tasks and publish the results, while the firms would focus on commercialization of a promising innovation. Even among the for-profit firms, the relationships vary and within the network and value chain, firms may occupy different positions which may define or restrict their participation. In some networks with systems innovations, there is often a co-ordinator or a system integrator, who takes care of the network and takes the responsibility towards outsiders as well.[8] A firm may be situated as a contract manufacturer (subcontractor), dependent on the main contractor, but nonetheless may contribute to the innovation process.

These co-ordinators and secondary innovators are not taken into consideration in IP law, as IP law recognizes only the rights of the first inventor and owners. As users and incremental innovators are not in the main focus of law, their incentives to innovate may yet need to be taken into consideration. The innovative contribution at the downstream may, often in the case of contract manufacturing, need to feed back to the upstream right holders. A manager of a system integrator company described its position: *"We more or less innovate. We catalyze the change but, of course, the parties can easily do it together. And, still, there are reasons to remain involved, and so that's a business model which is becoming more difficult."*

As the networks and collaborative innovation is dynamic, participants may change. Firms may change owners and a subcontractor may become a competitor. IP law does not regulate the change in the ownership structure of the industry of the network, but only the change of rights holders. Depending on the jurisdictions, the licensee may or may not survive the change in the ownership of the underlying IP. Thus some jointly agreed mechanism for encountering contingencies and changed circumstances within the network of collaboration is recommendable.

Change also affects parties unevenly and may lead to a more favourable result of one collaborator compared to the others. One dilemma of co-operation is an uneven distribution of benefits because of changed circumstances. When there is a danger of copying, leaked knowledge may reach a local competitor, which may then later threaten the collaboration. One interviewee noted that "... *we have not yet encountered it, but maybe someday we will face a massive epidemic of copying . . . but for instance like India, however, there is maybe even a problem worse than copying . . . that some local deliverer, and it does not necessary actually copy . . . it just borrows some common knowledge from these deliverers and then it simply does everything locally so extremely cheap. This is the problem. It's not even the machinery which is not really a copy that was the main problem, but the fact that it is just done in some corner with one euro per hour salary, where it does not cost nearly anything. The problem is that it may give a local buyer an attractive alternative. At least in India it goes like this. But as I have already said, in the software part we have not really been met with this problem, but software is different and luckily we have not met with anything bigger.*" If change was triggered by the leaked knowledge, the firm in this scenario may be able to affect the course of change by controlling the leak. On the other hand, as the example shows, copying was minimal and the change was rather triggered by the economic developments in the market resulting in the possibility of local sourcing for the buyer. These changed circumstances cannot be controlled by contractual clause or by law.

The need for open and dynamic communication makes innovation networks vulnerable to opportunism. Selective disclosure is not only prevalent but sometimes even encouraged. As a result, it is possible that collaborating partners are hiding information from each other in order to free ride on others' contribution and claim the entire innovation process. To prevent this, early information flow, especially outside the network, may have to be discouraged, as this may result in loss of IP altogether. At the same time, IP law does not protect incomplete and initial ideas as such, but protection has to be based on self-help and informal means. Firms use informal methods in protecting innovations and ideas. Such methods can be prohibition for competition, recruitment freeze, limiting the access of the circle of knowing about the innovation, defensive publishing and making the innovation rhythm faster to be ahead of the competitors (see Table 1.1 in Chapter 1).

In sum, while there is a need to seek non-IP based means of providing incentives for various collaborators and to protect against opportunism, the dynamic nature of the collaborative innovation makes it difficult to regulate this with one instrument alone. Flexible contracts may help and informal means of protection may also provide alternative solution to IP. However, as seen in the above example, private ordering also means that it is necessary to take the regulatory context of the IP into consideration.

Non-disclosure Agreements Shaping Collaborative Networks

Non-disclosure agreement (NDA) is a common method of protecting confidential knowledge. NDAs are becoming more important in networked innovation to keep the dynamic flow of information within the agreed framework. Our interviewee, for example, noted how common it is: "*We make them and quite often when we do something together with a client, perhaps also when there are not necessarily other parties, we may make some NDAs, and with subcontractors we have NDAs as well. It is typical that during co-operation, when it requires getting acquainted with each other's systems and everything, that you cannot use that information. This is the typical content of a NDA. There are standard forms and it is a routine, a NDA is not a terribly strange issue. And I guess it isn't for our clients or co-operation partners either. They (NDAs) are quite common.*"

Although NDAs are common, not everybody wants to sign them. Furthermore, the scope of NDAs varies from a simple non-disclosure of the received knowledge to a full scale non-competition clause in the same industry for a given period. When the NDAs are unreasonable considering the benefits of collaboration, firms may choose not to agree on the terms of non disclosure. For example, "*so the NDA states that we cannot work for others before a certain period of time has passed. Sometimes I don't sign them, because they want to block us for everything, for example we were working for a bakery machinery factory, and we were doing some . . . consultancy, just for 100 hours, and they wanted to block us for five years, not allow us to do anything in that industry. I don't think that's realistic, so I didn't sign it then. But sometimes they just include certain companies, especially those who are very competitive, and say that you cannot work on the same subject. But, yeah, we don't have a problem working for companies at the same time actually. We don't look for it though . . . Of course it's very interesting to maybe look at the competition as well, the competition of our customers, because you already have joint experience in that area.*"

NDAs are made to remind us about the confidential nature of information and knowledge exchange. Naturally they cannot prevent all human errors and mistakes. Sometimes a firm policy may favour not wanting to share all the knowledge. One manager observed: "*. . . don't have a CA* [confidentiality agreement] *at all. Some people in our company advocate this, they say don't do a CA.*" Not having a NDA makes it easy to collaborate but also to prevent claims of idea contamination. Another interviewee notes that: "*The reason is that, it's not only that you're afraid of . . . that your own IP leaks away, but you also don't want to be contaminated with IP from others. Because, if in such a brainstorm somebody comes up with a brilliant idea, maybe it's already being done in your lab, you could even have issues where they say, well we thought about it in that meeting, so now it's ours. So, it's really, it's very important that you protect yourself.*" Absence of trust may lead to hiding of information: "*don't do it* [a NDA] *! I have to decide what comes out of the workshop, no IP, or keep it isolated.*" When this policy is applied, collaboration will stay on a superficial or general level. Not wanting to sign NDAs may also create distrust among collaborators that the shared information is not valuable and signal the quality and level of co-operation.

On the other hand, there may exist pressures for publishing and making information on an innovation public, and this complicates the obligation of confidentiality. One of our interviewees downplays this pressure with the example for publicity: "*there have not been such challenging problems but sometimes it has happened that our own sales organization would have wanted to publish unfinished information* [and signal to] *the market . . . even before we can grasp the whole area where we are moving around. So we do not want to give competitors any hint on where our development is heading, but the marketing* [department] *of course wants to be innovative and offer clients new solutions too early, but we actually haven't had other pressures of this type.*"

In contrast to this, if open source software code is used, publication of the derivative codes is an obligation based on GPLs. The conflict may be real for open source software firms who offer open source based solutions to their client who may insist on a NDA. Similarly, in projects between university and industry R&D publication of the university research effort may create tension for the industry partners.

In the above-mentioned circumstances of pressure on new innovative ideas, human mistakes can easily be made. Statutory or contractual remedies may function as threats, but do not cover the damage done. Use of NDAs should be combined with educating the personnel who work with potential trade secrets. Agreeing and going jointly through the agreed rules emphasizes the significance of the agreement much more than only signing and perhaps not even reading the contract. As not all informational exchange can be subject to NDAs, the control that NDAs aim for cannot be achieved.

In collaborative innovation networks the value of contracts increases as the collaboration would result in beneficial outcomes in the future. Keeping the aims and needs of the network needs to be in balance with creating and maintaining trust. As IP law may fail to provide protection, contracts and promises may also be broken. The problem with collaborative innovation is the uncertainty of the outcome. The risks of network innovation should therefore be understood beforehand and taken consciously. Chapter 5 discusses more on sharing costs and benefits of collaborative innovations in contracts.

Dual and Strategic Use of Openness

Firms use openness as well as networked innovation strategically in a dual way. They may use networks for searching for solutions outside the boundaries of firms. This exchange across the boundary of a firm is what Henry Chesbrough has expressed with the idea of open innovation.[9] The rapid pace of technological developments and market-driven changes make it nearly impossible even for a large corporation nowadays to rely solely on their own R&D department as sources of innovation.

Even in a relatively closed inventive process, it is not uncommon to use external scientists and collaborators in the inventive process leading to the grant of the right, and during the commercialization. In the innovation process, openness can be introduced in the conception and creation of the innovation, in the production/sourcing of the innovation, and in the use and distribution of innovation. Likewise, firms do not necessarily practice openness at the stage when it is not desirable for the firm such as when it would cost the firm to lose the claims to the inventive idea. Literature documents that the result of the innovation is that innovative products themselves may incorporate openness in the product design by allowing open access to the underlying product information technically and legally, or encourage improvements by user innovations.[10] Any of these approaches may be combined to achieve a desirable degree of openness in the innovation process and in the product.

Firms which have realized the importance of open innovation also actively work for developing communities and the rules that govern them. Such firms are also active in networks and invest in developing the contractual models and a basis for collaborative innovations. As some open innovation or collaborative innovation communities and platforms allow users to set the rules, this leads to an interactive community development, and active firms may influence how collaborative innovation can be done in a given platform.

Additionally, some firms defend their "freedom to operate" on a certain technology or industry sector and therefore, for instance, aim to publish information as soon as possible to prevent their competitors from patenting the knowledge before them. The network can then be engaged for that purpose. Free revealing or disclosure of information does happen in non open source communities, especially in industries where competition for patents is fierce. As a defensive measure, firms may reveal information with the intention of defeating a rival firm's patent application. This strategy is often used together with patent opposition filing against rivals in order to defend the freedom to operate. Our case firms seem to recognize the need for protection and utilize various means beyond IP (such as recruitment freeze, prohibitions of competition, limiting the access to the circle knowing the innovation, publishing, or making the innovation rhythm faster). At the same time they are not always aligned with IP strategies or in some cases stricter rules on confidentiality may lead to a failure in collaboration. This kind of defensive use of openness (publication) is an interesting interface where a method of closed innovation (patent race) meets with open innovation strategy.

Formal or Informal Exchange?

IP rights and law not only provide incentives for innovation and protect them as property, but also co-ordinate the modes of their exchange. At a most obvious level, innovation can be embodied in the tangible products and services that the firms offer. A more intangible aspect of innovation is the processes and routines of a firm. Firms utilize their capabilities in internal or external exchanges of intangibles. They may also utilize the knowledge, which they have generated, for the internal efficiency of the organization and improve the general organizational capabilities. On the other hand, if there are demands from the market/customer, industry structure, and technological features, and if the regulatory contexts and the general capabilities of the firm can support it, firms may choose to extract values by commercializing them.

Not all commercially valuable knowledge can be isolated and belong to the firm and be protected as IP. Some of the knowledge collectively resides with the firm, based on their past experiences, and some with individual employees. This includes the collective tacit knowledge of the organization, or aggregated knowledge that belongs to the engineers of the firm gathered through their experiences in the firm. This dual nature of the intangibles makes it crucial to isolate this capability from other *ad hoc* or personalized management of the protection and transactions of intangibles in a firm. Intellectual property rights in law is one means of isolating intangible and valuable knowledge. At the same time it is possible to physically and/or contractually control and isolate the knowledge. Utilizing organizational processes to regularly transfer the knowledge from R&D personnel to the organization and contractually bind them to non-disclosure obligations is one such example.[11]

When firms introduce openness in their innovation process, this dual nature of knowledge becomes manifested. If the knowledge was to be treated only as property, a firm's internal policy on IP alone would be sufficient to implement and introduce openness in the innovation process. However, duality of knowledge makes it important not only to implement IP policies, but also other means to control and protect the knowledge sharing may also have to be considered. A confidentiality clause, which is often regulated with firm internal policies and through non-disclosure agreements of the collaborating parties, is often used to complement IP policies. Additional means include prohibition of competition, recruitment freeze, limiting the access of the circle knowing about the innovation, defensive publications, and making the innovation rhythm faster to be ahead of the competitors.

Formal and informal exchanges deal with this aspect of knowledge. Formal exchange would function best in the context where the knowledge is most formalized as concrete legally protected IP. Thus, formal IP based exchange (i.e. buying, selling, and licenses) is used widely in branches of industry and technology where IP is an important means of competition. Formal IP based exchange is only possible when all the collaborating partners can be identified. Protection of confidential information formalizes the informational exchange as well. Open innovation or collaboration in this industry setting is likely to be transactional in character where the networks are platforms to exchange IP which are units of transaction.

Informal exchange would promote exchange of non-IP-based knowledge. At the same time, informal exchange works when there are good rules concerning the framework and network or platform itself laying the most important rules for co-operation (i.e. the aim of collaboration, the process for IP over inputs and output). Ground rules concerning the framework may be created by framework agreement (contracts), community norms, and trust. Informal exchange is beneficial only if there are clearly understood rules of the community or the network, as uncertainty as to the collaborative input and outcome would subject the entire collaborative network to opportunism and free-riding. As the informality of the exchange also makes it easy for a collaboration party to exit, rules on exit and consequences of non-collaboration should be clearly understood at the outset. In innovation networks in business to business exchanges the most used informal exchange is supported by contracts, which can be regarded as the most formal of the informal methods of protecting knowledge (see Table 1.1 in Chapter 1).

Since IP law does not target innovation from networks, contracts remain the most formal form of private ordering on collaborative and network innovations. Private ordering here is not an attempt to escape or circumvent mandatory legislation but rather an effort to remove uncertainties and provide co-ordination. Developing contracts with co-operative partners within private governance requires a lot of work and energy from firms, who try to create a well-functioning framework of collaboration.[12] More recent literature in law seems to advocate the superiority of the private ordering means over legal reforms to provide means of co-operation and govern use of intangible resources.[13] Reforming legislation means that the law needs to incentivize actors to introduce more openness taking the multiple claim holders and their heterogeneous interests as well as openness in communication into consideration. This is more challenging. For example, one way of introducing openness in the innovation would be through the use of specific limitations or exceptions in the IP law.[14]

Two such obvious examples could be posited as an exception to disclosure before the acquisition of a patent (i.e. novelty rules on patent) and as an exception to infringement for the sake of "open innovation" in patent law. The first example would call for introducing a longer or more extensive "grace period" to preserve the novelty of the invention. At a glance this would promote open discussions and sharing in a given forum. At the same time, this would defeat the users of defensive publication. Introducing a more extensive grace period would have to be carefully approached. Providing exceptions is more difficult. Arguably introducing research and experimental use exceptions to patent infringement for example would not necessarily promote openness in the innovation because this will only benefit researching actors who are participating in the process.[15]

In other words, the dynamic and heterogeneous nature of the actors makes it difficult to introduce an actor or behaviour-specific limitation or an exception in IP law for open innovation. However, to protect the interests of joint collaborators, one potential doctrinal element that would empower open innovators may be own invention defence for own use against the claims of infringement. It may be useful and needs to be carefully explored. Most patent laws, however, do not provide this defence. In sum, given the current legal context, in the absence of IP law revisions, to prevent disputes, we find proactive private ordering necessary to interface IP laws with open innovation.

Despite the importance of contracting, contracts are still ignored, especially in the beginning phase of networked innovation processes. The reason for ignoring contracts is that they are regarded as formal legal devices, preventing free flow of innovation. However, one interviewee expressed a completely opposite view according to which contracts are worth the trouble: "... *the thing that goes wrong is that ... where a potential collaboration does not start when you can't find agreement on the terms. But I'm not sure if that was wrong. Maybe it's better that they don't start. So ... I mean, it's the negotiations about contracts etc. ... they can be very time-consuming and lead to delays in getting something started, but I don't think we've made any big mistakes or have had any bad experiences with something that we have put in place, so far. Is that the wrong answer?"*

Seen from an empirical approach contracts are regarded both as a method to strengthen statutory protection and an alternative to statutory protection. The dynamic nature of collaborative innovation and co-creation and the heterogeneous interests of the partners make it difficult to uniformly govern it with IP law alone. In the absence of a proper legal safeguard for own collaborative input, open and collaborative innovation requires firms to more actively and strategically involve in the governance of IP and knowledge, not just in terms of acquiring and defending them, but also to use the rights and to generate values. As contracts and contracting are more than NDAs and licenses, managers of collaboration need to acknowledge the role of contracts as a means of governance. Based on this the next chapter explores the role of the contract as a tool for collaboration.

Conclusions: IP Law and IP Management in Networks

IP rights and law provide incentives for innovation and protect them as property. IP rights and law, however, are designed for protecting innovations without multiple stakeholders. Open and networked innovation challenges the principles of IP law in two ways:

(1) Multiple claim holders who (may) have heterogeneous interests, and
(2) Openness in the communication in their exchange.

Accordingly, IP law gives considerable support to transactions of existing IP from one actor to another as an input for new business development or as an enabling factor of business offering. IP law, however, gives less support for the co-creation of new knowledge and business with two or more actors. It supports possible transactions related to the input and output knowledge of co-creation, but the actual innovation process of co-creation is not sufficiently well backed by the present IP legislation. Although IP laws do regulate the question of co-inventor, co-creator and co-owner, they do not regulate how these rights may be co-ordinated or managed, in what hierarchy, and how to handle possible conflicts of interests among the stakeholders during the life cycle of IP. Openness between the stakeholders

Table 4.1.   Modes of IP exchange in networked innovation.

	Inbound	Outbound
For Profit Transaction/ Exploitation	Acquire/Buy/Contract In/ License In	Sell/License Out/ Contract Out
For Profit Access	Cross License & Pool	
Not for Profit Co-creation/ Exploration	Take (formal & informal)/ Open Source/Crowdsourcing	Disclose (formal & informal)/ Contribute & Publish

in innovation should also be managed. That can only be done formally, through formal governance means, i.e. contracts, or informally, through community norms and trust.

We have summarized the conclusions of the chapter in Table 4.1. The table has a strong link to the discussion on collaboration models and knowledge management in Chapter 3. While the discussion in Chapter 3 was focused on the classification of collaboration models, Table 4.1 addresses the modes of IP exchange supported by IP law in networked innovation. The table considers both inbound and outbound directions of business value chain. The words "for profit" and "not for profit" underline direct business interests in question. In the transaction of existing knowledge, the business interests are directly involved in the exchange, but in the co-creation of new knowledge the business interests may be indirect and in the future. The table also includes special cases of IP transactions, namely cross-licensing of IPs and creating of IP pools.

Notes

1. [Samuelson, P. (1954). The Pure Theory of Public Expenditure, *Review of Economics and Statistics*, MIT Press, Vol. 36, pp. 387–389.]
2. [Lee, N. (2007). Toward a Pluralistic Theory on an Efficacious Patent Institution, *John Marshall Review of Intellectual Property Law*, Vol. 6, pp. 220–249.]
3. [Lee, N. (2009). Exclusion and Coordination in Collaborative Innovation and Patent Law, *International Journal of Intellectual Property Management*, Vol. 3, pp. 79–93.]
4. [Lee, N., Nystén-Haarala, S. and Huhtilainen, L. (2010). 'Interfacing Intellectual Property Rights and Open Innovation', in Tokkeli, M. (ed.), *Frontiers of Open Innovation*, Faculty of Technology Management, Department of Industrial Management, Research report 225. Lappeenranta University of Technology, pp. 121–140. Also available online at http://www.ssrn.com/astract=1674365 (Accessed on 23 February 2012.)]

5. Open source software refers to GNU, General Public Licenses of different variations (LGPL, AGPL, FDL), or Unix licences. GNU created the "copyleft concept" meaning that distribution of modified versions must occur on the same royalty-free term as distribution of the original. Unix-based open source licenses (Linux Kernel) such as BSB, which originated at the University of California for Berkeley Unix, permits the user to do essentially anything with the software, as long as the licensor's copyright notice is retained. See Phillips (2009) and the Open Source Initiative. [Phillips, D.E. (2009). *The Software License Unveiled. How Legislation by License Controls Software Access*. Oxford University Press, p. 232; Open Source Initiative, http://www.opensource.org/licenses (Accessed on 22 February 2012.)]

6. See for example, Lee (2009) 3, and Hagedoorn (2003). [Lee, N. (2009). Exclusion and Coordination in Collaborative Innovation and Patent Law, *International Journal of Intellectual Property Management*, Vol. 3, pp. 79–93; Hagedoorn, J. (2003). Sharing Intellectual Property Rights — An Exploratory Study for Joint Patenting Amongst Companies, *Industrial and Corporate Challenge*, Vol. 12, pp. 1035–1050.]

7. See for example, Art. 27,1 confirming these as minimum standards in the WTO member states. [WTO Agreement on Trade-Related Aspects of Intellectual Property Rights (1994). Art. 28, 15 April, 33 I.L.M. 81.]

8. [Paasi, J., Valkokari, K., Rantala, T., Hytönen, H., Nystén-Haarala, S. and Huhtilainen, L. (2010). Innovation Management Challenges of a System Integrator in Innovation Networks, *International Journal of Innovation Management*, Vol. 14, pp. 1047–1064.]

9. [Chesbrough, H. (2003) *Open Innovation: The New Imperative for Creating and Profiting from Technology*, Harvard Business School Press, Boston.]

10. [Strandburg, K.J. (2008). Users as Innovators: Implication for Patent Doctrine, *University of Colorado Law Review*, Vol. 79, No. 2. Also available online at http://ssrn.com/abstract=1141386 (Accessed on 23 February 2012.)]

11. [Lee, N. (2008). 'From Tangibles to Intangibles — Contracting Capability for Intangible Innovation', in Nystén-Haarala, S. (ed.), *Corporate Contracting Capabilities, Conference Proceedings and Other Writings*, Publications of Legal Studies of the University of Joensuu 21, pp. 33–50.]

12. Lee *et al.* (2010), and Vlaar *et al.* (2006). [Lee, N., Nystén-Haarala, S. and Huhtilainen, L. (2010). 'Interfacing Intellectual Property Rights and Open Innovation, in Torkkeli, M. (ed.), *Frontiers of Open Innovation*, Faculty of Technology Management, Department of Industrial Management, Research report 225. Lappeenranta University of Technology, pp. 121–140. Also available online at http://www.ssrn.com/astract=1674365; Vlaar, P.W.L, Van den Bosch, L., F.A.J. and Voberda, H.W. (2006). Coping with Problems of Understanding Interorganizational Relationships: Using Formalization as a Means to Make Sense, *Organization Studies*, Vol. 27, pp. 1617–1638.]

13. Examples of such literature are O'Connor (2009) and Van Overwalle (2010). [O'Connor, S.M. (2009). 'IP Transactions as Facilitators of the Globalized Innovation Economy', in Dreyfuss, R. *et al.* (eds), *Working within the Boundaries of Intellectual Property*, Oxford University Press, Oxford, pp. 203–228. Also available online at http://ssrn.com/abstract=1465004 (Accessed on 23 February 2012.); Van Overwalle, G. (ed.) (2010). *Gene Patents and Collaborative Licensing Models — Patent Pools, Clearinghouses, Open source Models and Liability Regimes*, Cambridge

Intellectual Property and Information Law Series, No. 10, Cambridge University Press, Cambridge.]

14. Lee *et al.* (2010). [Lee, N., Nystén-Haarala, S. and Huhtilainen, L. (2010). 'Interfacing Intellectual Property Rights and Open Innovation, in Torkkeli, M. (ed.), *Frontiers of Open Innovation*, Faculty of Technology Management, Department of Industrial Management, Research report 225. Lappeenranta University of Technology, pp. 121–140. Also available online at http://www.ssrn.com/astract=1674365 (Accessed on 23 February 2012.)]

15. Lee *et al.* (2010) *ibid.*, and Strandburg (2008) *ibid.*

Chapter 5

Contract and IP Management in Networked Innovation

In business, a contract is often understood as a written document,[1] which is concluded in order to bind the two or more contracting parties and safeguard them from risks or inconvenient contingencies as well as opportunistic behaviour of the other party. Contracts, however, can be very different from each other depending on the business model in question. For instance, in ordinary sale of goods the rights and duties of contracting parties are contradictory, while in collaboration contracts the parties have joint targets. Oral agreements can be as binding as written ones, and written contracts can contain a lot of important appendices. Contracts can also be chained with other contracts (subcontracting) or be connected in a business network. Some contracts are multilateral having a lot of contracting parties. Contract law, however, has been developed for transaction contracts, the model of contract law being ordinary sale of goods, where interests of the (mostly two) parties are contradictory.[2] As intellectual property law is designed for protecting clear innovations without multiple interests or multiple stakeholders, contract law is also designed for clear transactions from one party to another. When the scope of a contract gets more complicated and the time period longer, the protection of contract law decreases. In the Bazaar of Opportunities it is crucial for collaboration partners to understand clearly what they actually have agreed both in written documents and in oral agreements. In Chapter 5 we take a closer look at contracts and contracting in networked innovation, especially from the standpoint of IP management.

The Role of Contracts and Contracting Capabilities in Networks

Even if contract law is too static and rigid for dynamic and flexible collaboration, it is mostly non-mandatory, making contracts and contracting a practical device for private ordering. Co-operation partners can design their contracts themselves for their own purposes and create their own rules differing from the default rules of non-mandatory legislation. Contracts can be enforced between the parties (self-enforced) even in situations in which the courts would not enforce them. In recent literature contracts are often regarded as a more effective way to protect IP compared to IP law when there are multiple interests and multiple stakeholders.[3] Private governance is more flexible and efficient compared to legislation. Private governance, however, calls for good capabilities in designing and applying good and well-functioning contracts.

Contracting for transaction networks and co-creation networks has differing logic as illustrated in Table 3.2 in Chapter 3. Contracts of transaction networks, such as licensing contracts, tend to express rights and duties of contracting parties clearly and share risks between known partners. They are usually fairly static and complete. Contracts governing co-creation networks, on the other hand, are, especially in the beginning phase of co-operation, dynamic and incomplete. It is difficult to share risks and benefits when you do not even know what will be the result of the joint innovation process. Uncertainty has a strong impact on co-creation contracting. At the beginning of co-creation, contracts are a frame in which parties can collaborate. The frame can be complemented gradually and new, more complete and definite contracts are made as well. In this volume we apply the concepts of incomplete and evolving contracts. In contract law such concepts are applied to contracts, which are difficult or even impossible to enforce by a court decision.[4] Some contract law scholars do not even regard incomplete and evolving contracts as contracts, because they are often only self-enforced[5] while there are other scholars who see contracts more as a framework for co-operation than a strict division of contradicting rights and duties of contracting parties strengthened with remedies.[6]

Transaction and co-creation networks are also dependent on the subsequent business models. In networks, companies may also have to deal with many different business models, and have to adjust their contracting with different purposes and roles. Especially in co-creation differing roles and motivations in co-operation complicate contracting (see Table 3.3). Seeing contracting as a dynamic and evolving process starting from the planning phase of the project (such as joint innovation or licensing IP rights) through negotiations, design, signing, implementing and finally ending the project in a well-managed way, helps in understanding the supporting role of contracting as a device of collaboration, not a document locked in a safe-box for potential court procedure.

Figure 5.1 depicts the idea of a contract being a process dependent on the subsequent business model. The idea can more easily be presented in transaction-type contracts,[7] thus Fig. 5.1 applies the idea to licensing contracts.

Figure 5.2 is a simplified process figure illustrating the evolving nature of contracting around innovations and their commercialization. Framework contracts may be specified on the way, and when the commercialization phase (offering) is reached, co-operation partners often have to agree on sharing profits again in the new circumstances. Ownership and especially use of IP has to be decided at some point of the process. The final point to agree on IP is right before the offering, but collaboration partners may decide on the main rules of IP use already at the beginning of co-creation.

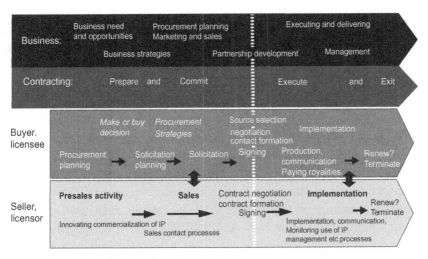

Fig. 5.1. Contracting and business processes applied to licensing agreements.

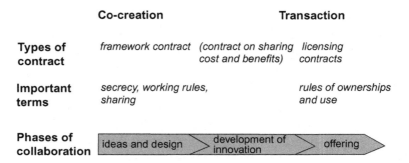

Fig. 5.2.   The evolving nature of innovation contracting.

Licensing agreements are most often applied to govern rules of use of an already commercialized innovation. (Cf. the figures on typologies of co-creation and transaction networks in Chapter 3.)

The role of contracts can be comprehended through their functions, the combination of which again depends on the applied business model. Transaction networks mostly require safeguarding, while co-ordination of co-operation and preparing for contingencies are more important for co-creation. Transaction and co-creation contracting also call for differing contracting capabilities; formal and detailed content of contract documents is more important in transaction networks, while co-creation calls for relational networking capabilities that rely on creating and maintaining trust between co-operation partners. In the commercialization phase co-creation contracts start to resemble contracts of transaction networks. Management of contract processes also differ in these two types of networking models.

When contracts are regarded as devices of private ordering, they are not studied *ex post* as in court procedure, but *ex ante*, proactively as serving the aims of business.[8] This chapter approaches contracts and contracting proactively as a means for enhancing successful and important relationships and performances, aiming at preventing problems from arising as well as managing conflicts when they arise within private governance without the need to take disputes into courts.[9] In this chapter we study the differences between contracting in transaction and co-creation networks requiring different contracting capabilities and fulfilling differing functions. The focus is on co-creation contracts, which do not have standard forms and do not always even fit in the standard (legal) understanding of contract.

Functions of Contracts in Transaction and Co-creation Networks

The difference between contracting in transaction and co-creation networks can be illustrated with different functions of contracts in these networks. Understanding why contracts are concluded helps to realize how they should be designed and managed. Figure 3.1 illustrates the decision making on why collaboration is needed, how interests and targets are decided and what the model of collaboration resulting from this process is. Yet, contracts are often regarded only as compulsory and dull evils that simply have to be made to be able to make the deal or start the collaboration. In other words, contracts are separated from the collaboration process. Approaching contracts from their functions, however, reveals a more complicated world of opportunities, offering competitive advantage for those who know how to design good contracts and align them with subsequent business models.

The idea of presenting contracts by their functions developed in organization studies to approach contracts from organizational learning and processes of change. Functions can be classified differently depending on the research aim and the types of contracts. Functions of contract of both transaction and co-creation networks can be illustrated in Table 5.1.[10] Some contractual functions are framework functions or prerequisites for co-operation or contracting while others are more practical functions.

These functions are discussed in the sections that follow.

Binding force and commitment

A contract is a commitment and the whole idea of contract law is based on the legally binding nature of contracts. If contracts are not performed, they can be enforced with the help of contract law in a court procedure.

Table 5.1. Functions of contracts.

Prerequisites	Parties bound or committed to the contract
	Value creation and appropriation (at least in the long run)
Practical functions	Safeguarding
	Co-ordination and control
	Preparing for contingencies
	(Dispute settlement)

Transaction network contracts usually represent this idea. When they are written in a formal way, defining rights and obligations explicitly and safeguarding for foreseeable risks, lawyers in court may interpret them in a more or less foreseeable manner. In co-creation, the commitment is in the beginning often only for working together in good faith. They may be self-enforcing, based on commitment, which cannot be enforced by court decisions. There are, however, also co-creation contracts obliging the co-operation partners to develop a product or solution together linking royalties to outcomes of results. No court can, however, force the partners to deliver an innovation. Nor can it in practice remedy the loss of the failure to innovate, information leaking out too early or secrecy commitments being broken. The commitment in co-creation networks is completely different than the one which contract law attaches to contracts. Self-enforced contracts rely more on other kinds of mutual commitment than contracts, which can be enforced in courts. They have to be aligned with complementary governance methods, such as trust or specific assets.

From this point of view, it is understandable that not all lawyers regard co-creation network contracts, expressing joint aims and good faith, as contracts at all. Legally they can be compared with letters of intent or gentleman's agreements, which in principle are not binding before court. However, in contract law there have been recent, gradual developments in commitment, rights and duties.[11] Soft self-enforcing contracts, which are not intended to be legally enforceable, may also include clauses such as limitations of competition and secrecy, which are also legally enforceable. Co-creation contracts are typically made for collaboration parties themselves to function within their private autonomy. They are intentionally only self-enforced. Sometimes, however, because the doctrine on indefinite contracts or contract as a process has blurred the earlier clear borderline between binding contracts and non-binding gentlemen's agreements, the court may find a contract legally binding and enforceable, which was intended to be only self-enforced.[12] Drafters of co-creation contracts thus need to be alert. All the participants in collaboration need to know what, if anything, is legally binding in their contracts, as well as what the commitment, the interests and the goals of other participants are, in order to be able to focus successfully on private governance of the contract. Disputes of co-creation contracts would only confuse judges and are not designed to be decided according to contract law rules and doctrines.

Transaction cost economics has developed an *ex ante* alternative for the commitment enforced *ex post* by contract law. Since the threat of opportunism is always present in networked innovation, as it generally is in all business, opportunism has to be turned into trust with tying the other parties into co-operation in such a way that opportunism will not pay. Transaction cost economics suggests the condition of asset specificity. A specific asset, which in joint innovation could be *ex ante* investment in networked innovation, works as a credible commitment to co-operation.[13] The contribution of transaction cost economics is in explaining how to tie other partners into co-operation and maintain their motivation and interest as well as prevent them from opportunistic behaviour.

Since promises are not always kept, a contract (even a legally binding one) is not an adequate commitment. It has to be supported with other mechanisms, such as asset specific conditions or relational governance relying on creating and maintaining trust. We will come back to the relationship between contracts and trust in the section "Network Capabilities and Trust in Network Contracting" in this chapter. Networked innovation can be governed with relation to specific investment *ex ante* and *ex post* renegotiation obligation, which both work as constraints of opportunism in different ways. Asset specificity conditions makes the firm think about potential loss of their investment. Relational governance, on the other hand, relies on reputational costs. In small business circles, such as in Finland and the Netherlands, where our research was done, losing reputation may serve as a considerable threat against opportunistic behaviour. Globalization of business, however, seems to tempt opportunistic behaviour, since a bad reputation does not spread as easily as in small national markets. Opportunism is also constrained by the rise of switching costs. When the relationship lasts for a long time and has been invested in, costs of switching to another partner will be high.[14]

Possibilities for applying these mechanisms to protect oneself from opportunistic behaviour are, however, not strategies, which are always available in the Bazaar of Opportunities. In rapidly changing business environments new business partners are frequently needed, and relying on only long-term relationships does not open enough new opportunities. Furthermore, both asset specificity and building on long-term relationships will be more difficult when there are more participants in collaboration. Possibilities to protect oneself from opportunism are not equal in all business models either. For instance, a contract manufacturer is vulnerable to opportunism of the contractor, who can transfer all the risks to the contract manufacturer and then find a new low-cost partner to manufacture the product, which the earlier contract manufacturer has developed further. Such a business model does not encourage innovation.

Value creation and appropriation

The other prerequisite of contracts along with commitment stems from the very nature of business. Business contracts are in general made to create and/or capture value. Co-creation contracts are used to create value, so that when the innovation is commercialized, contracts capture value in a similar way to transaction network contracts. The motivation disappears and commitment weakens when the collaboration turns out not to be profitable. In business this prerequisite is self-evident, while in courts the binding nature and contractually expressed commitment itself play a more important role. Sometimes judges may underestimate or even ignore the business reason and the purpose for which the contract was originally made and treat contracts separately according to contract law rules.[15] Getting rid of non-profitable commitments should therefore be made possible with rules, which are proactively laid down in contracts.

The difference between transaction and co-creation contracts is, however, that value capturing can often be clearly calculated beforehand in transaction contracts, while co-creation is in the beginning usually based only on hopes and vague expectations of profit or other kind of benefits. It is not always that the innovation is really developed, let alone commercialized in a profitable way to all co-operation partners. Thus, co-creation contracts are also businesswise not always "real" contracts, but simply options. However, not all co-creation is unpredictable. There are situations in which the co-creation has a predictable end during a predictable time period. Commercial results can in those circumstances be more easily shared beforehand or at least divided between the parties with a few options.[16]

Practical functions of contracts: Safeguarding, co-ordination and change management

While framework functions are prerequisites on the background of contracting, more practical functions are discovered in the contract contents, processes, and network dimensions. (See Fig. 5.3 which depicts contracting capabilities in designing documents, arranging contractual processes, and applying network capabilities.) Quite often contracts are seen as tools for risk management and the main function of a contract as safeguarding from risks. Lawyers are particularly criticized for focusing too much on safeguarding, as they are experts on contract law, the *ex post* approach of which increases risk aversion.

In more traditional exchanges, where rights and duties are clear, risks are easier to manage with safeguarding contractual terms. Limitation of liability is a typical way to approach risks, and remedies for a breach of contract are typical safeguarding. In co-creation safeguarding is more challenging. Who is to bear the risk of a failure and on what grounds? Firms sometimes apply formal hard terms to prevent opportunism by introducing purchase obligations and time limits to ensure returns of the innovation.[17] Too intensive safeguarding may, however, function as limiting the efforts in collaboration and letting others take care of the costs and other inputs. In this way a strong safeguarding oriented attitude is not fruitful for co-operation, but represents opportunistic behaviour.

Protection of IP is especially challenging in networked co-operation as discussed in Chapter 4 of this volume. If there is no IP to protect or IP is not going to be protected according to the ideology of open source, protection of networked innovation is not an issue in contracting. In practice, however, there is a need for some kind of protection of IP in networked innovation. More recent literature (Henkel *et al.*[18]) suggests technological methods, such as modularity. When a product or process design is modular with respect to IP, firms may better capture value in situations where knowledge and value creation are distributed across many actors. Sharing information in such circumstances may appropriate a large share of jointly created value. At the same time, however, a firm with no protected resources can only earn competitive returns, not superior returns. Those cases may need an intermediary strategy in which some knowledge is shared while other knowledge remains protected. Modularity allows for the partition of knowledge in discrete "chunks" which receive different IP treatments. According to Henkel *et al.* the main principle is that knowledge, which has relational value, should be shared, while knowledge, which has positional value, should be protected by IP rights or secrecy. The interviews of our research show that in practice it seems to be difficult to decide what should be shared and what should not. Uncertainty of what should be revealed easily leads to holding back information and mistrust among collaboration partners based on this behaviour. The reason for uncertainty on disclosing of information may be that firms have not really thought about their strategy towards co-creation (see Chapter 6).

The most common way to protect shared information, and to protect against leaks outside the network, is a NDA (non-disclosure agreement). For 70% of the companies in our interview study, a confidentiality agreement was one of the most important tools in protection of knowledge in inter-firm relations (see the section "Non-disclosure Agreements Shaping Collaborative Networks" in Chapter 4 and "Firms' Practices of IP Management in the Bazaar of Opportunities" in Chapter 6). Safeguarding information with contracts is typically not enough without other additional methods of protection such as educating personnel and other relational methods (see Table 1.1). Breaching confidentiality is legally sanctioned both by NDAs and by most countries' legislation (as commercial secrets). Sanctions, however, do not cover the damage done. Secrecy clauses can function as a threat or a reminder of the importance of secrecy, but cannot give a full safeguard against opportunism or careless human behaviour.

Safeguarding connected with IP is currently a complicated area. In transaction networks, where all the contracting parties are known, IP inputs and outputs can usually be defined and their ownership can be arranged. Open source may, however, complicate ownership of IP, since it may be difficult to separate open source and further developed innovations based on open source, or if technology which has been bought by a license is mixed with solutions acquired by an open source license. The typical clause in exchange of products and services making the seller responsible for potential violations of IP rights of the sold product, service, or solution, can turn out to be a trap in developed technology with multiple claim holders with obscure rights. Thus limitations of liability (for consequential losses) are recommended for such clauses, since damages can otherwise rise into astronomic spheres.[19]

In an empirical research study on business alliances in the German automobile industry, it was found out that in long-term contracts the amount of safeguarding clauses diminishes compared to co-ordination, control, and contingency clauses.[20] Co-ordination functions are important in co-operation. In transaction network contracts co-ordination appears to be more control. In co-creation contracts co-ordination includes for example terms of division of roles and responsibilities, contract management, control, and communication as well as project management with timetable, reporting and so on. Paying attention to co-ordination will add discipline in co-creation, where unclear joint rules may be understood differently and cause confusion.

Co-ordination of the information flow is challenging in co-creation networks. Tacit knowledge and sharing information play an important role in co-creation challenging the protection of IP and tacit know-how. Since networked information requires communications and a free flow of information, information should in the beginning flow as freely as possible to encourage creativeness. Thus, framework contracts, which govern co-creation often emphasize non-disclosure of information to outsiders. The circle of information should be defined as clearly as possible to help the participants make a difference between outsiders and insiders. Co-ordination of innovation processes also requires clear, transparent mechanisms. These mechanisms, although they are a management issue, should be described in contract documents as well. Aligning documents with management processes increases clarity and trust between the collaboration parties.

In co-ordinating as well as controlling contract processes contract life-cycle management is crucial. Every project should have "an owner" in every participating organization and a project manager to ensure smooth and flexible life-cycle management. Co-creation is often controlled by a consortium, which has to be aware also of contracting issues, including the content, the processes and relational aspects of contracting (see Fig. 5.3). Unfortunately, contracts are easily given to lawyers or to someone "who understands about contracts" in the organization. On the contrary, managers tend to write contracts on their own without any knowledge of, for example, the governing law. Two problems seem to occur in these vague contracting management practices in companies. Firstly contracts are made too tight and thus shrink the prospective innovation process. Secondly, contracts become discrete from real life and follow neither the innovation process nor the business processes. Both of these vague contracting practices ignore the empowerment of a joint contracting process as well as the tacit knowledge and information of the people whose operation the contract governs.

Change management can be understood as a separate function of a contract, even if it quite often is connected with risk management and safeguarding for risks. Dealing with change management as a separate function emphasizes the fact that contingency planning is not only done for safeguarding for threats, but also for orienting to new possibilities. Change management represents the idea of flexible or agile co-operation and contracts. In business models such as service business, alliances and networks, which are created for long-term co-operation, change is a rule, not an exception.[21] This is also the case to a great extent with networked innovation. Traditionally business contracts have included *force majeure*, price change or even a *hardship* clause in the contract documents. *Force majeure* is an exceptional impediment beyond the control of the contracting party. In such cases, delivery may be delayed or not happen at all without remedies. *Hardship*, on the other hand, refers to economic impossibilities to deliver.[22] They often lead to re-negotiations. A typical relational mechanism, which is applied in co-creation contracts, is simply a duty to renegotiate in case of hardships or other contingencies. More detailed mechanisms of change are rare in contract documents.

In transaction networks the above-mentioned traditional clauses may be enough and correspond to the idea of exchange of IP. In co-creation networks, there is a need for more precise change mechanisms. However, quite often contract documents lack such clauses, but they only refer to renegotiations. Network capabilities are then challenged without any real support of the document. A co-operational document can describe the contract and project management processes and steps to take in case of contingencies. A contract document covering change mechanisms is a good road map or a tool for co-operation. Unfortunately there are very seldom models of change management clauses available, and therefore they are ignored when contracts are designed. Developing such mechanisms without previous examples increases immediate transaction costs of contracting, although in the long run with recurrent co-creation transaction costs will decrease with proactive change mechanisms.

Dispute settlement is sometimes defined as an own function of contracts. The reason may be the traditional clauses on litigation and arbitration;

nowadays, mediation is increasingly used in business contracts. Settlement of disputes can also be seen as a part of contingency management or co-ordination. Private governance of co-creation contracts prefers negotiations and bilateral means of settling disputes. Litigation is a dangerous alternative not only because IP or other protected information may leak out in public litigation, but also because the whole logic of court procedure differs too much from the idea of co-creation networking. Litigation and other costly third party dispute settlement means can, however, also be used as a reminder or a learning process preventing disputes or allowing them to be settled in private governance. A contractual clause on litigation or arbitration builds mutual knowledge of the propensity to reciprocate.[23]

The content of co-creation contracts can be described as consisting more of soft and vague terms than hard and precise ones. Hard terms represent traditional contract law type of governance, while soft terms represent relational governance within private ordering. Such "soft" contracts do not resemble the model of contract of traditional contract law any more.[24] Their aim is to express and support co-operation and good will as well as align aims, rights and duties, instead of defining contradicting rights and duties between partners. They are soft and incomplete contracts. Table 5.2 illustrates the general development of the use of contract terms in business. Flexibility becomes more important in contracts of new business models. Old terms, such as limitation of liability and indemnification will stay on the list of important terms, but their role will be less significant than earlier compared with change management.

Developing Contracting Capabilities

Developing contracting strengthens co-ordination and use of innovations and even encourages creative collaboration. Contracting requires capabilities which reach far beyond simply finding suitable contractual terms for each contract. Instead of special legal technical capabilities, contracting can be seen as an organization's learning process. This learning can be understood as a part of organizational capabilities, which can be developed as contracting capabilities.[26] The concept of contracting capabilities was developed in organization studies, which defines capabilities as a unique capacity of a firm to allocate resources[27] to the study of business contracting.

Table 5.2.   Top ten negotiated terms today and in the future (IACCM survey).[25]

Top 10 today	Top 10 in the future
1. Limitation of liability	1. Scope and goals
2. Indemnification	2. Change management
3. Price/charge/price changes	3. Responsibilities of the parties
4. Intellectual property	4. Communications and reporting
5. Confidential information/data protection	5. Service levels and warranties
6. Service levels and warranties	6. Price/change/price changes
7. Delivery/acceptance	7. Delivery/acceptance
8. Payment	8. Limitation of liability
9. Liquidated damages	9. Dispute resolution
10. Applicable law/jurisdiction	10. Indemnification

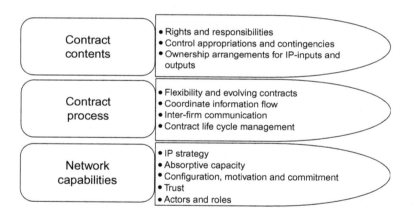

Fig. 5.3.   Contracting capabilities in three dimensions.

Figure 5.3 illustrates contracting capabilities applied to innovation management in three dimensions. These three dimensions should not be considered separately, as they have an effect on each other and support each other. The core of contracting capabilities is actually in finding a right balance between the different capabilities.

Contract content capabilities on top of the figure are related to drafting the documents applying contract templates and instructions and the contract policy of the company. Safeguarding, co-ordinating and change management clauses have already been discussed in the previous section of this chapter. Contract content, however, includes a lot more than just the visible terms of contract. A contract always contains regulations of non-mandatory legislation filling the gaps of the documents or complementing contractual clauses.[28] There is also a lot of mandatory legislation, which cannot be agreed differently in a contract, and which therefore has to be known and applied. Knowledge on legislation concerning competition law and IP law is important information in drafting both transaction and co-creation contracts. Even if IP law is quite international, every national legal system has its own regulations, for instance, for employer invention setting the minimum requirements for contracts with R&D employers. Rules on patentability vary and may set special requirements for co-creation (see Chapter 4). Competition law may also limit co-creation between competitors. Knowledge of legislation and skills of lawyers are in this respect vitally important for the contracting capabilities of a firm. Drafting contracts should neither be left only for lawyers, nor should lawyers be separated from the contracting process. Harnessing the best capabilities for contracting requires co-operation and aligning skills and knowledge of different professionals participating in the process.

Co-creation contracts should actually be comprehended as a process of an evolving contract (see Fig. 5.1). When commercialization of the innovation will approach, the amount of hard terms dividing costs and benefits will increase gradually changing the type of governance of contracting. Management of contracting processes is therefore also challenging and requires flexibility. In governing contracting processes an approach understanding contracting starting from the preparation phases of the project reaching until its successful exit could benefit contract management and alignment of evolving contracts with subsequent business models (see Fig. 5.2). Seeing contracting as an evolving process is a new dynamic approach to contracting.

According to our case studies, the contract process in firms is understood to begin from the negotiations, not from the preparation phases suggested by the approach presented in Fig. 5.1 above. Yet, managers explained that, for instance, training and teaching the project managers or the salesmen for the selling event has to be done in advance. This again follows from the basic principle that different kinds of strategies have to be adapted for different suppliers. In some cases there are suppliers that *"want to be supported, for the certainty and continuity, and then they also have the aim and desire of further developing the products, supporting the development project in many ways: the price, know-how, development, etc."*. Secrecy policies, which are a part of contracting strategies, also have to be controlled from the beginning of the contracting process. Aligning strategies and policies with contracting processes requires an approach to contracts as an evolving process. Too little attention seems to be paid to management of contracting processes and contracts are too often regarded as a separate process from the actual collaboration. Arranging management of the contract process, aligning it with strategies, policies and business models, is an investment spending transaction costs. In the long run savings are however made with smooth and efficient co-ordination and control.

Network Capabilities and Trust in Network Contracting

The legally binding effect of a contract shields the parties especially when rights and duties are clearly defined in a contract document, and breached contracts and broken promises can be taken before court. Although litigation works as a threat against breaking promises, businesses try to avoid legal disputes for many reasons. Firstly, disputes are costly. Apart from the direct litigation costs, there are a lot of indirect costs, reputational costs being the most difficult to anticipate. A company which gets a litigator's reputation may begin to be avoided as a collaboration partner. Secondly, legal sanctions seldom cover all the losses. Broken secrecy is a typical example of the weakness of legal sanctions. Damages cannot cover the loss of business or business relationships, let alone the lost reputation because of leaking personnel or unreliable security systems of the company. For these reasons firms prefer private governance of disputes.

Trust is an important prerequisite for well-functioning private governance. Trust is also important in transaction networks, because you would avoid, for instance, licensing contracts with companies which you do not trust. In co-creation networks creating and maintaining trust is even more crucial. However, network capabilities (Fig. 5.3) are often not regarded as capabilities connected with contracts at all, but contracts and relational capabilities, especially creating and maintaining trust, are seen as opposites of each other. Stewart Macaulay's famous article discussed how businessmen wanted to deal without (written) contracts, because formal contracts may show a distrust of the collaboration party.[29] In other works, they relied on reputational rather than legal sanctions.

The opinions of Macaulay's businessmen still seem to exist in business, although researchers have also found several other attitudes towards contracts.[30] In our case studies we also met with opinions in favour of trust without written contracts. According to some R&D personnel contracts kill enthusiasm for collaboration and threaten the atmosphere of trust. It, however, turned out that with contracts they meant formal, precise, and hard contracts. Their fear for formal contracts was also connected with the fear for lawyers, who start to raise contradictions when it is important to create trust between the collaboration partners.

The idea of creating trust with contracting was new to most people in our case studies. They seemed to regard contracts more as a necessary and unavoidable safeguarding mechanism. Some empirical studies align with our understanding that when contracts are soft, co-operational and emphasize joint aims, they will more likely increase trust rather than show distrust among parties of collaboration.[31] Negotiating and discussing the starting points and aims of co-creation will also give information about the interests of other co-operation parties. It is vitally important to advance from assumptions to knowledge of the interests of others. A contracting process may function as a test of the credibility of the co-creation partners. Information about each other also helps in defining the roles and interests of each co-creation partner and in this way enables collaboration (see Fig. 3.3). Unwillingness to discuss risks and rules of co-operation may be a sign of unpreparedness for collaboration. Trust, if it is built on vague or even false assumptions, is not worth nourishing, since it may easily change into disappointment. Not wanting to agree on rules may also be a sign of a reckless attitude, rather than a sign of trust. When collaboration partners change frequently and methods which can be used in long-term relations such as asset specificity and tested relationships are not available, the contracting process can actually function as a reliability test of a new partner. Willingness to discuss their own interests and write them into the contract document will show reliability and create trust. Furthermore, when the starting points and aims of co-creation are laid down in a contract document, applying network capabilities gets easier and aligned with contracts. Therefore, we dare to claim that this effort will probably also in the long run save transaction costs.

Even if soft framework contracts are found to increase trust, hard contradictory contracts with legal remedies still seem to be the prevailing device even between collaboration partners. It seems to be typical that even long-term co-operation contracts are concluded according to the traditional hard model applying limitations of liability, liquidated damages, and other remedies for not delivering or performing (see Table 5.2). Poppo and Zenger report that formal contracts and their remedies are set aside when collaboration partners negotiate about how to deal with contingencies. Change management and strict (hard) contracts are separated from each other, although Poppo and Zenger interpret that they complement each other.[32] The case studies in the CCC research project also support prevailing of this policy. Managers explained that a good solution can be found with good will and trust on each other in spite of the contract.[33] Such contracts rely on network capabilities and the possibility of finding a softer solution in co-operation.

To our mind such "hard" contracts do not support collaboration but rather contradict it. In private ordering, documents contradicting real practices may cause misunderstandings and disputes. If the dispute finally had to be taken before court, the decision would be taken the written rules of the formal contract as a starting point. Practices contradicting the formal document may, however, puzzle the judges and dilute the hard terms of the document. In other words, the different practices may be interpreted as having changed the contract. All in all, the result can be totally unpredictable. Contract documents, which are aligned with real co-operation practices, policies and strategies of the firm, will create trust with their consistency. The reason for separating strict contracts from flexible change management may be the lack of examples of softer change mechanisms in contract documents. For the the same reason, contracts are regarded only as safeguarding methods and safeguarding is not understood to work without threatening with sanctions.

Advocating for only soft contracts in order to create trust in co-creation would, however, be naive. Likewise, trying to avoid conflict may not be the most efficient and rational option.[34] Good contracts are a combination of hard and soft terms. They evolve during the collaboration, and the amount of hard terms increases the closer commercialization of the innovation gets. Flexible network capabilities also cover capacity to move from "open" relational governance to sharing the results in the commercialization phase of the co-created innovation. Softer contractual clauses pay attention to sharing, but cannot prevent "the baker of the cake" losing its share when moving to the commercialization phase. Therefore hard terms to ensure "a piece of the cake" for the baker as well are needed.

Collaboration in a competitive environment, which is also apt to opportunistic behaviour, is always a challenge. Trust is a prerequisite for successful co-operation, but in some situations too much trust may be as bad as too little. Contracts are a practical device in supporting trust, but also in safeguarding from opportunism.

A rapidly changing business environment was regarded as the most dangerous threat for trustful co-operation in our case studies. Trust is usually understood as personal trust functioning between individuals. People change their jobs and move to different positions and the trustful relationship may vanish into air with the change of a key person. Trust can also be created between organizations, although managers in our case studies seemed to believe that "organizations are still run by people". Even when trust is laid on the organizational structures, changes in the ownership of the firms may ruin the foundations of co-operation and confidential information and innovations may leak out to competitors. Contracts containing rules of sharing costs and benefits can also be of use in such situations.

Trust is vulnerable, promises can be broken and litigation cannot bring back the lost investments, let alone lost reputation. Trust alone is not enough, as contracts alone are inadequate. There is no safeguard for all the potential risks. Co-creation may still be profitable in spite of all the risks involved. Trust and contacts should be applied in support of each other.

Conclusions: Developing Contracting Capabilities within Private Governance

The *ex post* approach of courts and contract law also complicates the attitudes of businesspeople in developing contracting within private ordering. Contracts, which could function as tools for collaboration, are developed as obligatory formal documents, which can be put into a safe box and hopefully never interpreted, because interpreting means that a dispute has led the parties to litigation or arbitration.

Development of new business models, such as networked innovation, challenges contract law and the capabilities of business people to design good contracts governing their operations in private governance. Contracts as tools for collaboration have functions other than traditional exchange contracts. They need to create trust, anticipate changes, and co-ordinate the flow of information inside the network as well as protect and safeguard IP from leaking out of the network. Although the proportional amount of safeguarding clauses diminishes compared to the amount of clauses governing co-ordination and change management, safeguarding does not lose its significant role in co-creation networks either. The contract only develops to be more flexible and relational. Co-creation contracts can also contain hard and very precise terms, especially when co-creation advances towards commercialization. On the other hand sharing of the results of the innovation can even be stipulated beforehand in the beginning phase of co-creation with several options. Contracts are always a mixture of hard and soft terms, safeguarding, and flexible change management. The mixture is drawn from the subsequent business model and circumstances.

Contracting capabilities also change their form when clear division of contradictory rights and responsibilities strengthened by remedies turns into enabling collaboration and maintaining trust and motivation. Contractual clauses of co-creation contracts will differ from transaction network contracts since they have different functions. In co-creation contracting processes require more co-ordination and the role of network capabilities becomes significant.

Table 5.3 below shows the main differences between transaction and co-creation network contracts. The differences are, however, shown between the two ends of these types of contract. It should be borne in mind that in reality contracts are a mixture of these two extremes. Transaction network contracts may include relational elements and co-creation network contracts can contain hard terms and hard governance mechanisms.

The role of contracts as such should not be exaggerated, however. They should also be complemented with tying co-operation partners into co-creation and/or with relational methods such as creating and maintaining trust and motivating to collaborate. Contracting capabilities, however,

Table 5.3. Differences of contracting between transaction and co-creation contracts.

Transaction networks	Co-creation networks
Complete, clear	Incomplete, evolving
Static	Dynamic
Safeguarding emphasized	Co-ordination and contingency management
Public governance available by IP and contract law	Only private governance realistic
IP protection (fairly) clear	IP protection vague

are still typically an underused resource of companies, and developing contracting capabilities could increase competitive advantage of business partners in the Bazaar of Opportunities.

Notes

1. According to contract law contracts can be concluded in many ways, not just by signing a formal contract document. Contracts can be oral, even implicit; they may develop gradually or be interpreted to have emerged in certain circumstances. Often business research focuses only on formal contracts either implicitly or explicitly. See Blomqvist *et al.* (2005) which explicitly focuses on written contracts. [Blomqvist, K., Hurmelinna, P. and Seppänen, R. (2005). Playing the Collaboration Game Right — Balancing Trust and Contracting, *Technovation*, Vol. 25, pp. 497–504.]
2. Nystén-Haarala (1998) compares the logic of contract law with that of business. The negative consequences of the sale of goods model of contract law for long-term contracts is the core of the contract law part of the book. [Nystén-Haarala, S. (1998). *The Long-term Contract, Contract Law and Contracting*, Finnish Lawyers Publishing, Helsinki.]
3. [O'Connor, S.M. (2009). 'IP Transactions as Facilitators of the Globalized Innovation Economy', in Dreyfuss, R. *et al.* (eds), *Working with the Boundaries of Intellectual Property*, Oxford University Press, Oxford., pp. 203–228. Available online at http://ssrn.com/abstract=1465004 (Accessed on 23 February 2012.); Van Overwalle, G. (ed.) (2010) *Gene Patents and Collaborative Licensing Models Patent Pools, Clearinghouses, Opensource Models and Liability Regimes*; Lee, N., Nystén-Haarala, S. and Huhtilainen, L. (2010). 'Interfacing Intellectual Property Rights and Open Innovation', in Torkkeli, M. (ed.), *Frontiers of Open Innovation*, Faculty of Technology Management, Department of Industrial Management, Research report 225, Lappeenranta University of Technology, pp. 121–140. Also available online at http://www.ssrn.com/astract=1674365 (Accessed on 23 February 2012.)]
4. Salbu's (1997) concept evolving contract is similar to dynamic contract, which is also applied. In Finland the concept dynamic contract is known from Vesa Annola's doctoral thesis (2003). The concepts incomplete or indefinite contracts are often applied in law

and economics research. See Scott (2003). [Salbu, S. (1997). Evolving Contract as a Device for Flexible Co-ordination and Control, *American Business Law Journal*, Vol. 34, pp. 329–384; Annola, V. (2003). *Sopimuksen dynaamisuus: talousoikeudellinen rakennetutkimus sopimuksen täydentymisestä ja täydentymisen ohjaamisesta.* Turun yliopiston oikeustieteellisen tiedekunnan julkaisuja. Yksityisoikeuden julkaisuja A: 107, Turku; Scott, R. (2003). *A Theory of Self-enforcing Indefinite Agreements*, University of Virginia School of Law, Law and Economics Research Paper, No. 03-2. Available online at http://ssrn.com/abstract_id=390763 (Accessed on 23 February 2012.)]

5. Scott (2003) *ibid* refers to American court practice. The same approach also prevails in the court decisions of countries with civil law legal systems.

6. Ian Macneil's (1978) relational contract suggests regarding relational contracts as a framework for co-operation. He separates them from discrete contracts, with which he means the sales contract model of contract law. Macneil sees contract law as advancing from classical to neoclassical and later to relational contract law. Neoclassical contract law seeks to find special solutions for relational aspects of long-term contracts, such as general clauses. Relational contract law would in the future find the starting point in relational aspects of contracts. Macneil's relational contract has inspired a vast relational contract literature. See e.g. Scott (2003), Goldberg (1985), Goldberg and Erickson (1987), Joskow (1988) and Goetz and Scott (1981). [Macneil, I. (1978) Contracts: Adjustment of Long-Term Economic Relations under Classical, Neoclassical, and Relational Contract Law, *Northwestern University Law Review*, Vol. 6, pp. 854–905; Scott, R. (2003). A Theory of Self-enforcing Indefinite Agreements, *Columbia Law Review*, Vol. 103, No. 7, pp. 1641–1699. Available online at http://ssrn. com/abstract_id=390763 (Accessed on 23 February 2012.); Goldberg, V. (1985). Price Adjustment in Long-term Contracts, *Wisconsin Law Review*, 527–543; Goldberg, V. and Erickson, J.R. (1987). Quantity and Price adjustments in Long-term contracts: A Case Study of Petroleum Coke, *Journal of Law and Economics*, Vol. 30, pp. 369–398; Joskow, P.L. (1988). Asset Specificity and the Structure of Vertical Relationships: Empirical Evidence, *Journal of Law, Economics and Organization*, Vol. 95, p. 101; Goetz, C.E. and Scott, R.E. (1981). Principles of Relational Contracts, *Virginia Law Review*, Vol. 67, pp. 1089–1150.]

7. The figure is developed from a figure in the final report of the research project consortium Corporate Contracting Capabilities (CCC) available at http://www.uef.fi/oikeustieteet/ccc (CCC report 2008) (Accessed on 23 February 2012).

8. *Ex post* (after the fact) refers to disputes in courts, where lawyers try to find out who bears the risks. *Ex ante* (beforehand) refers to drafting contracts anticipating how risks could be prevented from occurring and how disputes could be avoided.

9. The authors of this chapter agree with the ideas of proactive or preventive law. See Haapio (2006), Barton (2009), Brown (1950) (a classic of preventive law), and Siedel and Haapio (2010). [Haapio, H. (2006). 'Introduction to Proactive Law from a Business Lawyer's Point of View', in Wahlgren, P. (ed.), *A Proactive Approach*, Scandinavian Studies in Law, Vol. 49, Stockholm Institute of Scandinavian Law, pp. 21–31; Barton, T.D. (2009) *Preventive Law and Problem Solving: Lawyering for the Future*, Vandepals, Lake Mary, FL; Brown, L.M. (1950). *Manual of Preventive Law*, Prentice-Hall, New York; Siedel, G. and Haapio, H. (2010). Competitive Advantage through Proactive Contracting, *American Business Law Journal*, Vol. 47, Issue 4, pp. 641–686.]

10. The table is developed based on different authors' views on contractual functions. [Argyres, N. and Mayer, K.J. (2007). Contract Designing as a Firm Capability: An Integration of Learning and Transaction Cost Perspectives, *The Academy of Management Review*, Vol. 32, No. 4, pp. 1060–1077; Eckhard, B. and Mellewigt, T. (2006). *Contractual Functions and Contractual Dynamics in Interfirm Relationships: What We Know and How to Proceed*, University of Padeborn working papers, No. 88. Also available online at SSRN http://ssrn.com/abstract=1289428 (Accessed on 23 February 2012.); Haapio, H. and Haavisto, V. (2005). Sopimusosaaminen — tulevaisuuden kilpailutekijä ja strateginen voimavara, *Yritystalous*, Vol. 2, pp. 7–16; Nystén-Haarala, S. (2008) 'Why Does Contract Law not Recognize Life Cycle Business? Mapping of Challenges for Future Empirical Research', in Nystén-Haarala, S. (ed.), *Corporate Contracting Capabilities, Conference Proceedings and Other Writings*, Joensuun yliopiston oikeustieteellisiä julkaisuja 21, Joensuu, pp. 18–32.]

11. In Scandinavian law this approach is called "contract as a process". See Grönfors (1987) and Pöyhönen (1988). The idea is the same as in evolving contracts or indefinite (incomplete) contracts (see end note 4). [Grönfors, K. (1987). *Avtalsgrundande rättsfakta*, Nerenius & Santérus Förlag, Gothenburg; Pöyhönen, J. (1988). *Sopimusoikeuden järjestelmä ja sovittelu*, Suomalainen lakimiesyhdistys, Helsinki.]

12. Scott (2003) *ibid* gives examples of what he calls misunderstandings of judges in finding binding effects in contracts which were not intended to bind. He blames the unclear doctrine of incomplete contracts for such mistakes.

13. Williamson (1985 and 1996) distinguishes six types of asset specificity, which all can be applied also in co-creation. *Site specificity* is in question, when for example successive stations are located in "a cheek-by-jowl" relation to each other to economize in inventory and transportation expenses. *Physical asset specificity* is, for example, specialized dies which are required to produce a component. *Human asset specificity* arises in a learning-by-doing fashion. *Dedicated assets* represent a discrete investment in generalized production capacity that would be made for the prospect of selling a significant amount of products to a specific customer. The fifth specific asset is *brand name capital* and the sixth is *temporal specificity* which is technological non-separability. [Williamson, O.E. (1985). *Economic Institutions of Capitalism*, Free Press, New York, p. 95; Williamson, O.E. (1996). *The Mechanisms of Governance*, Oxford University Press, New York; Oxford, p. 105.]

14. [Gilson, R.J, Sabel, C.F. and Scott, R.E. (2009). *Contracting for Innovation: Vertical Disintegration and Interfirm Collaboration*, Columbia Law and Economics Working Paper, No. 340; Stanford Law and Economics Olin Working Paper No 368. Also available online at SSRN, http://ssrn.com/abstract=1289428 (Accessed on 23 February 2012.)]

15. Law and economics emphasize that economic efficiency should govern court decisions. Law and economics is quite widely accepted in the United States, but not in Europe. Ugo Mattei (1996) has discussed the reasons for this difference. [Mattei, U. (1996). 'Economic Analysis in European Legal Scholarship', in Simoni, A. and Cameron, I. (eds), *Dealing with Integration*, Iustus, Uppsala].

16. [Gilson, R.J, Sabel, C.F. and Scott, R.E. (2009). *Contracting for Innovation: Vertical Disintegration and Interfirm Collaboration*, Columbia Law and Economics Working Paper, No. 340.]

17. *ibid.*

18. [Henkel, J. and Baldwin, C.Y. (2010). *Modularity for Value Appropriation — How to Draw the Boundaries of Intellectual Property*, Harvard Business School Finance Working Paper 11-054. Also available online at SSRN, http://ssrn.com/abstract=1340445 (Accessed on 23 February 2012.)]

19. There are firms called patent "trolls", often non-producing firms that enforce patents, often acquired ones, against firms that use the technology covered by the patent. Often patent trolls wait until the IP-related product or process is successful before filing suit, thus maximizing the value of any future damages of settlements. [Golden, J.M. (2007). "Patent Trolls" and Patent Remedies, *Texas Law Review*, Vol. 85, pp. 2111–2162; Henkel, J. and Baldwin, C.Y. (2010). *Modularity for Value Appropriation — How to Draw the Boundaries of Intellectual Property*, Harvard Business School Finance Working Paper 11-054. Also available online at SSRN, http://ssrn.com/abstract=1340445 (Accessed on 23 February 2012.)].

20. [Eckhard, B. and Mellewigt, T. (2006). *Contractual Functions and Contractual Dynamics in Interfirm Relationships: What we Know and How to Proceed*, University of Padeborn working papers, No. 88. Also available online at SSRN, http://ssrn.com/abstract=899527 (Accessed on 23 February 2012.)]

21. In the CCC research based on case studies, managers of firms co-ordinating export projects emphasized the importance of flexibility, and experienced business lawyers highlighted that there is a gap between rapidly changing reality and static contract doctrine. [Nystén-Haarala, S., Lee, N. and Lehto, J. (2010). Flexibility in Contract Terms and Contract Processes, *International Journal of Managing Projects in Business*, Vol. 10, Issue 3, pp. 462–478.]

22. Contract law has developed doctrines for exceptional changes from the main principle of *pacta sunt servanda*, according to which contracts bind in the form in which they were concluded. Exceptional contingencies are typically unforeseen natural disasters or insuperable orders of state agencies. For instance the Convention on International Sale of Goods recognizes only an impediment beyond control (Article 74). Other contingencies allowing changes in contract have to be stipulated in the contract itself. Some countries' also recognize hardship or economic impediment. The same is true with international sets of principles, which can be included in the contract by referring to them. Examples include Principles of European Contract Law and UNIDROIT principles. Although they are not binding rules, judges and arbitrators may find guidance from them in the absence of contract terms or in order to interpret contract terms.

23. Arbitration is often presented as a private means for settling disputes, since it is separated from state courts. Arbitrators, which the disputing parties can choose, make the decision (arbitral award) which is final. The parties take care of costs of arbitration. Arbitration can, however, become very costly and most arbitrators are lawyers. [Gilson, R.J, Sabel, C.F. and Scott, R.E. (2009). *Contracting for Innovation: Vertical Disintegration and Interfirm Collaboration*, Columbia Law and Economics Working Paper, No. 340; Stanford Law and Economics Olin Working Paper No 368. Also available online at SSRN, http://ssrn.com/abstract=1289428 (Accessed on 23 February 2012.)]

24. The difference between hard and soft terms and their interaction concerning contracting in new business models is discussed in Nystén-Haarala *et al.* (2010). [Nystén-Haarala,

S., Lee, N. and Lehto, J. (2010). Flexibility in Contract Terms and Contract Processes, *International Journal of Managing Projects in Business*, Vol. 10, Issue 3, pp. 462–478.]

25. [IACCM, http://www.iaccm.com (Accessed on 23 February 2012.)]
26. [Williamson, O.E. (1999). Strategy Research: Governance and Competence Perspective, *Strategic Management Journal*, Vol. 20, pp. 1087–1108; Argyres, N. and Mayer, K.J. (2007). Contract Designing as a Firm Capability: An Integration of Learning and Transaction Cost Perspectives, *The Academy of Management Review*, Vol. 32, No. 4, pp. 1060–1077.]
27. [Teece, D.J. (2007). Explicating Dynamic Capabilities: The Nature of Microfoundations of (Sustainable) Enterprise Performance, *Strategic Management Journal*, Vol. 28, No. 13, pp. 1319–1350.]
28. Nowadays complementary and contradicting mandatory and non-mandatory regulations are abundant. In international business there are both national and international public and private regulations available. Typically the amount of international private regulation, such as standards for NGOs, is increasing. Although such an environment increases transaction costs of firms, it allows them to navigate and choose the best regulations for themselves. See, for example, Michaels (2005). [Michaels, R. (2005). The Restatement of Non-state Law: the State, Choice of Law, and the Challenge From Global Legal Pluralism, *The Wayne Law Review*, Vol. 51, pp. 1209–1258.]
29. Stewart Macaulay's famous article "Non-contractual relations in business" claimed that businessmen avoid (written) contracts and prefer informal methods when "making deals". [Macaulay, S. (1963). Non-contractual Relations in Business, *American Sociological Review*, Vol. 28, pp. 55–67.]
30. Blomqvist *et al.* (2005) found that trust complements contracts. They disagree with the earlier literature claiming that contracts become less important when complementary governance mechanisms such as trust exist. They claim that trust is needed because of the incompleteness of contracts and that trust can also be seen as a result of collaboration. Contracting can overcome the lack of information and can be valuable in creating trust. [Blomqvist, K., Hurmelinna, P. and Seppänen, R. (2005). Playing the collaboration game right — balancing trust and contracting, *Technovation*, Vol. 25, pp. 497–504.]
31. *ibid.*
32. Poppo and Zenger (2002) suggest that relational capabilities often complement formal ("hard") contracts. Change management is dealt relationally in spite of the formal contract. The contract document is thus not aligned with real practice. [Poppo, L. and Zenger, T. (2002). Do Formal Contracts and Relational Governance Function as Substitutes or Complements?, *Strategic Management Journal*, Vol. 23, pp. 707–725.]
33. Corporate Contracting Capabilities (CCC) report, 2008, is available online at http://www.uef.fi/oikeustieteet/ccc.
34. [Jeffries, F.L. and Reed, R. (2000). Trust and Adaptation in Relational Contracting, *Academy of Management Review*, Vol. 25, No. 4, pp. 873–882.]

Chapter 6

IP Strategy and Collaboration

Why is there the need to attach the word "strategy" to issues concerning IP management when dealing in the Bazaar of Opportunities? As discussed in the previous chapters of the book, the creation and management of knowledge inside and outside of a company as well as knowledge between companies involves many decisions, the impact of which can be permanent or long term at least. At first, creation of new knowledge is a time-consuming and costly process, while it is only too easy to lose that same knowledge in a short time due to, for example, ill-conducted collaboration, vaguely worded contracts, or with loss of key company employees. Yet, in the typical stylistic depiction of open innovation in the literature, the innovation funnel, illustrated in Fig. 2.1, knowledge transfer can perhaps too easily be understood as simple symmetric one-off transactions in and out of the company. Secondly, as we have already said: "... *open innovation is all about sharing* ..." It means that IP management in the context of open and networked innovation is not only about protection of knowledge, but it is also about controlled sharing of knowledge. We also recall that **in the Bazaar of Opportunities the term "intellectual property" may not only include IP rights that are granted and protected by the laws, but also the knowledge and other intangible resources whose use may be controlled by contracts, policies, organization and process routines and norms, both physically and technically**.

There are numerous ways in which competitive or corporate strategy can and has been viewed in the literature.[1] In addition, the word strategy itself can — or so often it seems — be linked to almost any kind of activity that is performed inside or between companies. Likewise, in the area of intellectual property management, strategy can refer to various topics. We view long-term and systematic processes as the key features distinguishing a strategic approach from an *ad hoc* basis. In this chapter, therefore, we broaden the examination of collaboration and networked innovation perspectives to IP management to the strategic level of view. The chapter, however, does not aim to be an all-encompassing treatise on strategy-level issues concerning intellectual property management. Rather, we seek to connect the ideas of networked innovation presented in the previous chapters to the discussion of higher-level objectives of IP management. We examine the impacts of increased interdependence and collaboration within the context of knowledge creation and transfer between companies, and highlight the resulting implications to IP strategy.

IP Strategy in the Context of Networked Innovation

Several differing definitions exist for IP strategy[2] or the somewhat narrower concept of patent strategy[3] but they all share the common view that the IP strategy guides the use of a company's IP in order to support a company's business vision[4] and strategy. The definitions given in the literature, however, focus solely on "closed innovation" activities — that is, they focus on innovation outcomes of their own R&D. Accordingly, they concentrate on the protection aspects of knowledge and pay little, if any, attention to the fundamental issues of open and networked innovation, namely multiple sources of innovation and openness as a behavioural norm. Thereby they give little support for successful navigation in the Bazaar of Opportunities.

In our definition for the IP strategy in the context of open and networked innovation, we pay attention to both the protection and to the sharing of knowledge and seek balance between them. We also seek to emphasize the relationship between IP strategy and overall business strategy and the business goals of the company. Accordingly, we define **IP strategy as a company's awareness about what knowledge is important for the company and how the IP should be protected, managed, or shared in order to support the business model and business strategy of the company**. IP strategy should link the company's own competencies with the objectives of business and technology strategies, identify and make visible their own IP and the relevant IP of others and enable systematic management of IP. In line with the broadened definition for IP itself, introduced in the beginning and used throughout this book, IP strategy focuses both on knowledge that can be controlled with formal intellectual property laws, and also knowledge and other intangible resources whose use may be controlled by contracts, policies, organization and process routines and norms, both physically and technically.

The broader definition of intellectual property is also well in line with our general theme of networked innovation. That is, companies need to consider and manage both those codified IP assets that are based on IP legislation as well as those, perhaps somewhat indefinite assets that can be controlled by contracts, policies, routines, norms, and other informal methods given in Table 1.1. This is naturally linked to the basic tenet of open innovation literature, i.e. the fact that much of the relevant knowledge and competences for companies exist outside of them. Thus, in tandem with the consideration of their own competences, knowledge, and capabilities, companies should do the same with respect to other relevant players in the industry, both potential partners as well as competitors.

In the context of open and networked innovation, the IP strategy of a company may look very different to traditional patent strategies of companies. The IP strategy should form the guidelines to decision making related to the "why?", "how?", and "what?" questions given in Fig. 3.1. That is, why create or acquire knowledge to reach the vision? How could that be done — internally within the firm or by the use of external actors? If by using external actors, what model of collaboration should be used? And finally, how should network co-ordination, business management, and legal details related to the chosen model of collaboration be arranged? All these are issues that are typically not supported by a patent strategy. However, they are issues of strategic importance in order to deal successfully in the Bazaar of Opportunities.

As an example of difference between traditional patent strategy and modern IP strategy, let us consider a company that has found it valuable for its business to use open source (OS) software in their products and services, and by this way to expand the knowledge resources of the company and make its own knowledge resources known to other actors. Strategy and practices related to the use of OS software are issues that should be given in the IP strategy. We have seen an IP strategy of an IT company whose content was nothing but a description of strategic principles and practices about how the company operates interactively in OS societies. And it was one of the best strategies that we have ever seen. The company had really realized what knowledge is important for them and how it should be protected, managed, and shared in order to support their business model and business strategy. For them, that happened through well-controlled interactive operation in OS societies. The given example is not to downplay the importance of patents in the IP strategy of firm, in general, but to underline the scope of modern IP strategy that should go beyond the formal protection of IP.

According to our interview study, however, it seems that a general IP strategy is partly or entirely missing in many companies. The following kind of answers seem to be quite common across a variety of companies in different branches of industry: "*There's no specific strategy regarding IP… we have a kind of plan, on which direction we have to go…*" and, "*No, we don't have our own IP strategy or anything like that. We go through those questions on a case by case basis… from time to time one actually wishes for more emphasis on those topics, as they are quite big issues in our industry, especially in international markets*". Furthermore, there are companies that have a document called IP strategy or patent strategy but the content of which just describes the company's process from the reporting of an invention to the filing of a patent without any strategic guidance to support the decision making in the process. While the lack of IP strategy itself does not necessarily need to imply a lack of long-term approach to IP management inside a company, the correlation seems strong. Thus, if a much more systematic approach towards IP management could be instilled in companies — whether such a concept would be called an IP strategy or something else — we believe that it would also be a step towards better and more profitable IP management decisions and better success in the Bazaar of Opportunities.

IP Strategy, IP Practices, IP Actions

Implementing IP strategy is perhaps one of the key practical challenges when integrating the networked innovation perspective to IP management. IP strategy works on a high level but it impacts lower-level functions of a firm through day-to-day IP management decisions. The discontinuity between the long-term high-level strategic planning and actual day-to-day decision making is one of the main reasons for the lack of systematic IP management in many companies. Even well thought out IP strategies are not very effective if they are not supported with good practices and resources to support day-to-day IP management actions. A representative of a technology company pointed out a disparity between strategic and action levels: *"Basically the dilemma is always between the short term and long term. In the short term, a unit can be under a lot of pressure and have lots of patents, which is costly. If we don't have the money at the moment to uphold the patents, we will have to drop them at the time. Short term I can understand it, but in the long term it might be bad for the corporation."*

In order to be flexible, a company's IP management procedures need to incorporate the high-level strategic IP objectives, the more practical policies and process-related issues, and the low-level methods to support decisions and negotiations regarding IP rights and collaboration in individual cases. In other words, firms need to specify how implementation proceeds from strategy level to practices, and from practices to individual actions and decisions. Additionally, the practices and also strategies may need to be revised due to, for example, increased experience, changes in the market conditions, or changes in actions of partners or competitors. Accordingly, we have divided the IP management into three interrelated levels of IP strategy, IP practices, and IP actions. This is illustrated in Fig. 6.1.

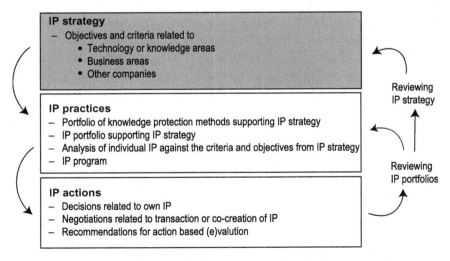

Fig. 6.1. IP strategy, IP practices, and IP actions.

In the framework of Fig. 6.1, the IP strategy level is understood as the high-level objectives and criteria related to business areas or target markets, technologies or other knowledge areas, and to other companies. These objectives for IP strategy are partly based on the company business strategy as a starting point. For each main business area, one should be able to see how the company makes business in those and how the IP is going to support that business. In some companies, these business areas might be different geographical market areas. In other companies, they might be completely distinct business models, such as consultancy, product sales, and related services. If objectives related to technologies are relevant to the company, the IP strategy should receive input from a company's technology strategy. The objectives should be based on reviewing those technologies or knowledge areas that are important for the company's businesses currently or in the future. Furthermore, when considering these technology areas, one should be able to answer how the company sees the development of those technologies, and in which additional technologies it needs to invest.

The defined strategic-level objectives work as a guideline for the IP practices level of Fig. 6.1. Each company has its own set of key knowledge, part of which is protected with IP. All important IP in a company cannot be formally protected due to the nature of knowledge. It is also the case that for some competences, IP protection is not even desirable. For example there may be high costs, the problem of a high speed of technological development in the field, or simply the objective of keeping them confidential. IP practices include the selection of a suitable portfolio of protection methods that supports the objectives set in the IP strategy. The portfolio may differ from one business area to another. A somewhat comprehensive list of potential different protection methods was listed in Table 1.1. As we mentioned in Chapter 1, we view the repertoire of possible protection methods as larger than those that are explicitly mentioned in law. Thus, in addition to formal protection methods such as patents and copyrights that suit well-defined knowledge and technology areas, IP can also be controlled by contracts, made between a company and its partners or employees, and by informal methods. Some contractual and informal methods of protection belong also to practices of human resource management as in the following example from the interview study: "*It* [our business model] *is very knowledge and people dependent... anyone could in principle copy our concept and do a brochure claiming that they can do the same things as we do, but we don't really need to worry about protecting that. They would need the right people to succeed in that, and they are in a very limited supply... but there is then the real risk related to our key employees, and we have tried to make necessary contracts with them.*" Additionally, a degree of protection may also be given by companies' internal processes, which seek, for example, to screen and limit the information that flows out of the company. IP practices also usually include other, process-related issues, labelled here under "IP program". This contains items such as employee roles and responsibilities related to IP, employee education regarding IP, confidentiality policies, reporting and reviewing of inventions, and monitoring IP activities of other companies. Last, but absolutely not least, the point made under the IP practices heading is regarding the analysis and valuation of individual IP against the objectives of IP strategy.

As already said above, IP assets typically have little intrinsic or market value and their real value comes indirectly from the business that is possible through the IP. This indirect impact of IP makes it difficult to valuate an individual IP. Firstly, there are many different ways in which a firm can create business value from an IP. The IP may allow unique features of the product or service which can increase sales or the price of the offering. The IP may also allow the firm to conduct business in strategically important markets without a risk of being sued for infringement. Both of these sources of value for IP are as valid in a closed innovation environment as in the open and networked Bazaar of Opportunities. In a networked environment the IP may be a direct source of additional revenue from licensing the IP for use in other companies. The IP may also increase the attractiveness of the firm as an innovation and business partner. The sources of value for IP are not limited to the four situations described above but they are, perhaps, the most common in the context of networked innovation. Secondly, the valuation of IP in a networked innovation is difficult because two actors of networked innovation seldom share the same opinion of a value of a single IP. That is because the actors seldom share the same view of the business potential that could be made possible through the IP: the actors may have different opinions about future markets and about the strategic use of the IP. All that has resulted in IP valuation being a hot topic both in academic and business discussion.[5] We will come back to the topic in Chapter 7.

The IP actions in Fig. 6.1 are operational-level day-to-day decisions related to a company's own IP, negotiations related to transaction or co-creation of IP, or recommendations for action-based evaluation of IP. The results and experiences from IP actions should give recommendations for decision makers about potential changes in future courses of action. With the arrival of new information about single IP assets or about the environment in which it is intended to be utilized, revisions of the relevance and value of the asset should be made to see whether the current approach towards that IP asset is still valid under the new conditions. A significant change in the internal or external conditions could also influence the IP strategy of a company and thus also the company practices regarding IP. One interviewee discusses the importance of this in the upstream and highlights a general tenet of open innovation[6]: *"My view is that our industry was rather open until 10–15 years ago, there weren't too many patents. You gave some [information] and got some and that was it. In the last ten years I think the number of patents has increased, each company looks at some aspects where they want to be, trying to have coverage of what they're doing. And in those fields they do not want to give it away. They want to have their own assets and not have to license them out or whatever."* This is an example of a field where openness among the firms in the business is decreasing and formal protection of knowledge plays an increasingly important strategic role.

Relationships Between Business, Technology and IP Strategies

Intellectual and intangible assets, such as knowledge and IP rights, typically have little if any intrinsic or market value but are valuable for the company because they allow the company to operate in its own competitive way. That is, the value of IP assets derives from the business that they allow. Thus, whatever impacts the IP strategy may have are ultimately shown in the success or failure of the company's businesses, usually well into the future, either as a source or lack of sustainable competitive advantage. Accordingly, we see a close link between IP and business strategies of the company, as our definition of IP strategy already implies. For companies where technology plays an important role in their business either in the form of their business offering (e.g. a product) or as an enabling factor of their business offering (e.g. a technology-based service), there is a third

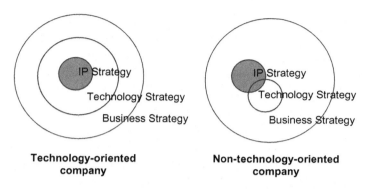

Technology-oriented company   **Non-technology-oriented company**

Fig. 6.2.   IP strategy in technology-oriented and non-technology-oriented companies.

strategy, namely the technology strategy, that should have an interplay with the IP strategy of the company. The business, technology, and IP strategies should all be aligned and support the business vision of the company. For a company, where technology plays just a supporting role in their business, the interaction between IP strategy and technology strategy, if this even exists, is less important. But the business and IP strategies should still be aligned. The two potential ways to view this interplay of business, technology, and IP strategies are given in Fig. 6.2[7] below.

The left part of the figure represents the ideal situation for a technology-oriented company. In such a company, competitive advantage is built on technological know-how, a core of which is typically protected with IP. Traditionally, this has meant intensive closed own development work and patent protection of the key technologies. Nowadays, when the companies have opened their boundaries to let external know-how and technology flow in and internal know-how and technology to move out in a controlled manner, the ways in which the technology strategy is realised using the IP strategy are more diverse than in the past. As we have defined, the IP strategy is broadly about the company's awareness about what knowledge is important for the company and how the IP should be protected, managed or shared in order to support the business model and business strategy of the company. In addition, the technology strategy is successfully executed through much more than traditional patent protection of key technologies. All that should be aligned with the business strategy driven by the business vision of the company. This is not to say that IP strategy (or the business strategy) should be rigid. Well-functioning strategy processes have both planned and emergent elements.[8] In a company with a culture that supports innovation, the business, technology, and IP strategies are not only aligned but also actively interplaying. A strong new and emerging IP may really lie at the core and influence the technology and business strategies of the company.

Intellectual property and IP strategy can also be a topical subject among those companies that cannot be labelled as technology-intensive or technology-oriented. Various kinds of content providers are good examples of non-technology oriented companies for which IP is important as a source of competitive advantage, rather than technology. Alignment of IP and business strategies is highly important for them but the alignment of IP and technology strategies (if they have them) is not so important. For example, a publishing company may have a technology strategy where it defines technological solutions through which it distributes its actual business offering, namely its IP, in accordance with its IP and business strategies. The actual IP strategy, however, has little if any interplay with the technology strategy. This is depicted on the right of Fig. 6.2.

The alignment and interplay of business, technology, and IP strategies also has an influence on the portfolio of protection methods used for the knowledge important for the company. IP strategy may define what knowledge should be protected and what knowledge could be shared in order to give the best support for the business strategy and business model of the firm. When it comes to the protection aspects of IP strategy, the portfolio of methods should go beyond the formal methods of IPR to also include contractual and informal methods to protect knowledge important for the company, as already discussed in Chapter 1 and Table 1.1.

Although in the protection of knowledge there is much in common between firms in different business, the actual IP strategies of firms may vary significantly from business to business. It is well known that patent strategies are dependent on the life cycle of technology used in the product.[9] For example, in life sciences (biotechnology and pharmaceuticals) patents play a very important role because of the long life cycle of the product in the business and the competitive advantage that they allow. On the other hand, for technologies whose life cycle is short, patenting may not be relevant. The patenting process typically takes 2–4 years and during that time the technology may become old in some fields of extremely fast development.

Companies are less eager on filing patents when chances to monitor and defend against infringements of patents[10] are highly limited. One example of such a field is the construction business. Monitoring of patent infringements often takes place through reverse engineering. One can do that for simple electronics but one cannot do that for buildings. Therefore, construction companies typically prefer other methods than patenting to protect their core knowledge (which does not, however, mean that construction companies do not have any patents at all). One more typical case where firms prefer other methods of knowledge protection than patenting are firms whose core competence is on the systemic level issues.

The formal methods of knowledge protection are important for the majority of firms. The actual set of methods used depends on business and may vary a lot between firms. The use of formal methods is also related to the alignment of business, technology, and IP strategies. Patenting is pronounced in fields of business where the technology life cycle is long and where the monitoring against infringements is relative easy. Patenting is also favourable for those technology firms that want to increase their visibility and value in the Bazaar of Opportunities through a strong formal IP portfolio. Trademarks are highly important in consumer business, but they are also actively used in business-to-business markets. Trademarks are used by all kinds of companies — technology companies, non-technology-oriented companies, service companies — to protect their business by preventing others from using identical or similar marks. Copyright plays a highly important role in some fields of business, especially for non-technology-oriented companies. The entertainment business is a good example of that. Their copyright may be a major source of income for content providers. The fundamental principles of open and networked innovation — openness as a behavioural norm of innovation and multiple source of innovation — seem to be well supported by the copyright legislation, both during the innovation work and after it as long as the IP protection is valid.

Contractual protection methods are important in the Bazaar of Opportunities, independently of the field of business. Innovation activities within the actors of the Bazaar are typically formalized through some kind of contract both in knowledge transaction and knowledge co-creation kinds of actions. The agreements between actors may include clauses on confidentiality, IP management including the ownership of IP and rights to use the IP, non-competition, recruitment freezes, etc. Agreements between actors in the Bazaar of Opportunities are, however, only one part of contractual protection of knowledge important for a firm. Another part is contracts between the firm and its key employees. Such contracts may include clauses on employee invention, confidentiality, and non-competition. The content of the clauses as well as with whom the firm makes such employee contracts depends on the business, technology, and IP strategies of the firm.

The use of informal methods of knowledge protection (Table 1.1) is more related to intra-firm IP management than to inter-organizational relations when dealing in the Bazaar of Opportunities. The use of informal methods is also more dependent on a firm's culture[11] than the field of business, or whether it is a technology or non-technology oriented firm. There are informal methods, such as publishing and fast innovation rhythm. These may be more pronounced in some fields of technology, but their use is still strongly affected by the firm's culture. Publishing of knowledge or technology, or alternatively sharing of it with a limited group of actors, are particularly used in fields where the core of the business is not exactly in a specific technology but in systemic level or in services related to the technology. By publishing the firm may create new markets, support the building of the business ecosystem,[12] and prevent others from protecting the knowledge or technology. Fast innovation rhythm is used for the protection of (knowledge) business, instead of patenting, especially in high-tech fields where the product life cycle is short. The firm may seek competitive advantage by launching new products or product updates frequently. Fast innovation rhythm is also commonly used in some service businesses where the protection of business against heavy competition would be otherwise difficult. Secrecy is an informal method of knowledge protection that is highly relevant and used when dealing in the Bazaar of Opportunities. Secrecy means here that key knowledge is kept secret either from some of the employees inside the company and/or from external co-operation partners such as customers and business partners. That means controlled sharing of knowledge. The IP strategy of a firm should define, in accordance with the business and technology strategies, what knowledge can be shared, and who it can be shared with, as well as the knowledge that cannot be shared.

How IP Strategy Could Support Navigation in the Bazaar of Opportunities

IP portfolios of firms fall typically under different technological or knowledge areas with varying degrees of importance. The technologies are used in different business areas, each having different characteristics with respect to the development of market size and market shares and each potentially requiring a different set of technologies from the firms intending to act in the market. IP is a tool for a firm to either enter a given market or get additional returns from the current market or from other actors. Accordingly, the sources of value for IP may be different in each business area. Furthermore, the portfolio of management methods for the protection and controlled sharing of knowledge in each technology or knowledge area may vary from one area to another. The IP strategy seeks to match the technological competences of the firm with the potential target markets and their future needs. A general illustration of that is depicted in Fig. 6.3.

The company should identify their core technological or knowledge areas. The company may want to own or have tight control of all relevant IP around these areas. The company may also need to invest more in these

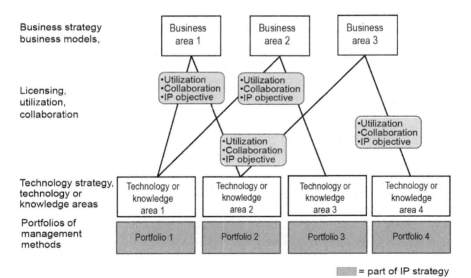

Fig. 6.3. Example of linking business areas and technology and knowledge areas with IP strategy.

areas. On the other hand, the company should also identify those areas in which IP need not be owned and could be licensed in. Thus, for the valuation of IP assets, the company should have an idea about the relative importance of the key technological areas and their future potential.

The company should also define its stance with respect to collaboration in different technological areas. Some technologies may only be accessed through collaboration, joint development, or IP transaction agreements. The company may prefer collaborating with certain partners due to their existing competences or past experience, or refrain from collaboration with some companies due to competitive issues or other highly conflicting interests.

As we have seen, companies should identify the current and potential technologies that they use or will use in the future, and define their importance. In the same way, the company should also analyse the potential business areas or business models. For the utilization of intellectual property, companies should have an understanding of what markets are of crucial importance, and which the company might want to serve directly, and which are more peripheral and can be served through, for example, licensing. The potential markets could be analysed, e.g. from the following viewpoints, some questions remaining the same as in the analysis of technology areas, but also looking for market viewpoints.

Companies typically use one or several technological areas in each business model. Or conversely, each technology is utilized in one or more business models. IP strategy should then define how each "link" between technology areas and business areas should be protected or managed and the corresponding tools or portfolio of protection methods that are used to reach this objective. In other words, just obtaining IP protection for a given knowledge asset does not necessarily yield any value for the company without defining how, where, and why that protection is going to be used (see also the discussion in Chapter 3 about Fig. 3.1). Moreover, IP strategy should help to define the business or technology areas in which the company needs technology from the outside, the areas in which the company is ready to transfer technology outside, or in which areas the company seeks collaboration with outside partners.

In the section "Collaboration, Open and Networked Innovation — Why?" in Chapter 1, we illustrated motivations for the transaction of IP and co-creation of IP (Figs. 1.1, 1.2, and 1.3). What is said above about

IP strategy and its alignment with technology and business strategies just deepens the discussion started in Chapter 1. The planned offering in Fig. 1.1 is something that belongs under business (and technology) strategies. The present knowledge of a firm represents the current IP portfolio of the firm (in accordance with the IP strategy). The question is how to fill the gap between the present knowledge and knowledge required for the planned offering. The possibilities are in-house R&D or IP transaction in one way or another, as discussed in Chapter 3. In the IP transaction one should also consider whether the aim is to own the IP or just acquire a license to use it. An example of the different possibilities for organizing the development and ownership of IP is given by this interviewee: "*We lacked a good proprietary technology. Instead of developing that ourselves, we decided to team up with another company. Five years earlier, we would have tried to develop it ourselves, but at that point we said no. We might have done that, but it would either take much longer or the end product would be inferior to the situation where we could team up with somebody. So what we did was, we signed a deal with them, defined a joint development program, and obtained an exclusive license.*" Here, one key technology is owned by an outside partner, but differentiation and competitive advantage is secured with an exclusive license contract.

The inbound transaction of IP does not require that the actors open and share their knowledge. Accordingly, the IP management related to the transaction is more straightforward than the IP management in co-creation with external actors where you have to open and share your knowledge to others. In the case of Fig. 1.2, where it is a question of unused existing knowledge of the company that does not support the planned offering of the firm under its own commercialization, one has to consider strategically the different possibilities for the unused knowledge: whether to strategically keep it in-house, but without making any direct profit on it; whether to sell or license out the IP; or whether to find a partner with whom to co-create a new offering based on the unused knowledge. Furthermore, the alignment of the decision with the business, technology, and IP strategies must be considered. From the viewpoint of IP strategy, the main focus is on costs related to maintaining IP and risks associated with making the IP known outside of the company. This is different from the technology and business strategy viewpoints, where the focus is on how the potential actions will influence the running of the business, or its future plans, as well as the problem of limiting resources in the firm.

The co-creation of IP in Fig. 1.3 is the approach that calls for the novel thinking of IP strategy in the context of open and networked innovation. The traditional patent strategies of firms do not give much support for the co-creation because they do not consider issues related to the controlled opening of knowledge, which is a prerequisite for successful co-creation followed by successful business offering. Furthermore, the co-creation of IP may call for flexibility and new thinking also from the business strategy level because there is a variety of different forms and models using which the results of joint innovation can be commercialized.

We have underlined above the strategic value of IP as an attractive asset for collaboration. Usually that really is the situation, but there are situations where owning IP might be a drawback in collaboration. The following quotation, in the words of a manufacturer, is an example of that: "*We had this concept development phase going on together with a customer, and found out an improvement that we could utilize in the customer's product. We then went forward to file a patent. We informed the customer about that, and that it would probably be a major improvement to their product, but they were not particularly interested… it actually turned out to be quite a sensitive and delicate situation with us owning a potential patent on our customers product.*"

Successful navigation in the Bazaar of Opportunities requires that the networked business case is considered as a whole. The strengthening of their own proprietary IP is not always beneficial in networked business and, therefore, IP strategy should give guidance to practices and actions related to the protection and use of an individual IP in the main technological and business areas of a firm. The importance of formal IP protection methods leading to proprietary IP can vary widely between firms in the same business area and between different business areas of a single firm. Sometimes non-proprietary contractual and informal methods of knowledge protection are more important in order to support the business strategy and model of the firm than formal proprietary IP. Consider, for example, an IT company that develops its own key technologies (software) but licenses them out with an open source license. This kind of approach combines two novel aspects of open and networked innovation. Firstly, the core technological knowledge is refined and improved in collaboration with outside actors, potentially even with competitors. Secondly, the protection of the created core knowledge does not rely on formal IP protection methods, but rather on tacitness of expert knowledge of the employees. And that special knowledge of the employees makes the actual competitive advantage for the company — not the technology (software) itself.

Firms may also want to patent their technology, process, etc., if their aim is to gain income through selling or licensing the IP of their innovation. This is an important strategic approach towards formal IP protection in the Bazaar of Opportunities. There are increasing numbers of firms and public research organizations whose aim is not to commercialize the developed technology themselves but, instead, gain revenues through selling or licensing the IP related to the technology to another actor whose interest is to commercialize it. All that is in accordance with the paradigm of Open Innovation.[13] Filing a patent means that it becomes public. In Europe that happens one and a half years after the patent filing. Accordingly, patent databases are excellent sources to gain worldwide publicity for your innovation if your intention is to sell or license the innovation. Firms who are searching for external knowledge and technology required for their planned offering are increasingly active in the search of such knowledge and technology in patent databases. Formal protection of IP also opens up a possibility to use IP inter-mediators[14] in the marketing of innovation. In the Bazaar of Opportunities, a published patent may also act as a calling card that attracts other actors in the Bazaar to have collaboration with the firm.

Firms' Practices of IP Management in the Bazaar of Opportunities

Firms in different fields of business have much in common when it comes to IP strategy in the context of open and networked innovation. Perhaps the main common issue in the Bazaar of Opportunities is related to what the firm can share with other actors and what it cannot. In the words of an interviewee: *"The only thing is, which I always point out at the beginning of the co-operation, that you have to figure out first, is what is absolutely core (unique) to you — something that you will never share ... We're not going to give that sort of IP away."* Firms do not share their absolute core knowledge. There may well be exceptions to this, but they really are exceptions. The core knowledge should be defined and communicated in a way that ensures that everybody in the firm understands what is their absolute core, something that they never share with their innovation partners. The absolute core knowledge of the firm, i.e. the knowledge that brings the special competitive advantage for the firm, however, may sometimes be found going in an unexpected direction. Above we talked about the IP strategy of an IT firm whose sole content was focused on interactive operation in open source communities. For them the absolute core knowledge was not in the software technology but, instead, in the processes how they could make value for their customers by using open source software. Technological (software) know-how was important for them, but that was not their absolute core.

Although firms do not to share their absolute core knowledge with other actors, in strategic alliances the sharing of knowledge with the strategic partner may become quite close to the core, if that is required by the strategic goals of the partners. As an example, Nokia Corporation and Microsoft Corporation announced in Winter 2011 a strategic alliance with a target to build a new global mobile ecosystem including a new generation of Nokia smart phones with a new Microsoft Windows Phone operating system developed for the new Nokia smart phones.[15] In order to do that, both companies needed to open up their knowledge and some key technologies to each other. This strategic alliance was a surprise for many. It was believed that the old operating system of Nokia mobile phones, Symbian, would be replaced by Meego, which had been under joint development between Nokia Corporation and Intel Corporation for a while.[16] Nokia, however, made a strategic decision to focus on Windows Phone instead of Meego as the future operating system in their smart phones. The argument for the decision was not a technological superiority of Windows Phone in respect to Meego but an expectation that the business ecosystem around Windows Phone would grow to become much larger than the business ecosystem around Meego. In the words used in this book, the top management of Nokia anticipates that there will be many more actors in the Windows Phone alley in the Bazaar of Opportunities than in the Meego alley of the Bazaar. The actors will create application software for the phones, offer mobile services, and other attractions for the users of smart phones that have an influence on the buying decision of a new smart phone. One may expect that Nokia will also share some technology and knowledge with the developers of applications and services in order to promote the growth of the business ecosystem. At the point of writing this book, it is too early to say whether the Windows Phone alley will become larger than the Meego alley and whether the strategic alliance with Microsoft Corporation was a vice strategic movement for Nokia or not. However, the strategic movement underlines the growing importance of the business ecosystem in many branches of industry. The building of an ecosystem and participation in it may require a new approach to a firm's IP strategy. It can no longer be only about formal protection of knowledge. It should also include aspects related to controlled sharing of knowledge. But if the business ecosystem is in line with the firm's business strategy, it is just about alignment of business, technology, and IP strategies in the context of networked innovation.

The interview study uncovered the fact that, independently on the field of business, companies see IP in broader terms, so that it includes not only formal IP rights (patents, trademarks, copyrights, etc.), but also knowledge that can be controlled by contracts, norms, and policy. Accordingly, firms apply contractual and informal protection methods widely to ensure knowledge protection, and a portfolio approach towards IP management was a common practice in the most of the firms. The interviewed managers were asked to select their three most preferred ways for protecting knowledge. Certain firms found this question difficult to answer. For example, some firms were so large and were applying many types of protection methods depending on the business sector, products, services, etc. Some smaller firms were using many semi-formal and informal protection methods simultaneously and so couldn't decide on their top three. A handful of protection methods were clearly preferred as important tools for knowledge protection (see Table 6.1). Patents, trademarks, confidentiality agreements, secrecy, and publishing were seen as being the most important ways to protect knowledge in inter-organizational relationships. Confidentiality

Table 6.1.   Most common methods of knowledge protection in open and networked innovation.

Formal protection methods	Contractual protection methods	Informal protection methods
— Patent	— Confidentiality	— Secrecy
— Trademark		— Publishing

agreements were most common — for 70% of the firms it was one of the most important tools. Patents, trademarks, secrecy, and publishing were each important protection methods for 30% of the firms.

For half of the firms in the interview study, patents were an important way to protect their knowledge, but only 30% thought that patents were in the top three preferred methods for knowledge protection. Approximately 20% of the firms did not believe that patenting would protect their knowledge. Patenting was generally considered to be too expensive and too complex a method of protection. Patents are seen as being difficult to defend and the patent application process makes any invention too public. The following comment by an interviewee opens up the dilemma related to patenting: *"The difficulty is, yeah, you can keep something secret or you can patent it, but if you patent it, the information is open, and how can you know that someone else isn't applying that know-how ... So that's the balance. On the one hand you want to protect it because you've invested in it; on the other hand, yes if you cannot prove it, if someone else is using it, there is no use in it. That is sometimes an argument to publish. That's one of the three ways we use it — patenting it, keeping it secret, or publishing it. And in fact patenting is also publishing, because it is public after one and a half years."* On the other hand, publishing was considered to be a way to prevent others from filing a patent. For 30% of the companies, publishing (an informal protection method) was one of the top three preferred methods. In the words of an interviewee: *"As I explained, there's always a choice of, you know, what do you apply to patent, when do you file for a patent, and when it's just common sense to not talk about it ... Publishing can be a good way to make sure that, you know, if we're not applying for a patent, we at least publish enough that you keep your freedom to operate, you clear the path ... So at least somebody else cannot put a patent there."* In co-creation actions publishing was a quite common method to guarantee the freedom of action for their own business based on the innovation outcome of a joint work. In addition to that, one could create markets for the business through publishing.

The interview study also underlined the importance of confidentiality agreements. For 70% of the firms, a confidentiality agreement was one of the three most important ways to protect their knowledge. Only 15% of the firms didn't see confidentiality agreements as an important and useful way to protect their knowledge. Those firms had, for example, long, established partnerships and "gentleman's agreements" were common.

What has been said above about IP strategy is very much general. We have written little about sectoral differences. That is because the practices of open and networked innovation seem to be quite generic.[17] There are sectoral differences, for example in the patent strategy of firms in different branches of industry like those described above, but the differences according to our interview study were much smaller than what we initially expected. One reason for this may be the fact that the offerings of firms seldom consists of a single technology but, instead, are more or less complex systems consisting of different technologies, software, and maybe services. The complexity of offerings certainly has an influence on the used IP strategy. In this book we do not go into more details about sectoral differences in the IP strategies of product companies, because there are authors that have covered the subject.[18] However, we will discuss in more detail IP management in service business. There have been studies done about knowledge protection in service business[19] but these studies have not identified differences between alternative kinds of service businesses.

IP Strategy in Service Business

Service involves a provider and a customer working together to create value. Accordingly, services have been defined as provider–customer interactions that co-create value.[20] Services are processes, performances, or experiences that one person or organization does for the benefit of another. Thus, one may say that service is a system of interacting parts that include people, technology, and business. Accordingly, a service system may be defined as a dynamic value co-creating configuration of resources, consisting of people, technology, organizations, and shared information.[21] Activities in a service system can be divided into two categories: front-stage and back-stage activities.[22] Front-stage activity is the actual part of the service where the interaction between the service provider and the customer takes place. All other activities related to the production of the service belong to the back stage. Service innovation is defined as the combination of technology innovation, business model innovation, social-organizational innovation, and demand innovation to improve existing or create new service value propositions (offerings or experiences) and service systems.[23]

A modern service system may consist of several actors in the value network of service offering, and innovations in a complex service system are more and more frequently a result of interaction between two or more actors in the network. Thus we can say that many service innovations take place in the Bazaar of Opportunities, or at least require dealing in the Bazaar. Accordingly, the protection of service business really needs the strategic approach of IP management in the context of networked innovation. Protection of services is challenging in several ways. Firstly, many services are intangible in their nature. The formal system for the protection of IP has mainly been developed to cater to the needs of industrial manufacturing of physical goods. The intangible nature of many service innovations creates challenges for the existing IP systems.[24] The challenge is that formal IP rights cover only some elements of service innovation, such as technology that enables the service and the brand for which trademarks may give some protection. Secondly, the fact that multiple actors are involved in the creation of service innovation adds an additional challenge for the IP management, which calls for the use of contractual and informal methods of knowledge protection.

In the interview study there were many firms whose main business was in services, or who had significant service business separated from their tangible product business. When speaking about innovations, the managers of these firms usually spoke about technological innovations (including software), and these technological innovations were often developed together with an external actor. The knowledge and technology related to the innovation were either transferred to the service firm through some form of IP transaction (see Chapter 3) or co-created together with a technology provider. The front-stage activities of the service were typically developed by the firm itself. There were also examples where the front stage was developed in a network of actors, but these remained a minority. Many interviewees mentioned customers (either firms or consumers) as an important source of ideas and feedback for innovations but only few considered customers as co-creators of innovations. In this sense the situation is analogous to that of product business. Innovative endeavors take place commonly nowadays in interaction between two or more actors, but designs of new innovations are often developed internally by individual firms that keep strategic control over their designs.[25] Customers give input for the innovation work but work as co-creators only in a minority of cases.

The interview study also revealed that there are differences in the strategic approach towards IP management between services firms, similarly to firms in product businesses. In the service business, however, we found any sectoral categorization towards IP management practices very difficult. Instead we found a knowledge-based approach more relevant. Let us consider, as an example, a firm in the sector of financial services which has three essentially different kinds of financial business services: classical banking service based on face-to-face interaction, novel online banking based on virtual interaction through a website or mobile application, and business incubation services. All of these services are essentially different and require different kinds of approaches towards IP management. In order to build an appropriate strategy for each kind of service, one should consider the actual service system, the value network of the service and the critical knowledge required to create and deliver the service in question. In the example above, they are very different in the classical banking, online banking, and business incubation.

In order to go deeper into the subject, we classified the services that the interviewed firms provide into four distinct categories according to critical knowledge in service innovations and the actual service business.[26] The categories were named as technology-based services, human-resources-based services, research and engineering services, and innovation support services (see Table 6.2). IP management and open innovation were considered differently in these categories.

Technology-based services are built on an enabling technology (software or hardware). Examples of technology-based services include internet and mobile services as well as expert services based on a special enabling technology. In this category, service innovations typically take place in

Table 6.2. Categorization of services according to critical knowledge in the service innovations and actual service business.

— Technology-based services
— Human-resources-based services
— Research and engineering type of services
— Innovation support services

the back-stage activities in the development of enabling technology. The enabling technology might also be co-created together with a technology provider. The special knowledge of firms in technology-based service systems is technology (including hardware, software, processes) as well as in their people, in their knowledge of customer needs and enabling technology. Accordingly, their IP strategy includes the use of formal, contractual, and informal methods of knowledge and IP protection. The emphasis among the three depends on the life cycle of service innovations. In the given example in the financial sector, online banking includes enabling core elements that belong under the category of technology-based services.

Human resources (HR) based services typically have strong and well-developed processes in the front-stage of service, which allow easy replacement of persons providing the service. Accordingly, the special and critical knowledge of firms offering HR-based services is in processes and service innovations are typically process innovations. Examples of HR-based services include cleaning and personnel services that firms have outsourced to an external service provider. The classical banking in the given example also belongs under the category of HR-based services. If the HR-based service could be standardized, the service firm tends to innovate alone and they use customers only to gain input for their innovation. On the other hand, if the service requires tailoring, a customer is typically a co-creator of innovation. It is case dependent how this co-creation is contractually arranged in respect of the results of innovation. Protection of knowledge and IP related to innovations of HR-based services takes place typically through contractual and informal methods, such as restricted access to information. The firms may also actively use trademarks.

Research and engineering services are customized one-time performances to solve a problem or need of a customer by using special expertise of personnel in the service firms. Accordingly, the critical knowledge of a research and engineering type of service provider is in its people. Secondarily it can also be in the processes of the service firm. The service typically creates new IP which often belongs to the customer, although the interest of the service firm could be different if their role in the creation of new IP has been significant. The service may be confined to the front stage, but it may include a large back-stage service network including one or more actors, as well. In the latter case, the service provider may act as a system integrator by integrating the knowledge and technology of third-party actors to create a desired solution for the needs of customer. In research and engineering services, contractual methods are emphasized in the protection of the knowledge. Confidentiality agreements are standard practice. Commission agreements are typically well defined and service firms tend to use their own model agreements for a commission which grants some rights also to the service firm (not necessarily directly to the generated IP but to know-how related to it).

There are also service firms that are in the innovation process of their customers, not as active innovators but by supporting knowledge-based services for the innovation and new business development or providing a platform for the customer for innovation. Examples of such service firms include innovation intermediaries and IP management service providers. In the given example in the financial sector, the business incubation services belong under the category of innovation support services. Services of firms that provide innovation support for other firms are standardized and based primarily on well-developed processes of the service firms and, secondarily, on the expertise of the personnel. Providers of innovation support services do not aim to create their own IP when working with their customers. That is an essential difference with the other three categories and, therefore, the innovation support service firms could be placed into their own category, although they have much in common with research and engineering firms and both are good examples of KIBS (Knowledge Intensive Business Service) firms. The own knowledge of the service firm is protected by a wide range of informal methods of knowledge protection.

Conclusions: IP Strategy and Collaboration

The classical objective of IP strategy has been to achieve maximum protection for the knowledge assets of the company. In today's business ecosystem, where firms have opened their boundaries and deal with numbers of known and unknown actors in the Bazaar of Opportunities and gain from their knowledge, IP, business relationships, visions, and opportunities, protection is not the core of IP strategy. In the Bazaar of Opportunities the objective of IP strategy is not to achieve the maximum protection for the knowledge assets of the company but to allow access to such knowledge and technologies that are necessary for the competitive advantage of the firm. For one firm this might be achieved through its own technological knowledge and formal protection methods, while for another the key IP might be developed and owned by other companies with the access to the knowledge managed through licensing. In short, formulating an IP strategy comes down to successfully supporting the business model and business strategy of the company. And as the business models of companies even in the same industry and with similar areas and levels of knowledge can be very different, a generic IP strategy is surely not a recipe for success. As one respondent from a technology development organization put it: *"One way [to commercialize and profit from the developed technology] could be to sell it with as high a price as possible, another option is to sell or license the technology itself at a low price for an actor that needs expert services related to the technology and then try to make the profit from the sales of services. There is really no single and right way to do these things."* We believe that most firms would benefit from more diverse ways of collaboration, although the degrees and methods of knowledge co-creation and transfer naturally vary from case to case.

What does open and networked innovation, as well as the broadened view of intellectual property, actually mean for the IP strategy of firm then? It means, firstly, that collaboration aspects, both knowledge transaction and knowledge co-creation, should be deeply built into the firm IP strategy and policy on all levels. Secondly, according to our view, firms' IP and expert knowledge are not commoditized assets in the sense that they can be simply traded with arms-length transactions in and out of the company. One may do that for a formal IP but not easily for the know-how required to make business using the formal IP. According to experience, formal IP alone is seldom adequate to create new business but one also needs know-how related to the formal IP.[27] That is an aspect that should be considered in the IP strategy. Secondly, even when knowledge transfer or co-creation option is available, it should not be taken on a whim. Linking the IP strategy to business and technology strategies is important in this respect, so that key proprietary knowledge is not inadvertently lost. On the other hand, by adhering to formal IP protection mechanisms and internal development and knowledge creation only, one significantly under exploits the many possibilities offered by the Bazaar of Opportunities.

Collaboration and co-creation as a key part of IP strategy are not areas where one can afford to be naive. One should carefully weigh the positive and negative sides of different IP strategies, related to, for example, where one could rely on trust to achieve better results and where tighter control of IP assets is needed. An interviewed manager stated: *"Trust certainly works in the short term and it's very important. But in the long term, companies are bought and sold, and people come and go. Trust is very volatile, it evaporates like nothing. And then the whole thing changes."* Mutually beneficial and long-lasting joint development partnership may turn into a headache when the partner is bought out by a competitor.

To summarize, a successful IP strategy should illuminate how the IP that the company controls, in one way or another, supports the business strategy of the company. At the same time such a strategy sets the guidelines and rules for collaboration from the IP perspective: What critical knowledge needs to be kept strictly in-house? What knowledge can be shared? And with whom and how? Which are the areas where IP can be subject to transactions in and out of the firm? Which are the areas where open co-creation between suitable partners is the most beneficial mode of operation?

Notes

1. For example, Mintzberg *et al.* (1998) divide strategy into ten different "schools of thought", each with a different view of what strategic management entails. [Mintzberg, H., Alhstrand, B. and Lampel, J. (1998). *Strategy Safari: The Complete Guide through the Wilds of Strategic Management*, Financial Times/Prentice Hall, London.]

2. In his paper discussing IP strategies of Japanese and UK companies, Pitkethly (2001) defines IP strategy as "The use of IP, either alone or in combination with other resources of the firm, to achieve the firm's strategic objectives" (p. 426). [Pitkethly, R.H. (2001). Intellectual Property Strategy in Japanese and UK Companies: Patent Licensing Decisions and Learning Opportunities, *Research Policy*, Vol. 30, pp. 425–442.]

3. Lex van Wijk (2005) describe patent strategy as "a framework of decision making processes and procedures that should ensure that a company's patent activities support the company's current business and that they will assist the company in realising its business vision" (p. 5). [van Wijk, L. (2005). *There May be Trouble Ahead: A Practical Guide to Effective Patent Asset Management*, Scarecrow Press, Oxford.]

4. The term "vision" is used to describe a mental image of a state where the organization and the business are headed. According to Bennis and Nanus: "To choose a direction, a leader must first have developed a mental image of a possible and desirable future state of the organization…which we call a vision. A vision articulates a view of a realistic, credible, attractive future for the organization…With a vision, the leader provides the all-important bridge from the present to the future of the organization." (p. 89)

[Bennis, W. and Nanus, B. (1985). *Leaders: The Strategies for Taking Charge*, Harper and Row, New York.]

5. The valuation of business and intellectual property has been a hot topic of discussion because valuation is considered as one of the most critical areas of finance. In 2004 Robert Reilly and Robert Schweihs compiled contributions from leading experts in the field into a handbook. The handbook, however, did not complete the discussion but instead stimulated more debate. An example of the academic and business discussions is the series of IP Valuation Symposia organized in Europe (Budapest 2008, Helsinki 2009). [Reilly, R. and Schweihs, R. (eds) (2004). *The Handbook of Business Valuation and Intellectual Property Analysis*, McGraw-Hill, New York.]

6. The general tendency in business seems to be that openness among the actors will increase when it is a question of innovation. Eelko Huizingh (2011) has predicted that within a decade the term open innovation will fade way because it has become "business as usual" — not because the concept has lost its usefulness. This is, however, not valid in every field of business. There are businesses where open communication between firms is decreasing and protection of knowledge nowadays plays more important a role than in the past. [Huizingh, E. (2011). Open Innovation: State of the Art and Future Perspectives, *Technovation*, Vol. 31, pp. 2–9.]

7. The figure on the left is modified from the figure "Alignment of strategies", in van Wijk (2005) where the smallest circle is labelled as "patent strategy". The term "IP strategy" used here corresponds to the broader approach to intellectual property used in our book. [van Wijk, L. (2005). *There May be Trouble Ahead: A Practical Guide to Effective Patent Asset Management*, Scarecrow Press, Oxford, p. 92.]

8. For a discussion of these two main approaches to strategy i.e. planned and emergent strategy, see for example, Mintzberg *et al.* (1998). [Mintzberg, H., Alhstrand, B. and Lampel, J. (1998). *Strategy Safari: The Complete Guide through the Wilds of Strategic Management*, Financial Times/Prentice Hall, London.]

9. See e.g. the review paper by Petr Hanel (2006) and the book by Michael Collin (2008) and the references therein for more details. [Hanel, P. (2006). Intellectual Property Rights Business Management Practices: A Survey of the Literature, *Technovation*, Vol. 26, pp. 895–931; Collin, M. (2008). *Driving Innovation — Intellectual Property Strategies for a Dynamic World*, Cambridge University Press, Cambridge.]

10. *ibid.*

11. Organizational culture has been defined by J.B. Barney (1986) as the specific collection of values and norms that are shared by people and groups in an organization and that control the way they interact with each other and with stakeholders outside the organization. [Barney, J.B. (1986). Organizational Culture: Can It Be a Source of Sustained Competitive Advantage?, *Academy of Management Review*, Vol. 11, pp. 656–665.]

12. James Moore (1996) has defined the term "business ecosystem" as "An economic community supported by a foundation of interacting organizations and individuals — the organisms of the business world. The economic community produces goods and services of value to customers, who are themselves members of the ecosystem. The member organisms also include suppliers, lead producers, competitors, and other stakeholders. Over time, they co-evolve their capabilities and roles, and tend to align themselves with the directions set by one or more central companies. Those companies holding leadership roles may change over time, but the function of ecosystem leader is

valued by the community because it enables members to move toward shared visions to align their investments, and to find mutually supportive roles." (p. 26) [Moore, J.F. (1996). *The Death of Competition: Leadership and Strategy in the Age of Business Ecosystems*, HarperBusiness, New York.]

13. According to the paradigm of Open Innovation, firms can and should use external ideas as well as internal ideas, and internal and external paths to market, as they look to advance their technology. [Chesbrough, H. (2003). *Open Innovation: The New Imperative for Creating and Profiting from Technology*, Harvard Business School Press, Boston.]

14. IP inter-mediator is an actor that helps firms to transgress their own boundaries and access external knowledge.

15. See more information about the strategic alliance between Nokia Corporation and Microsoft Corporation from the blog of Nokia's CEO Stephen Elop and Microsoft's CEO Steve Palmer at http://conversations.nokia.com/2011/02/11/open-letter-from-ceo-stephen-elop-nokia-and-ceo-steve-ballmer-microsoft (Accessed on 23 February 2012). Additional information can be found on the Microsoft website at http://www.microsoft.com/presspass/press/2011/feb11/02-11partnership.mspx (Accessed on 23 February 2012).

16. Meego is a Linux-based open source mobile operating system project originally announced by Nokia Corporation and Intel Corporation in February 2010. See more information about Meego at http://en.wikipedia.org/wiki/MeeGo (Accessed on 23 February 2012).

17. van de Vrande *et al.* (2009) studied open innovation in SMEs in various fields of business and found that differences between practices in product and service focused firms are diminishing. [van de Vrande, V., de Jong, J., Vanhaverbeke, V. and Rochemont, M. (2009) Open Innovation in SMEs: Trends, Motives and Management Challenges, *Technovation*, Vol. 29, pp. 423–437.]

18. See e.g. the review paper by Petr Hanel (2006) and the book by Michael Collin (2008) and the references therein for more details. [Hanel, P. (2006). Intellectual Property Rights Business Management Practices: A Survey of the Literature, *Technovation*, Vol. 26, pp. 895–931; Collin, M. (2008). *Driving Innovation — Intellectual Property Strategies for a Dynamic World*, Cambridge University Press, Cambridge.]

19. See e.g. papers of Miles *et al.* (2000) and Päällysaho and Kuusisto (2008). [Miles, I., Andersen, B., Boden, M. and Howells, J. (2000). Service Production and Intellectual Property, *International Journal of Technology Management*, Vol. 20, pp. 95–115; Päällysaho, S. and Kuusisto, J. (2008). Intellectual Property Protection as a Key Driver of Service Innovation: An Analysis of Innovative KIBS Businesses in Finland and the UK, *International Journal of Services Technology and Management*, Vol. 9, pp. 268–284.]

20. On 14–15 July 2007 the University of Cambridge Institute for Manufacturing (IfM) and International Business Machines Corporation (IBM) organized a symposium on service science, management and engineering in Cambridge (UK) where leading experts in the field discussed the new discipline of service science. The symposium resulted in a discussion paper where (among other issues) the terminology of service business was defined. In this book we follow the definitions agreed in the Cambridge Service Science,

Management and Engineering Symposium. [IfM and IBM (2007). *Succeeding Through Service Innovation: A Discussion Paper*, University of Cambridge, Cambridge.]

21. *ibid.*

22. The division of services into front-stage and back-stage activities has been described in detail by J. Teboul (2006) in his book about service business. [Teboul, J. (2006). *Service is Front Stage: Positioning Services for Value Advantage*, Palgrave Macmillan, New York.]

23. [IfM and IBM (2007) *ibid.*]

24. The study of Miles *et al.* in 2000 pointed out that many service firms do not patent and that the major reason for this is that the patent system has largely been developed to deal with tangible innovations while many services are intangible in nature. The protection of service business, however, is as important as the protection of tangible product business. Therefore, service firms are actively using other methods (contractual, etc.) to protect their business, as found in the study of Päällysaho and Kuusisto in 2008. [Miles, I., Andersen, B., Boden, M. and Howells, J. (2000). Service Production and Intellectual Property, *International Journal of Technology Management*, Vol. 20, pp. 95–115; Päällysaho, S. and Kuusisto, J. (2008). Intellectual Property Protection as a Key Driver of Service Innovation: An Analysis of Innovative KIBS Businesses in Finland and the UK, *International Journal of Services Technology and Management*, Vol. 9, pp. 268–284.]

25. Openness in innovation in different branches of business has been studied by many researchers in recent years. Good examples of the early works are the papers of Christian DeBresson (1999), Elliot Maxwell (2006) and Keld Laursen and Ammon Salter (2006). [DeBresson, C. (1999). An Entrepreneur Cannot Innovate Alone: Networks of Enterprises Are Required, *DRUID Conference on Systems of Innovation*, Aalborg, Denmark; Maxwell, E. (2006). Open Standards, Open Source and Open Innovation. Harnessing the Benefits of Openness, *MIT Press*, Issue 3, pp. 119–176; Laursen, K. and Salter, A. (2006). Open for Innovation: The Role of Openness in Explaining Innovation Performance among UK Manufacturing Firms, *Strategic Management Journal*, Vol. 27, pp. 131–150.]

26. This categorization seems to apply well for the empirical data of the study, but there may well be services that do not fit very well into any of these categories. Therefore, we do not present this categorization as a theoretical proposition, only as an early hypothesis for further studies. Furthermore, the analysis does not include IP strategy for services that are add-ons for tangible products. The IP strategy of such offerings should be treated as a whole.

27. See the article by D.J. Teece (1998) for a broader discussion about the transfer of explicit knowledge (or formal IP). [Teece, D.J. (1998). Capturing Value from Knowledge Assets: The New Economy, Markets for Know-how, and Intangible Assets, *California Management Review*, Vol. 40, pp. 55–79.]

Chapter 7

Bridging Networked Innovation, Intellectual Property, and Business

In the earlier chapters of this book we discussed open and networked innovation, IP management and strategies in the context of networked innovation, and the role of contracting in the various forms of networked innovation. Firms that have been successful in the Bazaar of Opportunities have managed to link these capabilities together and with their business. A reader may already have noticed how deeply the perspectives of networked innovation, IP management, contracting, strategies, and business are connected together. In this chapter we continue the discussion about the combined view of network, IP, contracting, and business perspectives and consider three separate topics where the perspectives have or should be strongly connected together, if the firm is going to be successful. At first, we consider the business of system integration. After that we discuss IP valuation in the Bazaar of Opportunities. Finally, we analyse the levels of openness in the Bazaar in more detail than in Chapter 2. All these three topics bridge networked innovation, IP, and business.

The Business of System Integration

Business offerings are nowadays increasingly complex, consisting of "pieces" from various suppliers. The "pieces" typically consist of both technologies (hardware) and software. In addition, the business offering may also include services. When the offering consists of "pieces" from various suppliers, we may speak about integrated business offering. In some fields of business people speak about integrated solutions or integrated systems[1] but the meaning is the same: integration of "pieces" from various suppliers into a single, complete, and ready business offering.

An actor who puts together the pieces into a ready offering is called a system integrator (SI)[2] in network management literature. A system integrator orchestrates the value network of a business offering that creates the value. Thus, system integration is much more than just assembly. It also includes the human interaction required to create the offering. The human interaction also includes communication with customers. It is the SI whose role it is to communicate with customers on behalf of the other actors in the network and to carry out customer relationship management. The terms "system integrator" and "system integration" are not widely used in practical business life, but as theoretical terms they are accurate descriptions of the role and actions of the orchestrator of business networks. Many of the world's leading corporations, including Apple, Boeing, Ford, General Electric, Hewlett-Packard, IBM, Nokia, Siemens, and Toyota, perform system integration as a part of their business.[3] However, system integration is not only for "business giants"; there are examples of medium-sized, and even small, enterprises that can be called system integrators. So the business of system integration is not so much related to the size of business but merely to the business offering itself.

System integration (i.e. the design and development of integrated business offerings) developed in the 1940s and 1950s in the military arena, and then spread to other capital goods and high-volume industries; especially to the automotive, consumer electronics, and telecommunication industries.[4] The products (business offerings) in those fields of industry had become so complex that vertical integration inside a corporation was no longer feasible to produce the offering in a competitive manner. A network of suppliers and partners was required to supplement the own work for the offering.

In the 1990s and 2000s, the pace of technological change became faster and faster, accompanied by the increasing breadth and depth of knowledge required to manufacture and deliver both consumer and capital goods. Accordingly, system integration developed rapidly in the production of product systems consisting of hardware, software, and services. Product systems of capital goods are typically, to some extent, tailor-made for each customer (i.e. they are low-volume systems), on the contrary to consumer products which could be either low- or high-volume products. Independently, whether it is a question of low- or high-volume systems, system integration is characterized by the fact that there are several suppliers whose offerings have been integrated by the SI into a main business offering (i.e. product system) that is offered to the end customer(s).

In the literature, system integration has been defined as the capabilities which enable firms and other agents to bring together high-technology components, subsystems, software, skills, knowledge, engineers, managers, and technicians in order to produce a product in competition with other suppliers.[5] Thus, we can say that the design and development of integrated business offerings (i.e. integrated systems) is about engineering, business management, and leadership.[6] Engineering skills are required in order to technologically design the system, to understand what technology (including hardware as well as software) is required, and how to integrate the different technologies together into a working system. Management skills are required in order to organize and manage the design and development work, manage the production of the offering, and for running the business. Leadership skills are required to put the various suppliers together, to encourage and keep their people motivated to innovate and work towards a common goal.

The design and development of integrated business offerings (i.e. integrated systems) calls also for good capability in both component assembly and knowledge integration.[7] The emphasis on the importance between different capabilities depends on the business in question. Good component assembly capability may convey a special competitive advantage in high-volume production. Low-volume system integration may emphasize the knowledge integration capability of SI because low-volume systems are often tailored solutions and tailoring typically requires some kind of joint-innovation activities at the interface between actors in the system integration network. The knowledge integration capability, however, plays an increasingly important role also in the design and development of high-technology systems for high-volume production.

The extant literature of business network management has mainly focused on how a SI is able to manage supply networks in order to integrate products.[8] The operational structure of networks is often described by two models according to how and by whom the network is managed.[9] In the so-called hub-and-spoke model the network is controlled by a hub company, which in system integration is the SI. Accordingly, in the hub-and-spoke model the SI typically has strong control over the activities in the business network of integrated offering. In the so-called multiplex model the firms in the network have more or less equal voice in controlling the network activities. In the multiplex model the role of the SI is still the orchestration of the integration of "pieces" from the other actors of the network as well as the design of new business offerings, but the SI does not have any dominant role compared to other actors of the network when making business decisions related to the integrated business offering.

The models of hub-and-spoke and multiplex controlled networks have successfully been used in characterizing and designing the operative structures of networks integrating existing products and systems. The increasing complexity in high-volume products as well as the increasing demand for tailoring in low-volume products, however, will emphasize the role of the SI as an orchestrator of networked innovation. In the orchestration of networked innovation the key issue of SI is how the SI is able to utilize and manage its innovation network in order to strengthen its position in the value network and thus create future business opportunities. One may argue whether the approach of focusing on the operative structures is the best approach in characterizing innovation networks for creating completely new offerings. We have said above that the SI needs good capability in both component assembly and knowledge integration. While improvement of capabilities related to component assembly can be supported by focusing on the operative structures of the networks, we argue that improvement of capabilities related to knowledge integration calls for a knowledge management based approach.

In Chapter 3, we presented two knowledge management based basic models to characterize networked innovation: transaction networks and co-creation networks. In the Bazaar of Opportunities, the transaction and co-creation types of networked innovation models play an important role in the business of system integration. Next we consider different viewpoints of both models from the perspective of a system integrator.

System Integration in the Bazaar of Opportunities

In the Bazaar of Opportunities, a SI needs to design and control the business as well as innovation activities of companies that are involved in the innovation and offering network of the integrated business offering. From the business perspective, the SI needs to control the activities of companies in its network in a way that the contribution of each company is as valuable as possible and that they are motivated to provide their best effort in the design and development of the offering (i.e. integrated system). The SI should take into account that the role and contractual situation of a firm in the network may influence how committed the firm is to the collaboration. For example, the same firm may be less committed for the same work as a (replaceable) subcontractor than in the role of technology developer (supplier). The SI needs also to ensure that the value from the integrated business offering is divided so that it is profitable for each company to participate in the collaboration. The business management challenges of the SI given above are not independent of the innovation management challenges of SI. In the Bazaar of Opportunities, business and innovation management are strongly coupled together.

Discussions with the case companies of the study behind this book (listed in Appendix III) revealed that two clearly different kinds of systems could be identified from the perspective of innovation management in system integration:

(1) systems where the innovation arises from a novel combination of more or less existing "pieces" (which could be hardware, software, or services), and
(2) systems where the innovation evolves at the interface between two or more "pieces".

The first kinds of systems (integrated business offerings) are produced, without exception, in a transaction type of innovation network where the SI has a strong role as the orchestrator of the innovation network. Essential networking capabilities of SI in the transaction network include a capability to identify all the necessary pieces of the planned system and to have a basic understanding in order to be able to integrate them. Serial production and low demand for tailoring clearly favoured SI's operation in the transaction type of innovation network. In the context of system integration, transaction networks are for situations where a SI integrates more or less existing "pieces", i.e. results of earlier innovation. In a transaction, the ownership and rights of IP are transferred to the SI responsible for the exploitation or commercialization of the results. From the SI's perspective, it resembles sourcing and, therefore, one may also speak about sourcing network as a synonym for transaction network.

The development of the second kind of systems requires "opening" of knowledge by both the SI and technology suppliers in order to co-create the missing pieces of the integrated business offering. The development of systems where the innovation evolves at the interface between two or more "pieces" calls for co-creation and may take place in "pure" co-creation types of networks (as described in Chapter 3). Demand for a high degree of tailoring favoured operation in the co-creation kind of innovation network. In a co-creation network, there are several options about how the management of IP is arranged. The SI may own the IP, like in the transaction network, but suppliers and technology developers may as well keep the IP that they have generated. In the latter case the IP owner and the SI agree on how the SI may use the IP in the integrated business offering.

In addition to "pure" co-creation kind of networks, co-creation for integrated business offering may take place in a hybrid form of a network including elements from both the transaction and co-creation types of networks. The hybrid form may not be an initial choice of collaboration model but merely a "consequence of actions". It was said by a few SIs and technology developers that: *"despite a shared interest in the beginning to innovate openly and co-create new offerings, it is very easy to go back to entrenched routines and attitudes as the process goes on."* When that happens, the resulting model is a hybrid form of innovation network that includes elements from both transaction and co-creation. We cannot say that a hybrid form is, in general, a poorer form than the pure co-creation type of network, but a successful management of it may be very challenging. Successful co-creation also requires that the actors reveal their tacit knowledge to other partners. However, an actor may not necessarily wish to be open enough, which in fact may hinder the use of the co-creation model of networked innovation. A good network management capability is required in order for the SI to create an atmosphere where the actors can share their knowledge with the other partners. A representative from a SI company said that *"heterogeneous interests with respect to the collaboration model make the coordinating of the network challenging"*. It is a significant challenge for a SI to communicate the agenda of co-creation network sufficiently clearly to all actors so that their interests become, and stay, aligned. That requires not only good management skills but also good leadership by the SI towards other actors in the Bazaar of Opportunities that belongs to the integrated business offering network of the SI.

The interest of a network actor in a collaboration model depends not only on the culture and history of the company in innovation and offering networks for integrated business solutions. The interest also depends on the business model of the actor and the incentives that the SI offers for the other actors in the network. Incentives for innovation in the transaction network are typically based on contractual single-compensation of the work done for the SI.[10] In the co-creation networks there are more options for how the costs and benefits of work will be shared between the actors. It is the challenge of a SI to fit the interests of the actors with the collaboration model and incentives. For example, the business model of engineering service firms is often based on single payment for their service, and this model fits well for transaction types of works. Such a firm, however, may be less eager to share the costs and benefits in any other way, which may often be required in co-creation networks. On the other hand, a technology firm aiming to create its own IP may be well interested in co-creation collaboration and the sharing of costs and benefits in some other way than the single payment if it allows them to strengthen their own IP. For them future business opportunities through their own IP may be more attractive than single payment just after the innovation work. For some other actors an adequate incentive for co-creation could even be non-monetary, such as reputation for the members of open source software community.

The situation is further complicated by the fact that actors in the innovation network may be in different phases of innovation with the pieces that they are offering to the integrated system, as described in Fig. 2.4. While some actors are in the design or in the development phases of innovation, some other actors are in the offering phase of their business, i.e. they are having ready and commercialized pieces for the system. The phase naturally influences the expectations that a firm has for the collaboration. A firm in the design phase may see the collaboration as an investment for the future that will make profit only in the long term. Such a firm may tolerate quite a lot of uncertainty during the design of integrated business offering, if they see high enough opportunities for the business in the future. For a firm in the offering phase, on the other hand, the collaboration may be business-as-usual and they may want to minimize all risks related to their business. Accordingly, they may not like to see the collaboration as an investment for the future which will make profit only in the future.

One of the main challenges for a SI is to understand the business models and interests of all actors in the innovation network and to align the actions of network orchestration with the business models and interests. Independent of the collaboration model, another challenge of a SI is how to commit its suppliers to long-term collaboration in a way which is beneficial for all parties. On the other hand, sometimes a SI may itself be uncertain on whether it wants short- or long-term collaboration with a supplier. An interviewed R&D manager said: "*We may not want to have a long term commitment with that supplier because we are a bit concerned with their possible activities with our competitors.*" Such an uncertainty obviously also had an effect on the chosen form of collaboration because successful operation in co-creation networks requires a good level of trust and shared interests from all actors in the innovation network.

Legal challenges of a SI in the Bazaar of Opportunities are mostly related to the IP management of the innovation outcome and to contracting. In the transaction networks, the ownership and exclusive IP rights to the innovation are transferred to the SI (and sometimes further to the customer), which has both pros and cons. In this way, the SI maintains strict control over the IP and can be sure that the IP cannot be used against the SI in the future, which could take place in two ways: at first, a supplier (if owning the IP) might get interested in supplying directly to the SI's customers, and, secondly, the IP (if not owned by the SI) might end up being owned by the SI's competitor, for example through a merger or acquisition of the supplier. On the other hand, the supplier may not be interested in further developing the technology if the IP related to the technology is owned by the SI (or SI's customer). This issue has compelled a couple of the case firms to change their strategy towards the ownership of IP created in collaboration.

In their new strategy, a technology supplier may retain the ownership of the jointly generated IP, but the SI gets exclusive rights to use the IP in specified markets. As a technology manager of a SI company said: "*In the past we wanted to own all IP that resulted from collaboration, but now things are different. Sometimes we are happy just to license the technology in and leave open the possibility for the supplier to use and further develop the technology in another business area that may not be of interest to us.*" The change in the IP management strategy is often the result of realizing what actually brings the special competitive advantage for the firm. It may be related to a change from the transaction to the co-creation type of innovation network operation, but the collaboration may as well be retained in the transaction type of network. Examples of joint ownership of IP between a SI and a supplier or a customer were rare. Joint ownership of IP was considered as being a complicated and risky situation. One patent engineer explained why: "*Twenty years* [which is a typical duration of patent] *is a long time and a lot can happen. There can be changes in the interests and ownerships of the firms. And that can make things very complicated.*"

According to the study behind the book, contracts between a SI and its suppliers are typically dyadic. In transaction networks, safeguarding elements of contracts play the main role (see the section "Functions of Contracts in Transaction and Co-creation Networks" in Chapter 5 for more details about the elements of business contracts), although such kind of contracts may not have adequate flexibility to react to external changes requiring innovation actions. In co-creation networks, the contracting strategy is to keep the contracts lean and equal for both parties. Co-creation contracts often include evolving elements that would allow further specifications at a later stage.[11] More than one SI said that "*paying too much attention to details of contracts at the very beginning of joint work kills innovation*". Signing a contract, however, was considered to be an important signal which shows that the parties are serious in their collaboration. And in such a way, trust is strengthened in the contracting process.

What is said above concerns the SI's activities towards suppliers and technology developers, that is, towards upstream actors of a business network. At least as important are the SI's activities towards its customers. All interviewed representatives of SIs emphasized the importance of customer relationship management in their role as a SI. Understanding and alignment of the business models of both the downstream (customer) and upstream (suppliers) actors with the business model of the SI is one part of the customer relationship management. However, that may not be easy, and sometimes not even possible. Some SI managers were concerned that *"customers will bypass us and buy directly from the suppliers"*. In the Bazaar of Opportunities, SIs need to find ways to be an irreplaceable link in the value network. To do that, a SI should understand the actual additional value that it brings to the network and the critical knowledge associated with this additional value.

The SIs, which are not brand owners of the integrated system, typically act in a sourcing role for their customers. Discussions with several SI managers led to an impression that the innovativeness of a SI is not at its best when the customer has a strong control over the IP related to the offering of the SI. As one SI said: *"Not all solutions that we provide are equal, and we are looking for alternative paths to capture value from our knowledge."*

To summarize then, what are the pros and cons of the networked innovation models in the context of system integration in the Bazaar of Opportunities? We can say that in transaction networks, relationships between the actors are simpler and the roles of the actors are clearer than in co-creation networks. As a result, it is easier for a SI to manage innovation in transaction networks than in co-creation networks.[12] The major challenge of transaction networks is associated with improving their ability in the renewal and development of technology. For example, further development may be difficult if the IP has been transferred from a developer to a SI, the developer is not interested to further develop that IP but saves their new ideas and best solutions to other situations where they could get higher value for their efforts, and the SI does not have the ability to develop the technology. If that happens, the SI becomes stuck with old technology. Retention of the ownership of IP by the developer and agreement on the rights of use of the IP could be one way to align the interests of the SI and developer so that the offering could be updated, if necessary.[13]

Co-creation networks can be agile in changes requiring innovation actions, especially when the innovation evolves at the interface between the knowledge of two or more actors and when there is high demand for tailoring. The challenge of successful orchestration in co-creation networks is that it requires aligned interests and shared vision for the future by all the actors in the network. A SI must establish a convincing development agenda and communicate the agenda and development path very clearly so that each actor will understand it correctly. We argue that in co-creation a SI needs to orchestrate a more dynamic network than in the case of transaction. The main reason for this is the fact that the innovation process is often fuzzy and long, during which the roles and interests of the network's members may change. The orchestration of co-creation networks also requires capabilities to gathering and managing information and knowledge in a multi-professional environment. It is possible to successfully orchestrate co-creation networks and to gain the benefits that they offer, but it requires better network orchestration capabilities from the SI than what a sourcing type of operation typically requires.

Aspects that support and hinder networked innovation in the context of system integration in the Bazaar of Opportunities are collected in Table 7.1 for transaction networks and Table 7.2 for co-creation networks.[14] We cannot say, in general, that one model is better than the other. Both ways have supporting and hindering aspects using which a SI may select a network model that would be suitable in a particular case.

Valuation of IP in the Bazaar of Opportunities

In the discussion of the business of system integration in the Bazaar of Opportunities, we underlined the importance of IP. In closed innovation, where a firm is innovating and developing a new business alone without any kind of collaboration or interaction with other actors, IP is important in order to protect the business. In the Bazaar of Opportunities IP is more than just for the protection of business. In the Bazaar, IP is a direct means of business. IP can be sold and bought, IP can be licensed in and out, IP can give the value of a firm to be sold or acquired. Accordingly, its valuation is an important, though difficult, part of business. In closed innovation the valuation of IP covers only formal IP, i.e. patents, trademarks, copyrights, etc. In the Bazaar of Opportunities, the scope of IP valuation is broader than in closed innovation and it covers all knowledge that can be the subject of transaction from one actor to another.

In Chapter 6 we mentioned that an IP asset typically has little intrinsic or market value itself, and its real value comes from the business or business

Table 7.1.   Aspects of transaction networks that support or hinder networked innovation in the Bazaar of Opportunities from the viewpoint of a system integrator.

Transaction networks	
Supporting aspects	Hindering aspects
Effective when the innovation comes from a novel combination of existing "pieces". The SI can then easily manage the network: • The SI does not have to reveal its knowledge to suppliers because the innovation is based on a new combination of existing pieces (and IP). • Initiatives for business renewal are in the hands of the SI (if the SI has rights to the IP used). • Clear control of IP through formal contracts and formal IP protection.	Management of innovation may be challenging if it requires innovation actions from other actors of network: • Further development of offering (technology) may be difficult if the IP has been transferred from a developer to the SI (and perhaps even further to an end-customer); the new ideas of developers may be exploited through another path and the SI may become stuck with old technology. • Depending on incentives used, suppliers and technology developers may not be encouraged to propose their best solutions for the use of the SI, but rather save them for other situations where they could get higher value for their efforts. • The network may not be sufficiently agile in reacting fast to external changes requiring innovation actions by the network, if flexible elements of contracts are weak.

opportunity that is possible through the IP in one way or another. Thus we can say that the value of an IP depends on the context and it is highly case and company specific. As such, it is difficult to establish a value for an IP asset based on general market metrics alone, such as market size, market growth and competition in the market. The valuation should also reflect a firm's objectives, objectives of other relevant firms, as well as the type of IP, the particular business case and the business model used in the case. Moreover, the source of value for different kinds of IP in the company varies. The major value may come from increased sales due to unique product features allowed by the IP. In some instances the major value comes from internal cost savings, in some other cases from profitable licensing agreements.

Table 7.2. Aspects of co-creation networks that support or hinder networked innovation in the Bazaar of Opportunities from the viewpoint of a system integrator.

Co-creation networks	
Supporting aspects	Hindering aspects
Effective when the innovation evolves at the interface between two or more "pieces" and when there is high demand for tailoring. Then the SI have several options available for: • Incentives of innovation for suppliers/technology developers so that they could be motivated to provide their best effort for the joint work and to further develop the technology. • IP management. • Introducing flexibility in contracts in order to be better prepared for changes requiring innovation actions.	Management of co-creation network, characterized by nested and interconnected relationships, requires good innovation network management capabilities from the SI: • Successful co-creation requires aligned interests and trust between the actors which may easily change along with the specific work. • The options for incentives of innovation for suppliers and technology developers are ineffective unless the SI is capable of effectively using these incentives and aligning the business models of the actors of the network. • Co-creation requires that the actors are willing to share their tacit knowledge with the other actors of the innovation network; this is not always the case. • Management of IP can be complicated if not well agreed beforehand or if trust is missing between partners.

The IP may also increase the attractiveness of a firm as an innovation and business partner. The main business value of a firm may also come from its IP portfolio.

A good example of challenges related to IP valuation is the acquisition of Motorola Mobility by Google Inc. in August 2011.[15] The business of Motorola Mobility had been declining for a few years. The patent portfolio of the company, however, was still strong, and Google saw that the patent portfolio of Motorola Mobility would strengthen Google's Android ecosystem. That was the main reason for Google to acquire Motorola Mobility. One of the most interesting issues of the acquisition was related to the valuation of Motorola's IP. The price that Google paid for Motorola included a premium of 63% compared to Motorola Mobility's stock market price.[16] The high price reflects how the value of Motorola's IP was seen in the context of Google's Android ecosystem. In the context of the Android ecosystem, Motorola's IP was seen to be much more valuable than in the original context of Motorola's own business.[17] The example really underlines the fact that the value of an IP does not come from the IP itself but the business or business opportunities that are made possible by the IP. The business or business opportunities based on the same IP would not be the same for two different kinds of firms.

The valuation of IP can be based on either relative or absolute methods.[18] In relative, score-based valuation, a single IP is assessed and scored against multiple criteria that could be weighted. The value of the IP is related to the sum of weighted scores. The advantage of this type of evaluation is its simplicity in comparing different alternatives, for example when making capital investment decisions in the design phase of innovation when the future business offering is not yet clearly defined. In the Bazaar of Opportunities, however, there is often a need to give a price for an IP and that is not possible when using relative valuation.

In absolute valuation, the value of IP can be seen as a representation of all the future benefits as a single payment.[19] The objective is to estimate the monetary sum representing the future incomes resulting from the IP. An IP is valued as equal to the expected future profits, additional revenues, or cost savings obtainable by exploiting the IP, discounted to the present value. The income-based valuation depends on the estimated length of the life cycle of the IP as well as on the risks associated with the IP. In order to measure the income from the IP, the future cash flows of all products, services, or processes that use the patents must be determined, which can be very difficult. Alternatively, instead of direct focus on products, services, or processes, one may consider target markets and business enabled by the IP and estimate directly or indirectly the impact of the IP on the business in the markets, and in this way to estimate the incomes due to the IP. There can be huge uncertainties related to both product- and market-based approaches. The uncertainties could be managed by considering different scenarios of the future and making the IP valuation for the different scenarios. Nevertheless, the absolute valuation of IP is very challenging in the Bazaar of Opportunities because two actors of networked innovation seldom share the same view of the business potential of an IP and, accordingly, they seldom share the same view of the value of IP. In this book we do not go any deeper into the absolute valuation of IP. We have just underlined issues that actors in the Bazaar of Opportunities should be aware of and take into account when making any business deals related to IP.

Sharing the Value of IP between the Actors of Innovation

In addition to the absolute valuation of IP, another IP valuation challenge that the actors must face in the Bazaar of Opportunities is how to divide the value of IP between different stakeholders that have been involved in the innovation. And that is not only the question about sharing of rights and benefits related to the IP. It is also a question of sharing the responsibilities and costs of the collaboration between the actors of innovation. There is no single and correct answer to these questions. The answer depends on many things, such as the role of actors in the value network (see Table 3.3), the power of actors in contracting, the business model of actors, the interests of actors, etc. For example, contract manufacturers, even very innovative ones, traditionally have had weak contracting power in IP related issues against their big customers. The same applies for many subcontractors. On the other hand, the business model of many firms acting in a subcontractor role only supports the traditional subcontracting kind of sharing of rights, benefits, responsibilities, and risks. In the traditional business model of subcontracting, the subcontractor is happy to receive a single payment against its innovation efforts with no further responsibilities and risks related to the success of the business due to the innovation and with no sharing of the development costs. The IP has been transferred to the principal against the single payment. There are many subcontractors as well as principals whose interest is just this. But things could be done differently, and there are many actors who actually are making arrangements differently in their principal-subcontractor works.

In the discussion about system integration in the Bazaar of Opportunities, we said that it is not always optimal for the system integrator (principal) if the IP of joint work is transferred from a technology developer to the SI. It may lead to a situation where the SI becomes stuck with old technology. Furthermore, the technology developer may not offer its best solution to the SI if they have to give away the IP of the solution to the SI. Therefore, there are increasingly more examples where the technology developer can keep the ownership of IP and (only) exclusive rights to use the IP in a specified field of business are granted to the SI (or principal), while the technology developer retains the rights to use the IP in another field of business. There are also increasingly more examples where the payment for the subcontracting work is not based on a single payment but connected to the sales of the final business offering. Naturally, this also means sharing of costs of the development work between the subcontractor and the principal. If the sharing of costs and benefits could be optimally agreed between the actors, the model for the sharing of costs and benefits may act as a good incentive for both actors to direct their best efforts for the joint work. This is not to go against the traditional business model of subcontracting — there are many firms who will be just happy with that — but to present an alternative for situations where the interest of a supplier is different.

To illustrate the sharing of costs and benefits in the Bazaar, we give a highly simplified example.[20] Company 1 is the principal who subcontracts a predefined development work to Company 2 (developer) so that the results of the work (i.e. the IP) are owned by Company 1 (owner). Company 1 then licenses the IP further to end-users, who are not involved in the development work. In this example we have supposed that it has been agreed between the actors that the ownership of the IP is transferred from Company 2 (developer) to Company 1, who then licensed the rights to use the IP to the end-users. Here the question is now, how should the costs and benefits be shared between the actors? In the traditional model of subcontracting, Company 1 gives a single payment to Company 2 for the IP. The single payment covers the development costs of Company 2 with a margin. At the same time, Company 1 takes future risks related to the IP, but also all future profits. If the business due to the IP proves to be highly successful, Company 2 will not gain any further profit on that. An alternative model of collaboration would be to connect the monetary compensation that Company 1 pays for Company 2 to the future profits due to the IP. That would mean sharing of costs, risks and benefits related to the IP between the companies. Instead of a single payment, the payment from Company 1 to Company 2 is connected to the profit resulting from the developed IP, i.e. licensing revenues from the end-users. In both models, the key issue is the monetary sum: in the former model the sum of the single payment is in euros; in the latter model the percentage of future profits from licensing revenues. Let us suppose here that Companies 1 and 2 have agreed to discuss a collaboration model where the monetary compensation would not be a single payment but a percentage α of the future profits (licensing revenues from the end-users). What should the α then be so that both companies would be happy?

In joint development projects between a principal and a developer, short-term monetary gains and the final payback from the project are often contradictory objectives. In a joint development project involving complex technology as well as tacit and specialized knowledge, it is difficult to assess how much effort has been put into getting the obtained results and whether the results could have been significantly improved with marginal additional contributions. That emphasizes the importance of agreeing about such win–win incentives that best possible end results are in the interest of each partner. Let us consider that in the example the development work is so complex that the developer (Company 2) can choose the quality of resources it commits to the development work. The developer can either perform a standard development work using its standard resources or, alternatively, utilize its best resources and knowledge in the project to significantly improve the results and the estimated future profits.[21] The downside for the developer in utilizing the best resources is the additional costs of using the best specialists and the potential opportunity cost of utilizing that expert knowledge elsewhere in some other business of Company 2. Due to the complexity of work, Company 1 cannot observe whether the best possible resources and knowledge of Company 2 has been used in the work and, accordingly, Company 1 cannot control the development work. Naturally, if Company 2 estimates that its share of the estimated future profits would not cover the expenses of the actual development work, it would decline the whole offer. Furthermore, if Company 2 estimates that utilizing its best resources would not yield enough extra benefits to offset the additional costs, it would complete the work using its standard resources only.

In the profit calculations of the simplified example, we assume that the cost of the development project for Company 2 using its standard resources is $10\,k\in$, which results in expected total profit of $100\,k\in$. The additional cost for Company 2 of utilizing the best resources instead of standard resources is $10\,k\in$, which would increase the total profit by $40\,k\in$. As supposed above, a percentage α of the total profit would be for Company 2 and $(100 - \alpha)$ would be retained for Company 1. The resulting profits for Company 1 (IP owner) and Company 2 (developer) as a function of percentage α for the two strategies of Company 2 are presented in Fig. 7.1(a). From the figure we can see that Company 2 should decline the offer of collaboration when α

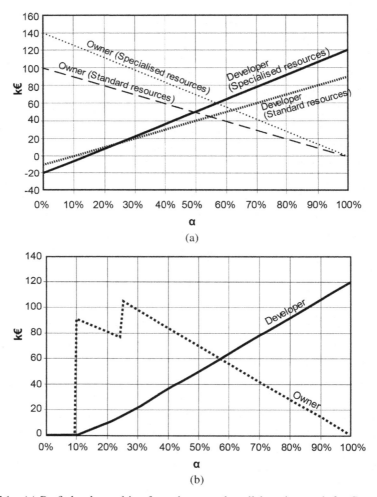

Fig. 7.1. (a) Profit levels resulting from the example collaboration work for Company 1 (IP owner) and for Company 2 (IP developer) as a function of profit sharing level α. (b) Net profit levels for Company 1 (IP owner) and Company 2 (IP developer) as a function of profit sharing level α when the resource use of Company 2 is optimized.

is less than 10%, which would yield a net loss. With α values between 10% and 25%, Company 2 would accept the offer but only utilize its standard resources. When α is greater than 25%, it would be optimal for Company 2 to utilize its best resources for the development work.

The optimal behaviour of Company 2 yields to the net profit curves depicted in Fig. 7.1(b). The result interestingly shows that Company 1 (IP owner) is actually able to increase its profit by sharing a greater fraction of it with Company 2. By focusing only on the direct costs of development, Company 1 could perhaps get Company 2 to accept the development work with 10% share of the future profits, in which case Company 2 would perform its standard work resulting in total future profit of 100 k€, of which 90 k€ would be retained by Company 1. However, if Company 1 would give 25% of the future profits to Company 2, the total profits would rise to 140 k€, 105 k€ of which would be kept by Company 1.

The example demonstrates that the structure of the rewarding mechanisms has a strong influence on the motivation of the actors. If the principal (here Company 1) is too short-sighted or cost-oriented towards the technology developer (here Company 2), the development work may lead to suboptimal results for all parties. In the example we did not consider the traditional subcontracting model of single payment, but it would have been obvious that in the case of the traditional model, Company 2 would have used its standard resources only, resulting in a total future profit of 100 k€ and, accordingly, a suboptimal total performance.

The example shows that the motivation and incentives of the actors should be understood and made sufficiently clear during the contracting process before signing and starting the actual joint work. However, one should not place too much emphasis on rigorous sharing of future profits before a clear idea about the future business and profits. *"One should bake the pie before dividing it"* was said by an experienced business manager in the interview study. If too much attention is paid to the sharing of profits before the actual joint work, the realization of the future profits may suffer. Experience has shown that, if all the parties are too risk-averse, they tend to avert extra profits as well.

In the example the ownership of IP was transferred from the developer (Company 2) to the principal (Company 1). Sometimes this arrangement leads to optimal results; sometimes another arrangement would be more beneficial. Independently of which company will own the IP, it is important that the ownership structures of IP reflect the interests of all parties involved. Otherwise a suboptimal performance could be expected sooner or later. For example, if the transaction of IP from the developer to the principal is not fully in line with the interests and business model of the developer, the developer may direct its best resources and solutions to other works and use only standard resources and "second best" solutions for the joint work. Or later on, the principal may become stuck with old technology if the developer is no more interested in improving the technology owned by the principal. There is no right answer about how the ownership of IP should be arranged. All that can be said is that in the Bazaar of Opportunities the interests of the actors in respect to IP ownership, its valuation, sharing of costs, risks, profits, etc., should be aligned. And they should be aligned not only before and during the joint work but also after that during the actual business, i.e. the offering phase of innovation.

We conclude this section of the chapter on the sharing of IP value with a few real cases taken from the interview study behind the book.[22] The focus of the cases is in the interest of the actors of innovation towards IP ownership and sharing of costs and profits related to the IP.

The first case is an example where the interests between the actors were well aligned during the design and development phases of innovation, but not so well during the actual business (offering) phase. In the words of a manager from the actor whose role in the partnership was to be the customer: *"We have strategic cooperation with a supplier which delivers a vital part of our product. We didn't pay them for the development. We have the IP but they have the first right for delivery and they amortise their development costs in the goods they supply. The downside is that we could make more profit if we could save a euro on materials, but that would require a new construction and a new development project with them (which is not of direct interest to the supplier in the model of collaboration we are using)."* This is a very common example of successful co-creation between a customer and a supplier where the rights of the joint innovation outcome were transferred to the customer. Through this IP transaction, the customer got full control to the rights of their product. However, at the same moment, the customer lost control for further improvements of the joint innovation. Obviously, this is an example of the non-optimized allocation of rights. On the other hand, the business deal and model of collaboration seemed to be pretty good for the supplier (but less good for the customer). An interesting thing in the case was that the customer obviously had good negotiation power during contracting but, nevertheless, did not succeed in making an optimal deal in the Bazaar of Opportunities.

The second case is an example of well-aligned interests of the actors of networked innovation where the allocation of rights promoted innovativeness on the part of both the customer and the supplier. In the words of the customer: *"We collaborate with a big material supplier. When they are developing new features for their materials, they sometimes provide us with samples for testing. Although we don't get IP rights to the materials, because we are a small company in comparison to them, the collaboration is very beneficial for us. It promotes our own product development and we gain a competitive advantage by releasing new products more quickly based on these materials on the market."*

The third case is an example of a novel way of innovation where the ownership of IP was well aligned with the business model used in the collaboration and where the business model defines the sharing of costs, risks, and benefits between the actors in a way that motivates both parties to direct their best efforts for the joint work. In the words of a manager of the customer firm: *"We lacked a good proprietary technology. Instead of developing that ourselves, we decided to team up with another company. Five years earlier, we would have tried to develop it ourselves, but at that point we said no. We might have done that, but it would either take much longer or the end product would be inferior to the situation where we could team up with somebody. So what we did was, we signed a deal with them, defined a joint development program, and obtained an exclusive license. Both companies benefit from it, because all the sales and the licensing revenues, we had opted for a licensing model, are shared between us. To me that is a modern example of how you do innovation, because you really derive a lot of strength from your partner, but you also bring very good things to the table."* As the interviewed manager notes, this is a good modern-day example of successful collaboration between a big company and a small technology supplier. An interesting point is how the exploitation of IP was made operational through a licensing model in which both parties gained revenues from the sales.

The fourth case is also an example of good fit in the interests and business model of the actors, but now in the words of a supplier: "*A lot of innovation comes from customers. Sometimes we have a promising technology and we work with a lead customer to generate the first application on that. But we typically arrange it in such a way that we also get the results back and we use that for other applications. It's a win–win situation, because the client can make use of our technology, but we also are able to use the results of that collaboration for different fields. So it's innovation with the customer for their product, but also to enhances other possibilities.*"

Unfortunately, not all cases in the Bazaar of Opportunities are as successful as the three previous ones. While the development phase of innovation may take place under shared interests, often the interests of the innovation actors will be less aligned during the business (offering) phase of innovation. The first case was already an example of that. Our fifth and final case is another one: "*It is often difficult to operate with a manufacturer. We want to have a new apparatus for our process. We know what we want to have, and they know how to make it. But they would like to make it for everyone, not just for us but for our competitor as well. But the joint innovation is between us and the manufacturer.*" That was the voice of a customer whose supplier is a large firm. There were also several cases in the study where the opposite occurred: a big firm that is in the role of the customer wants to own all the rights to joint innovation so that it can seek out alternative suppliers for the innovation.

The examples of this section underline the fact that the alignment of interests related to innovation increases the chances of success in co-creation partnerships in the Bazaar of Opportunities. The key interests in innovation relationships include issues related to IP management as well as to business objectives and business model.[23] In other kinds of business relationships where innovation is not so important, the alignment of interests may be less important, but such business relationships are outside the scope of this book.

Openness of Innovation in the Bazaar of Opportunities

In the section "Openness of Innovation (Process)" in Chapter 2 we introduced five levels of openness in open and networked innovation. The levels were named as "closed", "available", "usable", "modifiable", and "public" (Table 2.3). Here we consider them in more detail and take a look at how the levels are realized in the Bazaar of Opportunities.

The level "closed" is perhaps the most common form of open innovation where two actors are involved in the innovation work. The name "closed" comes from the way the actors open up the actual innovation work (process) to each other. In the level "closed", they tend to share their knowledge with the other actor as little as possible during the actual development work. All interaction is based on contractual transaction of IP that is used as an input for the actual (closed) development work. The transacted IP may include not only formal IP rights, but also other kinds of explicit knowledge that could be transacted from one actor to another (we refer here back to Chapter 3 and the discussion about the strategic dimensions of knowledge for more details). The former kind of transacted IP includes buying and selling of patents and other formal IP, as well as licensing of patents. The latter consists of subcontracted (sourced) expertise work with minimum interaction between the principal and the agent.

A major focus of open innovation literature is the buying or licensing of external IP as an input for a firms own, closed development.[24] It is the form discussed in the pioneering book on open innovation by Henry Chesbrough.[25] Companies are searching for external technologies that could be integrated into their planned business offering, as described earlier in this chapter when we discussed system integration, or they are searching for external technologies on which they could build a winning business model and then to commercialize the technology, etc. There are also lots of technology developers who are searching for partners to commercialize their technology. Companies are also searching for special expertise knowledge to be used as input for the closed innovation development work inside the company. And there are lots of firms that are offering such research and engineering services, as described in the section "IP Strategy in Service Business" in Chapter 6. When the innovation work between the provider of research and engineering services and the principal takes place with minimal opening of tacit knowledge to each other during the work, we can speak about IP transaction only and the work belongs to the openness category of "closed". When the innovation work is accompanied by an opening of tacit knowledge during the process, we speak about openness level of the "usable" or "modifiable". In the Bazaar of Opportunities, the actors can meet and negotiate about the possibilities and conditions for an IP transaction. They can discuss the value of IP, structures of IP ownership, business model, including the sharing of costs, risks, benefits, etc. When the interests of the actors are sufficiently well aligned, a business deal and the contract of IP transaction will take place and the principal may start or continue the (closed) innovation development work, in accordance with conditions agreed in the contract.

The level "available" has much in common with the level "closed". In both levels the actual innovation process is more or less closed and the openness is restricted to the input for innovation. There are two major differences between the levels "available" and "closed". Firstly, in the level "available" there can be more than two actors involved either through bi- or multilateral (consortium) contracts of collaboration. Secondly, the input does not have to be based on a transaction of IP from one party to another but sharing of input knowledge with other parties of collaboration without a necessity for changes on the ownership structures of the input IP. An example of practical innovation work under the category of "available" is a contractual establishment of a common knowledge platform above which the partners of the consortium could independently develop and commercialize their own applications. That is, the parties agree about strategic collaboration in order to build a common knowledge base in order to support proprietary development and commercialization of their own IP using the common knowledge base. The common knowledge base could be created either by sharing (making readable) their own existing knowledge of the principal actors or by jointly sourcing the input from a third party. Innovation works that could be categorized under the level "available" are not as common as the works under the other four levels of openness.

When moving in the direction of increasing openness, the next level in Table 2.3 is called "usable". The level "usable" represents a wide range of common models for the co-creation kind of innovation works between two or more actors, typically having bi- or multilateral contractual relationships for the innovation. In innovation works under the category "usable", the input (background material) for the development can be freely utilized within the actors in the consortium during the development work. The actors agree on the conditions under which they can use the input after the work in the consortium agreement. Co-development between some or all members of the consortium is characteristic for the actual development work. The members also have the right to observe each other's development work. So we can say that the innovation process is open for the members of the project consortium. In order for the development work to be successful, there must be a good fit in the roles of the actors participating in the work as well as sufficiently well-aligned interests towards the outcome of innovation. The IP management related to the outcome must also be agreed before the development work. The development costs are often shared in a way in which each party takes care of its own costs. Innovation works under the level "usable" typically ends in proprietary (closed) IP owned by an inventing actor or, alternatively, an actor who has the best potential to successfully commercialize it. The other members of the consortium typically have rights to utilize the IP, the licensing conditions agreed either before or after the development work. Although the process will end up to proprietary IP, it does not necessarily mean that the owner of the IP will have all the future profits due to the IP. The actors of co-creation may agree on how the future profits will be shared. It depends very much on the roles and interests of the actors as well as business model(s) used in order to commercialize the IP. For example, a material supplier may profit from a jointly developed product by having the first right to deliver the material required to manufacture the product. It may also be the case that the owner of the IP is only interested in commercialization in a specific field of business. As a result, other member of the consortium may get exclusive rights to commercialize the IP in alternative fields, if agreement was reached by the partners in the consortium. Such an arrangement naturally underlines the good fit in the roles and business interests of the actors in the consortium and careful design in the building of the project consortium.

"Modifiable" is the most open form of innovation that could take place within closed relationships. In this case we can speak about truly open innovation with known actors, where the input for innovation, the actual innovation process, and the innovation outcome are open only for the members of the closed consortium. The level "modifiable" differs from the level "usable" in two senses. Firstly, the innovation leads to joint

IP (joint ownership and utilization). The joint ownership, however, may not necessarily mean joint patenting. Instead, it may mean a contractual arrangement where the structures of IP ownership and rights to utilize the IP are contractually arranged in a way where the members of the network will have equal rights to utilize, modify, and build business above the jointly developed IP.[26] Secondly, the openness related to the input and the process is more controlled in the level "usable" than in the level "modifiable". In the level "modifiable", the input (background material) is freely modifiable within the actors, the actors take part in each other's development work, which means sharing of tacit knowledge with each other, and the results of co-development work are shared between the actors. Basically, the principles are very similar to those of open source societies, with the exception that the participation of the work is not open but takes place within closed bi- or multilateral relationships.

Innovation works that fit under the category "modifiable" have a wide range from bilateral innovation relationships to large consortia with 20–30 partners. They are often pre-commercial in their nature meaning that the innovation is explorative leading to results that cannot be directly commercialized. The joint work may end up in a common knowledge base which the members of the network can use at a later point to independently develop their own products and services to be commercialized. Pre-commerciality, however, is not a characteristic feature in the level "modifiable". There are also innovation works whose outcome finds out directly its place in a business offering. Such works can be bilateral co-creation that takes place at the interface of the firms. They can also be open source projects where the participation, however, is limited to known actors defined at the beginning of the work. The motivation to run open source projects within a closed consortium is the fact that then the actors know who are involved in the project and by this way they have better control over the knowledge that they share with the consortium. In this way they can be sure that their competitors are not directly or indirectly involved in the work, which makes a big difference to what they can and will share with the other members of the innovation network.

All interviewed project managers who have experience in innovation works under the level "modifiable" said that these kind of open innovation projects are challenging because, in order to be successful, the actors must really share the view on the objectives of collaboration and the degree of openness required to reach the objectives before, during, and after the project.[27] That may not be easy. The actors, if not used to innovation works having the openness level "modifiable", may be so stuck with innovation models under some other level of openness that the openness required to successful co-creation may not be realized in practical project work between the actors of the network. The projects under the level "modifiable" are also sensitive for the free-riding problem meaning that, especially in a large consortium, there can be actors who are not sharing their knowledge with others in sufficient depth but are just picking up the shared knowledge from the other members of the consortium.

The openness level "public" is the ultimate form of open innovation. In this level, not only the input, the process and the outcome are open, but the whole work is available, accessible, and modifiable by everyone; that is, the work is public. The fact that it is public and open for all, however, does not mean that there are no limiting conditions for the accessibility and modifiability of the work. Typically there are well specified rules for the accessibility and modifiability of the work. Open source projects are a good example of that. In open source projects the participation is open but controlled and, in order to utilize the results, one must accept the license conditions of the open source project. Open source software projects are the most common but not the only examples of "public" open innovation projects.

The main motivation to make a software project a public open source project is the chance to enhance the resources that are working on the project. In theory, there is an unlimited number of experts who could work for an open source project, if it is attractive enough. Such projects represent the famous slogan of open innovation, "not all the smart people work for you", at its best. Secondly, successful contribution to open source works give great merit for the contributors. There is an increasing number of both firms and individual experts that have found new customers by active contribution to open source works. So for them, open source may serve as the main marketing channel for their IT services.

The public status of open source projects enhances available resources working for the project, but the public openness may also limit what you can do in an open source work. A R&D manager of an IT company said: "*You must be careful as to what you show and give for an open source because of your competitors. They are probably there, too.*" It may also be challenging to direct the open source work. "*It is quite a democratic community. The work may develop in a direction where you would not like to go*", said another IT manager. There are also open source projects that are under a strong control of few people. The development of standard Linux kernel was a good example of open source work with strong control. It was Linus Torvalds who had the ultimate authority to decide on what new code is incorporated into the standard Linux kernel.[28]

Successful "public" innovation projects are typically works that can be digitized and then shared through the world wide web. Digital information products can be created, modified, and distributed at virtually no cost without diminishing their availability to others.[29] Participating in such works does not require heavy investments in equipment or facilities. It is basically just about sharing your own working effort (resources) with the community involved in the open project. There are few examples of successful public open source innovation projects in the manufacturing industry, that is, open source hardware projects, although there are several open source hardware projects running in different fields of industry.[30] Open source hardware projects often remain in a concept or prototype stage. A possible reason for this is that, if you have to make real investments for the development work (as you must do in the manufacturing industry), you are then less keen on making the results fully available, accessible, and modifiable by everyone else. Instead, you would probably be more interested in collaborating with known actors using a collaboration model with some other level of openness.

The five-level categorization of the levels of openness in innovation gives structure for the design and management of practical innovation projects in the Bazaar of Opportunities. The systematic categorization of openness levels would help project managers, contract and IP management designers in gaining a shared view of openness in a particular innovation project. This shared view will lead to contracts that actually support the co-ordination of open and networked innovation works during and after the development project. The shared view also helps the project co-ordinator to create a convincing development agenda and to communicate it clearly to each partner in the innovation work.

Conclusions: Bridging Networked Innovation, IP and Business

In Chapter 2 we introduced the example of New Factory in Tampere: a novel way of bridging networked innovation and IP in order to create new business. The New Factory has its roots in the subcontracting kind of networked innovation but, instead of subcontracting, it has reformulated the models of networked innovation from a transaction type of operation to co-creation kind of collaboration where the different actors of the innovation network will all win and, accordingly, will be motivated to direct their best efforts for innovation. That has required an establishment of a new business model for the New Factory apparatus as well as new kind of mindset towards IP management and openness in innovation. Furthermore, if compared to classical subcontracting, there is a new network actor in the process, namely an innovation inter-mediator that co-ordinates the process. Although single projects in the New Factory (as well as the start-up companies that are results of successful projects) are small, the total impact of the New Factory to the city of Tampere is considerable because the number of start-ups is significant.

We highlighted the New Factory in Tampere as an example of a novel era in designing and developing new business. Nevertheless, we believe that the New Factory kind of innovation platforms and communities are instruments that supplement, not replace, new business development by established firms and business networks. We do not believe that they will come as the main drivers of innovation in business. That role will remain for innovative firms.

The New Factory kinds of platforms are suitable for the development of business where there is no need for heavy investments during the R&D or piloting the business. ICT and service business are examples of businesses where it is possible to design and develop new business with moderate costs. In more traditional industries, new business development often calls for significant investments. Therefore, firms in traditional industries may look for other novel forms of designing and developing new business than the New Factory. For them system integration may offer an attractive alternative path to develop new business offerings. System integration has much in common with the New Factory: networked innovation and new mindset towards IP management in order to create new business.

202 Bazaar of Opportunities for New Business Development

There are several ways to successfully bridge networked innovation, IP, and business. A firm in the Bazaar of Opportunities should find the right way for its particular case. In the right way, the interests of the actors in the value network of innovation are aligned and directed to give their best effort for the success both during the development work and after it during the offering phase of innovation.

Notes

1. The term "integrated solution" is used in the service and IT businesses. The term "integrated system" is used especially in automotive, electronics, and telecommunication industries.
2. See the paper of Hobday *et al.* (2005) for a more detailed discussion on the role of a system integrator [Hobday, M., Davies, A. and Prencipe, A. (2005). Systems Integration: A Core Capability of the Modern Corporation, *Industrial and Corporate Change*, Vol. 14, pp. 1109–1143.]
3. See the book *The Business of System Integration*, edited by Prencipe, Davies, and Hobday (2003) for examples. Although the book was first published in 2003, its content is not outdated. What has changed since the year 2003 is that the importance of system integration is nowadays even more important than in 2003. [Prencipe, A., Davies, A. and Hobday, M. (eds) (2003). *The Business of System Integration*, Oxford University Press.]
4. See for example the studies of Sapolsky (2003), Davies (2003), Becker *et al.* (2003), Hobday *et al.*, (2005), Möller *et al.* 2005, and Dittrich and Duysters (2007) to review the development of system integration from the late 1940s to the present. All the authors do not address the term system integration or system integration in their papers but the meaning is the same. [Sapolsky, H.M. (2003). 'Inventing Systems Integration', in Prencipe, A., Davies, A. and Hobday, M. (eds), *The Business of System Integration*, Oxford University Press, pp. 15–34; Davies, A. (2003). 'Integrated Solutions: The Changing Business of Systems Integration', in Prencipe, A., Davies, A. and Hobday, M. (eds), *The Business of System Integration*, Oxford University Press, pp. 333–368; Becker, M., Johnson, P.H. and Ruijsenaars, N. (2003). *Collaborative Product Development — Case Study within the Swedish Automotive Industry*, Lund Institute of Technology; Hobday, M., Davies, A. and Prencipe, A. (2005). Systems Integration: A Core Capability of the Modern Corporation, *Industrial and Corporate Change*, Vol. 14, pp. 1109–1143; Möller, K. and Rajala, A. (2007). Rise of Strategic Nets — New Modes of Value Creation, *Industrial Marketing Management*, Vol. 36, pp. 895–908.; Dittrich, K. and Duysters, G. (2007). Networking as a Means to Strategy Change: The Case of Open Innovation in Mobile Telephone, *Journal of Product Innovation Management*, Vol. 24, pp. 510–521.]
5. The definition was given by Hobday *et al.* (2005). [Hobday, M., Davies, A. and Prencipe, A. (2005). Systems Integration: A Core Capability of the Modern Corporation, *Industrial and Corporate Change*, Vol. 14, pp. 1109–1143.]

6. Management and leadership are both managerial skills. Leadership is defined by Wikipedia as "organizing a group of people to achieve a common goal" [http://en.wikipedia.org/wiki/Leadership (Accessed on 15 March, 2012)]. Management has a broader scope, and in addition to organizing people, it also involves planning, directing, and controlling. Often, when one wants to distinguish between the social and administrative sides of management, as in this paragraph, the term "leadership" is used to emphasize the social side of management and the term "management" is used to emphasize the administrative side of management.

7. These two major capabilities were first addressed by A. Prencipe (2003). [Prencipe, A. (2003). 'Corporate Strategy and Systems Integration Capabilities: Managing Networks in Complex Systems Industries', in Prencipe, A., Davies, A. and Hobday, M. (eds), *The Business of Systems Integration*, Oxford University Press, pp. 114–132.]

8. See e.g. Hobday *et al.* (2005) and the references therein. [Hobday, M., Davies, A. and Prencipe, A. (2005). Systems Integration: A Core Capability of the Modern Corporation, *Industrial and Corporate Change*, Vol. 14, pp. 1109–1143.]

9. For more details about the models of hub-and-spoke and multiplex controlled networks see the book by Y. Doz (2001). [Doz, Y. (2001). *Clubs, Clans and Caravans: The Dynamics of Alliance Memberships and Governance*, Carnegie Bosch Institute, Berlin.]

10. In the transaction network, where the relationships are usually dyadic between the SI and a supplier, the situation can be stated as a contract design problem. The problem is studied extensively in the principal-agent literature (for a review, see Eisenhardt, 1989), where a contract is made between the principal (such as the SI) and the agent (such as a supplier) about work to be done by the agent on behalf of the principal. However, the information asymmetry where the principal cannot completely observe the quality of the agents work gives rise to moral hazard and adverse selection. One alternative to diminish these unwanted effects from the SI's point of view, and to align the incentives of the SI and the supplier, is to contract for the outcomes (the desired result of the contracted work) rather than agent behaviour (the work itself). Such an approach, however, transfers more risk to the supplier agent from the SI principal because the outcome of an agent's work is not only a function of the quality of the work, but is also dependent on uncertain factors outside the agent's control. Another alternative that would help to diminish the undesirable effects is repeated collaboration. In longer-term relationships, past performance and company reputation decrease the potential for agency problems. [Eisenhardt, K.M. (1989). Agency Theory: An Assessment and Review, *Academy of Management Review*, Vol. 14, pp. 57–74.]

11. See reference 4 in Chapter 5 for references and a discussion about evolving contracts.

12. The statement corresponds to findings in network management literature where closed business nets have been found to be more easily managed than open networks: Möller *et al.* (2005) and Järvensivu and Möller (2009). [Möller, K., Rajala, A. and Svahn, S. (2005). Strategic Business Nets — Their Type and Management, *Journal of Business Research*, Vol. 58, pp. 1274–1284.; Järvensivu, T. and Möller, K. (2009). Metatheory of Network Management: A Contingency Perspective, *Industrial Marketing Management*, Vol. 38, pp. 654–661.]

13. The finding has been suggested also by Teece (2000) and by Leiponen (2008). [Teece, D.J. (2000). *Managing Intellectual Capital: Organizational, Strategic, and*

Policy Dimensions, Oxford University Press, New York; Leiponen, A. (2008). Control of Intellectual Assets in Client Relationships: Implications for Innovation, *Strategic Management Journal*, Vol. 29, pp. 1371–1394.]

14. Tables 7.1 and 7.2 are modified from the original tables of Paasi *et al.* (2010). [Paasi, J., Valkokari, K., Rantala, T., Hytönen, H., Nystén-Haarala, S. and Huhtilainen, L. (2010). Innovation Management Challenges of a System Integrator in Innovation Networks, *International Journal of Innovation Management*, Vol. 14, pp. 1047–1064.]

15. The press announcement of Google Inc. can be found at http://googleblog.blogspot.com/2011/08/supercharging-android-google-to-acquire.html (Accessed on 23 February 2012).

16. The press announcement by Motorola is available at at https://mediacenter.motorola.com/Press-Releases/Google-to-Acquire-Motorola-Mobility-3797.aspx (Accessed on 23 February 2012).

17. Although here we are saying that the price premium reflects the value of Motorola's IP in the context of Google's Android ecosystem, we are not claiming that it was the only reason for the premium. Business agreements are always a result of multiple issues, but here the IP clearly seemed to be a major one.

18. See *The Handbook of Business Valuation and IP Analysis* (Reilly and Schweihs, 2004) for more details. [Reilly, R. and Schweihs, R. (eds.) (2004). *The Handbook of Business Valuation and Intellectual Property Analysis*, McGraw-Hill, New York.]

19. For more information, see Smith and Parr (2000) and Reilly and Schweihs (1998). They divided monetary IP valuation methods into cost-, market- and income-based approaches. Cost-based approach equates the value of IP with the development costs or costs of inventing around. Market-based approaches seek to base the value of IP on values of comparable traded assets. In income-based approaches, the IP value is determined by the estimated future incomes resulting from it. From these approaches, the income-based approach is the most important in the Bazaar of Opportunities and, therefore, only that approach is discussed in this book. [Smith, G.V. and Parr, R.L. (2000). *Valuation of Intellectual Property and Intangible Assets*, John Wiley & Sons, New York; Chichester; Reilly, R.F. and Schweihs, R.P. (1998). *Valuing Intangible Assets*, McGraw-Hill, New York.]

20. The example is a summary of the original example by Henri Hytönen and Jaakko Paasi (2010). For full discussion about the example, see the original work. [Hytönen, H. and Paasi, J. (2010). 'Motivation and Intellectual Property in the Context of Open Innovation', in Torkkeli, M. (ed.), *Frontiers of Open Innovation*, Department of Industrial Management, Research report 225, Lappeenranta University of Technology, pp. 25–38].

21. This is another example of the contract design problem discussed already in reference 10 of Chapter 7.

22. The case examples are taken from the original paper of the authors about IP management in customer–supplier relationships (Paasi *et al.*, 2010). [Paasi, J., Luoma, T., Valkokari, K. and Lee, N. (2010). Knowledge and Intellectual Property Management in Customer-Supplier Relationships, *International Journal of Innovation Management*, Vol. 14, pp. 629–654.]

23. Our findings are in line with the findings of Bader (2006) and Chesbrough and Schwartz (2007). Bader studied IP management practices in R&D collaborations in service

business. The focus of Chesbrough and Schwartz was on business models in co-development partnerships. [Bader, M.A. (2006). *Intellectual Property Management in R&D Collaborations: The Case of the Service Industry Sector*, Physica-Verlag, Heidelberg; Chesbrough, H. and Schwartz, K. (2007). Innovating Business Models with Co-development Partnerships, *Research-Technology Management*, Vol. 50, pp. 55–59.]

24. For recent literature reviews on open innovation see the papers of Dahlander and Gann (2011) and Huizingh (2011). [Dahlander, L. and Gann, D.M. (2010). How Open is Innovation? *Research Policy*, Vol. 39, pp. 699–709; Huizingh, E. (2011). Open Innovation: State of the Art and Future Perspectives. *Technovation*, Vol. 31, pp. 2–9.]

25. [Chesbrough. H. (2003) *Open Innovation: The New Imperative for Creating and Profiting from Technology*, Harvard Business School Press, Boston.]

26. In his book Martin Bader (2006) discussed arrangements related to jointly developed IP and gave examples of practices used at IBM Corp. in their R&D collaborations. [Bader, M.A. (2006). *Intellectual Property Management in R&D Collaborations: The Case of the Service Industry Sector*, Physica-Verlag, Heidelberg.]

27. In the interviews we did not show Table 2.3 to the interviewees or speak about the characteristic levels of openness. The statement of the managers was placed here because what the managers said about co-creation innovation projects was best suited to the openness level that we call "modifiable".

28. The early development of open source has been reviewed by Henrik Ingo (2005) in his book. The book includes several examples of open source communities in the 1990s and early 2000, with a good insight into Linux community. [Ingo, H. (2005). *Open Life: The Philosophy of Open Source*, Ingram, http://openlife.cc/files/OpenLife-aa.pdf (Accessed on 23 February 2012.)]

29. A quite broad discussion about pros and cons as well as implications of open source and openness in innovation has been given by Eliot Maxwell (2006). [Maxwell, E. (2006). Open Standards, Open Source and Open Innovation. Harnessing the Benefits of Openness, *MIT Press*, Issue 3, 2006, pp. 119–176.]

30. A list of open source hardware projects is available on Wikipedia [Wikipedia, http://en.wikipedia.org/wiki/List_of_open_source_hardware_projects (Accessed on 23 February 2012.)]

Chapter 8

When is Dealing in the Bazaar
of Opportunities Beneficial?

In Chapter 3 we presented three questions (see Fig. 3.1) which can be used by a firm to consider if dealing in the Bazaar of Opportunities for New Business Development would be beneficial for them:

(1) Why? That is, analysis concerning knowledge required to reach the target, which could be, for example, an identified opportunity for really a new business or a renewal of existing business.
(2) How is it possible to obtain the knowledge, and what criteria should we use to assess how we obtain it? That is, could the knowledge be generated internally through a firm's own R&D, or should we consider the using of external partners, and, if using external partners, with whom should we collaborate and could their interests and targets be aligned with us?
(3) What would be the collaboration model to be used in innovation? That is, negotiations with potential actors about the details of collaboration model, including among other things, choice between different collaboration and business models, levels of openness, issues related to IP management, sharing of costs, risks and benefits.

We view these three questions as important at guiding the dealing in the Bazaar of Opportunities, while on the other hand, accept that the Bazaar should not be taken as an automatic self-evident solution to gain any necessary missing knowledge. In-house R&D is a good solution in many situations. And the Bazaar of Opportunities seldom replaces a firm's own R&D. Typically dealing in the Bazaar should be taken as an opportunity to supplement the firm's own R&D and, in this way, to expand their own possibilities and to create business opportunities that would not be feasible alone.

Firms will also face many risks when being and dealing in the Bazaar of Opportunities that they would not meet if making the new business development alone. In this book we have not explicitly focused on those risks, although the book will give guidance in order to manage the risks. Instead, we have paid our attention to the opportunities that the Bazaar will offer for firms. The reason for this is that new business is seldom created by focusing on risks related to the business. Much more often business is initiated through an identified opportunity of a new attractive business.

In this concluding chapter of the book we will deepen the discussion around the following important question: when is dealing in the Bazaar of Opportunities beneficial for a firm?

One Plus One is Three

"Because any collaboration starts simply with one plus one is three."

"To me that is a modern example of how you do innovation, because you really derive a lot of strength from your partner, but you also bring very good things to the table. Together you are really more powerful than any of the individual parts would have been."

"Ideas typically surface at the interface. I mean, when you interact, you both bring in. So it's like, hey, I have this idea, now describe your specific situation to me. That will lead to attempting the idea, evolving it, building on it, and then you get the great idea. But it's a dialogue, and they're always at the interface, the great ideas."

These three quotes from three different managers describe why increasingly more companies are operating and dealing in the Bazaar of Opportunities. It is because of an expectation that together actors are more powerful than any of the individual parts would have been. In the Bazaar, when successful, one plus one is much more than two. Naturally success is not axiomatic.

In the Introduction to this book we wrote that to be successful in the Bazaar, an actor must understand his or her own role and interests as well as those of the opponents, know the value of the offering in question, be creative and skilful in negotiating and agreeing, understand the business model in question and what opportunities and limitations that it will create, etc. In this sense the situation is the same if compared to dealing in the traditional oriental bazaar. In Chapter 7 we discussed more about knowing the value of the offering in the Bazaar of Opportunities where the offering may mean a complete business solution or a piece to be integrated into the complete solution. We also talked about how the roles and interests of the actors should be aligned with each other, with the business model, and with IP management used in the collaboration. We discussed openness of innovation in the Bazaar of Opportunities, and how the understanding of different levels of openness may guide the project co-ordinators to align the innovation actions of all actors involved in the particular innovation work. Failure in any of the issues listed above or inadequate capability in these subjects will have a negative impact on the results. How negative depends on the case. It may not necessarily be catastrophic for the actors, but the result may not be "one plus one is three" or "win-win". Instead, the result may be that only one party will "win" and another party or parties will not. Or nobody will win. So a prerequisite for beneficial dealing in the Bazaar of Opportunities is that an actor is prepared to be there.

All the issues above are related to capabilities of an actor where the actor can improve their skills. This book, as well as references given in the end notes of each chapter, contains lots of information that can be used to improve those skills. The internal capabilities of actors are necessary but not adequate factors influencing to the success in the Bazaar of Opportunities.

When is Dealing in the Bazaar of Opportunities the most Beneficial?

There is still a perspective related to the question "when is dealing in the Bazaar beneficial?" that has not yet been discussed in this book. The perspective is related to factors that are external to a firm. External factors are such to which a single firm has marginal, if any, control. In the context of the question, the external factors are related either to technology or markets of current or targeted business. Changes concerning the technology can be either slow with more or less predictable changes, or fast including disruptive changes in technology. In the former case we can speak about technologically stable environments and in the latter case about dynamic environments. Similarly we may speak about stable and dynamic markets. In dynamic, turbulent markets, changes in the needs and behaviour of customers are difficult to predict. In dynamic markets the competitive edge and the competition may also change rapidly. In stable markets, the changes are slow and can be more easily anticipated.

The role of open innovation strategies in different environmental settings and correlation between open innovation strategies and the success of innovation have been recently studied in the literature.[1] Clear evidence has been found that open innovation is more beneficial in dynamic than in stable environments, and that different environmental settings require the integration of different types of external resources. Under fast technological changes firms should primarily integrate suppliers into the innovation process. Similarly, under fast market changes firms should primarily integrate customers into their innovation works. These do not mean that firms should not have customer involvement in innovation under technological turbulence, or supplier involvement under market turbulence. It just means that the business of firms benefits more from open and networked innovation with technology suppliers than with customers under technological turbulence, and vice versa under market turbulence.

If thinking about the findings reported in the literature about the open innovation strategies and the success of innovation, there is nothing surprising. Under technological changes, firms are forced to actively search for new technological solutions. Few firms have resources to make that in-house with sufficient depth and speed. Then collaboration with external technology developers is often highly beneficial. Under market turbulence, on the other hand, firms may lose their understanding of customers, their needs and behaviour. In such a situation, it would be highly beneficial to have them integrated into the innovation process of the firm. In stable environments firms typically do not see so much need to integrate external knowledge into their innovation, especially if they are happy with the business in the stable environment.

Stable environments are often accompanied with competition. In the book *Blue Ocean Strategy*,[2] W. Chan Kim and Reneé Mauborgne encouraged firms, operating in markets having heavy competition, to create completely new markets where the competition is weak. The creation of new markets may take place with the help of new disruptive technology (R&D domain), with a completely new business model for old technology (business model domain), or with the combination of both new technology and a new business model. In their book they do not speak about open or networked innovation in the creation of new markets. But we believe that readers of *The Bazaar of Opportunities for New Business Development* have learned that there are actors in the Bazaar with whom one could create such a new market and develop offering(s) to the market. So dealing in the Bazaar is beneficial not only under dynamic business environment but also in a stable environment when one is aiming to cause turbulence to the environment through innovation.

Concluding Remarks

We have now come to the end of *The Bazaar of Opportunities for New Business Development — Bridging Networked Innovation, Intellectual Property and Business*. We have discussed open and networked innovation, collaboration models and knowledge management in the Bazaar, IP in networks and the role of contracting in the various forms of networked innovation, IP strategies and IP valuation in the context of open and networked innovation. We have discussed different levels of openness in innovation works in the Bazaar, and how the protection and sharing of knowledge should be considered differently in these levels of openness. Firms that are successfully doing business in the Bazaar of Opportunities either as traders, dealers or buyers, have managed to bridge these capabilities together and with their business.

In the Bazaar of Opportunities, there are technology developers and suppliers that are searching for partners with whom to make new "killer" applications. There are providers of research and engineering as well as innovation support services that could help in the development of the business offering. There is IP looking for a buyer or a licensee. There are customers who are searching for new technology, new solutions,

212 Bazaar of Opportunities for New Business Development

and solution providers for their needs. And there is enough information and knowledge available in order to deal successfully in the Bazaar of Opportunities.

We started the book by thinking about a place where we can find the missing piece in order to complete the offering related to our business opportunity. Thinking about a place where we can find other actors that share our vision and are willing to open and share their knowledge with us in order to jointly explore new business opportunities and build business offerings. Now at the end of the book, we may be much closer to such a place than what we had thought about before. So why shouldn't we explore what the Bazaar of Opportunities could offer for us?

Notes

1. We refer here especially to the studies by Fiona Schweitzer *et al.* (2011) and Irina Savitskaya (2011). [Schweitzer, F., Gassmann, O. and Gaubinger, K. (2011). Is Open Innovation an Effective Method to Embrace Turbulent Environments? Paper presented in the 2011 ISPIM Conference, Hamburg; Savitskaya, I. (2011). Environmental Influences on the Adoption of Open Innovation: Analysis of Structural, Institutional and Cultural Impacts, *Acta Universitatis Lappeenrantaesis* 439, Lappeenranta University of Technology, Lappeenranta.]
2. [Kim, W.C. and Mauborgne, R. (2005). *Blue Ocean Strategy — How to Create Uncontested Market Space and Make the Competition Irrelevant*, Harvard Business School Press, Boston.]

Appendix I

List of Publications from the IPOB (Intellectual Property in Open Business Models) Project

Journal Articles

Lee, N. (2009). Exclusion and Coordination in Collaborative Innovation and Patent Law, *International Journal of Intellectual Property Management*, Vol. 3, No. 1, pp. 79–93.

Luoma, T., Paasi, J. and Valkokari, K. (2010). Intellectual Property in Inter-organisational Relationships — Findings from an Interview Study, *International Journal of Innovation Management*, Vol. 14, No. 3, pp. 399–414.

Nystén-Haarala, S., Lee, N. and Lehto, J. (2010). Flexibility in Contract Terms and Contracting Processes, *International Journal of Management of Projects in Business*, Vol. 3, No. 1, pp. 462–478.

Paasi, J., Luoma, T., Valkokari, K. and Lee N. (2010). Knowledge and Intellectual Property Management in Customer-supplier Relationships, *International Journal of Innovation Management*, Vol. 14, No. 4, pp. 629–654.

Paasi, J., Valkokari, K., Hytönen, H., Luoma, T., Nystén-Haarala, S. and Huhtilainen, L. (2010). Innovation Management Challenges of a System Integrator in Innovation Networks, *International Journal of Innovation Management*, Vol. 14, No. 6, pp. 1047–1064.

Valkokari, K., Paasi, J. and Rantala, T. (2012). Managing Knowledge Within Networked Innovation, *Knowledge Management Research & Practice*, Vol. 10, No. 1, pp. 27–40.

Conference Papers

Huhtilainen, L. (2010). Contracting in Open Innovation, *Proceedings of the 3rd ISPIM Innovation Symposium*, Quebec.

Huhtilainen, L. and Nystén-Haarala, S. (2011). Contractual Coordination and Control in Innovation Networks, *Proceedings of the ISPIM 2011 Conference*, Hamburg.

Hytönen, H. and Paasi, J. (2010). Motivation and Intellectual Property in the Context of Open Innovation, *Proceedings of Open Innovation Research Seminar*, Kouvola, LUT Research report 225, pp. 25–38.

Lee, N., Nystén-Haarala, S. and Huhtilainen, L. (2010). Interfacing Intellectual Property Rights and Open Innovation, *Proceedings of Open Innovation Research Seminar*, Kouvola, LUT Research report 225, pp. 121–139.

Luoma, T., Paasi, J. and Valkokari, K. (2009). Intellectual Property in Inter-organisational Relationships — Findings from the Interview Study in Finland and in the Netherlands, *Proceedings of the 2nd ISPIM Innovation Symposium*, New York.

Luoma, T., Paasi, J. and Valkokari, K. (2010). Barriers to Innovating Openly, *Proceedings of the ISPIM 2010 Conference*, Bilbao.

Paasi, J. and Rantala, T. (2010). Services, Open Innovation and Intellectual Property, *Proceedings of Open Innovation Research Seminar*, Kouvola, LUT Research report 225, pp. 141–156.

Paasi, J., Valkokari, K., Erkkilä, J., Hakulinen, J., Kirveskoski, K. and Räisänen, V. (2011). Levels of Openness in Open Innovation, *Proceedings of the ISPIM 2011 Conference*, Hamburg.

Paasi, J., Valkokari, K., Hytönen, H., Luoma, T., Nystén-Haarala, S. and Huhtilainen, L. (2010). Innovation Management Challenges of a System Integrator in Innovation Networks, *Proceedings of the ISPIM 2010 Conference*, Bilbao.

Paasi, J., Valkokari, K., Rantala, T., Hytönen, H., Nystén-Haarala, S., Huhtilainen, L. and Lee. N. (2010). Knowledge and Intellectual Property Management in Networked Innovation, *Proceedings of EBRF 2010*, Nokia.

Valkokari, K., Paasi, J., Luoma, T. and Lee, N. (2009). Beyond Open Innovation — Concept of Networked Innovation, *Proceedings of the 2nd ISPIM Innovation Symposium*, New York.

Theses

Lee, N. (2010) *Exclusion and Coordination of Fragmentation. Five Essays Towards a Pluralistic Theory of Patent Rights, Doctoral Dissertation*, Publications of the University of Eastern Finland. Dissertations of Social Sciences and Business Studies, Joensuu.

Appendix II

List of the Organizations in the Interview Study

Organization	Industry/products/services	Personnel (2008)
ABN Amro	Finance, banking	50000
Arcusys	IT services	12
Blancco	Software, ICT	37
Consolis	Construction industry	9000
Corus Group	Steel industry	42000
Damen Shipyards	Shipbuilding industry	2100
DSM	Chemical industry	23000
Dun Agro	Agriculture	3
Forcit Defence	Chemical industry	5 (Forcit 220)
Fugro	Technical consultancy, geospatial industry	13000
Image Wear	Clothing industry	500
Imtech WPS	Parking technology systems	150
Kolster	IP Management services, patent and trademark office	200
Koppert	Biological systems — pollination systems and integrated pest management	250
KPN	Telecommunication and ICT services	43500
Krohne Altometer	Technology products and measurement solutions	315
Laitosjalkine	Textile and footwear industry	80
Medisize	Manufacturing industry	1000
Metso Automation	Industrial automation industry	1500
Nammo	Defence industry	1800
National Board of Patents and Registration of Finland (NBPR)	Government services, IP industry	500
Nederlands Vaccin Institute (NVI)	Healthcare Industry	400

(*Continued*)

215

Organization	Industry/products/services	Personnel (2008)
Nokia Research Center	Telecommunication	500
Norit X-Flow	Water purification systems	1600
Outotec	Metals and mining industry	2000
Philips Lighting	Lighting industry	40000
Rabobank	Finance, banking	60000
River diagnostics	Measuring and testing equipment, healthcare and medical industry	26
Sandvik Mining and Construction	Mining and construction	17000
Stevens Idepartners	Engineering and designing	10
Strukton Rail	Railway construction and maintenance services	3500
Tamlink	Technology transfer	70
ThyssenKrupp Accessibility	Accessibility industry	1100
Tremco Illbruck	Building material industry	1000
UPM	Forest industry	24000
Vaisala	Measuring and testing equipment	1100
Vebego	Cleaning, facility and personnel services	30000
VTT	Research and development	2700
Wihuri Oy Wipak	Plastics industry	3600
Xsens Technologies	3D motion measurement systems	40

Appendix III

IPOB Industry Project

In parallel with the IPOB research project, there was an industry-driven IPOB project where a consortium of six firms applied and customized the generic research results of IPOB research to their specific development needs. The work was supported by the experts of the research project (i.e. the authors of this book), thus providing a practical case study environment to test ideas and theories developed in the research project in real business environments of the firms.

The firms of IPOB Industry were:

Arcusys — a SME specializing in expert IT services and information system solutions (www.arcusys.fi)

Blancco — a medium-sized enterprise specializing in professional data erasure solutions (www.blancco.com)

Medisize — a large contract development and manufacturing partner in the healthcare market (www.medisize.com)

Outotec — a worldwide technology leader in minerals and metals processing (www.outotec.com)

Sandvik Mining and Construction — a part of Sandvik Corporation that manufacturers and delivers equipment and services for rock quarrying and materials handling (www.sandvik.com)

Tamlink — a SME offering innovation and technology transfer services (www.hermia.fi)

In the IPOB industry, the common main goal of the firms was to improve their capabilities in successfully applying open innovation in their new business development. Specific tasks included (among others):

- creating an IP strategy for the firm, or updating the IP strategy of the firm so that it welcomes and guides opportunities offered by open and networked innovation,
- improving models used in customer and supplier collaboration related to innovation and new business development,
- improving model contracts used in open and networked innovation projects, and
- enhancing the commercialization of IP through external partners.

Index